The Three Graces
Companionship, Discretion, Passion

Paul Monk

with original artwork by Ingrida Rocis

echo BOOKS

First Published in 2022 by Echo Books
Echo Books is an imprint of Superscript Publishing Pty Ltd, ABN 76 644 812 395
Registered Office: Suite 401, 140 Bourke St, Melbourne, VIC, 3000
www.echobooks.com.au
Copyright ©Paul Monk
Creator: Monk Paul, Author
Title: The Three Graces : Companionship, Discretion, Passion.
ISBN: 978-1-922603-97-5 (softcover)

 A catalogue record for this book is available from the National Library of Australia

Book layout and design by Peter Gamble, Canberra
Set in Garamond Premier Pro Display, 12/17, Bon Vivant and MinervaSmallCaps.

Cover image: *Companions at St Moritz*. Original artwork by Ingrida Rocis.
Original artwork copyright remains with ©Ingrida Rocis.

for Pasiphae Seferis

*με ευγνωμοσύνη για την παρέα σας σε αυτό το ταξίδι μέσα από το λαβύρινθο της αγάπης
και το υψηλό εγχείρημα της ποίησης*

and

for the three muses of this book

I crave an ivy wreath. The kind that poets,
If so crowned, believe puts them among the gods.
I love lyric inspired by the muses and composed
Among satyrs and nymphs, in a secret grove.

(Horace *Odes* I.1)

The poet

Contents

Preface   xv

Proem

    Temple ritual   xxxiii

Part one: Companionship. A: Darkness Over Love   1

1. We karyotes   3
2. Nutcracker man   4
3. Fire and the wheel   5
4. Circles in the dust   8
5. Lucullus to Clodia   9
6. Cave and woman   10
7. Aztec verses   11
8. Hymn to Ometeotl   12
9. Dance me on down from Toledo   13
10. Macondo mambo   15
11. The dream   16
12. Lara   17
13. The poet's bell   18
14. You walk away   19
15. Your architect   20
16. Proust and prolexia   21
17. Staying Seine   22
18. So that you will hear me   23
19. Leaning into the long afternoons   24
20. We have lost only a possible twilight   25
21. Losing Neruda   26
22. Manuela, my love   28
23. The bell and the choir   29
24. Thanks for the thread, Ariadne   32
25. Lullaby for Junius   34
26. Fusion   35
27. Ovid's metamorphoses   36
28. Orpheus among the stones   38
29. Sappho and Alcaeus   39
30. Cleis Scamandros   40

Part one: Companionship. B: The Seven Songs of Queen Nefesh — 43

1. Song of friendship — 45
2. Song of joy — 46
3. Song of comfort — 47
4. Song of knowledge — 48
5. Song of religion — 49
6. Song of love — 50
7. Song of healing — 51

Part one: Companionship. C: Lyrical Epigrams — 53

Prologue — 55

1. How to use our tongues — 57
2. Hamlet and then some — 58
3. The long summer — 59
4. Emily Dickinson — 60
5. Extrafloral nectars — 61
6. Before they cleaned you up — 62
7. Treasure magazines — 63
8. Uncanny gift — 64

Section one — 65

1. A Pageant of History — 67
2. The taste for books — 68
3. Report card — 69
4. Little Marco — 70
5. Beyond the borders — 71
6. Christina Hardyment's novel houses — 72
7. Enchanted by Tinuviel — 73
8. Book bindings — 74
9. Book of revelation — 75
10. The Wind in the Willows — 76
11. The river banker — 77
12. The piper at the gates of dawn — 78
13. Thomas Hardy, April 1914 — 79
14. Elspeth and Constance — 80
15. James Cook, voyager — 81
16. Render unto Caesar? — 82
17. The merest waste of time — 83
18. My private 4th of July — 84
19. Tokyo blond, 1985 — 85
20. Gaius Petronius Arbiter — 86

21.	Lord Byron's travels	87
22.	Pantheon	88
23.	Notitiae	89
24.	Being in Rome	90
25.	The City falls	91
26.	Colosseum	92
27.	If, at Babi Yar	93
28.	Gordion knots	94
29.	Abel, my little brother	95
30.	Salvadoran oligarch	96

Section two — 97

1.	Ana Gloria Hirleman	99
2.	Childhood awe	100
3.	Juvenal's spite	101
4.	Synesius	102
5.	The last of the Romans	103
6.	Trapped on the Aventine	104
7.	Love among the ruins	105
8.	On some lines from Kulikowski	106
9.	The life I live	107
10.	Our Ringstrasse moment	108
11.	Proust's way	109
12.	The ink pot and the quill	110
13.	Percy Bysshe Shelley	111
14.	Are we tempting fate?	112
15.	Evelyn Waugh's Oxford	113
16.	For you I wrote a villanelle	114
17.	My Apricot	115
18.	Erotic autonomy	116
19.	Margaret Island, Budapest	117
20.	El Prado	118
21.	Charon on the Styx	119
22.	Museum in Taipei	120
23.	A Taste of Freedom	121
24.	The trial of Wei Jingsheng	122
25.	In praise of Liu Xiaobo	123
26.	Martin Bodmer's books	124
27.	At the restaurant Casanova	125
28.	Considered as artists	126
29.	Return to Tipasa	127
30.	Anna Politkovskaya	128

Section three   **129**

1. Lead and Polonium 210   131
2. If they come for you   132
3. No water on Avila, Hugo   133
4. Doomsday machine   134
5. No irony Keegan   135
6. Sergei and Zinaida   136
7. All we can retrieve   137
8. The secret key   138
9. Sils Maria   139
10. The pact we've formed   140
11. Our hermeneutics in Zurich   141
12. Gormenghast and my past   142
13. Carneades, critical thinker   143
14. Volcanic texts   144
15. Philodemus and I   145
16. Chartwell with and without you   146
17. Festival of promise   147
18. Virginia and sex   148
19. Mansion and mind   149
20. Shrovetide   150
21. Finding the clearing   151
22. We are not reasonable   152
23. Kafka and Brod   153
24. Archaic Earth   154
25. Andromeda   155
26. Tractatus Logico-Poeticus   156
27. Boltzmann and Nietzsche   157
28. Jefferson's library   158
29. Wine at the Tree House   159
30. McGurk's lament   160

Section four   **161**

31. Gimme shelter   163
32. Coffee with the old historian   164
33. Fermi's paradox   165
34. Karl Kraus in love   166
35. Franz Brentano and us   167
36. The freedom to aspire   168
37. Whatever is out there   169
38. Transcendent conversations   170

39. Zarathustra and us	171
40. Museo Larco	172
41. Agreement over piña coladas	173
42. Heading to Tocumen	174
43. Imagining the Alcantara	175
44. Giles Sparrow's Cosmos	176
45. Sao Paolo on foot	177
46. Flight to Morocco	178
47. Without a prayer	179
48. Marrakesh maze	180
49. If you see her	181
50. High Atlas	182
51. Tangier	183
52. From Frankfurt to Singapore	184
53. Aleph was a breathing stop	185
54. Gestures, marks and signs	186
55. Rhythm's roots	187
56. The making of these signs	188
57. Treatise, tale or ode	189
58. Robert Graves on Mallorca	190
59. In Jerusalem last week	191
60. Easter Someday	192

Epilogue — 193

1. True companion	195
2. Time and Naipi's hair	196
3. Blue velvet bag	197
4. Corngold's Kaufmann	198
5. Reading *Orlando*	199
6. Our string quartet in C sharp minor	200
7. Listening to Chopin	201
8. This book is Chauvet Cave	202

Part two: Discretion. Delphic Deixis — 203

1. Secret poem	205
2. Hannah at Marburg	207
3. Fruitful thoughts	208
4. Rilkean lullaby	209
5. Gnossiennes 3	210
6. A Greek bearing doubts	211
7. Mercurial beauty	212
8. Ithaka and I	213

9.	Not for me	214
10.	Princess and stranger	215
11.	Old heroes	216
12.	Bishop's 'Insomnia'	217
13.	Sextus Propertius and Cynthia	218
14.	You embodied several ghosts	219
15.	Crystallization	220
16.	Mistaken about something	221
17.	Delphic deixis	222
18.	Daphne and Apollo	223
19.	Epicurean wisdom	224
20.	Eugene Onegin	225
21.	Actually, I am Tatiana	226
22.	Kraus, Rilke, Sidonie	227
23.	Nisreen of the orange blossom	228
24.	Beckett's maxim	229
25.	Prolepidoptera	230
26.	Honesty is the worst policy	231
27.	After Vygotsky	233
28.	The ancient rules	234
29.	Rovelli and reality	235
30.	Silence is toxic	236
31.	Six hours in conference	237
32.	Hardly Keats	238
33.	Saigon Secret	239
34.	Re-education camps	240
35.	Satie, again and again	241
36.	Beyond Hanoi	242
37.	Imogen and Paul	243
38.	Rational actors	244
39.	Quickly forgotten experiences	245
40.	Pas de deux	246
41.	A clinical case	247
42.	De Clerambault syndrome	248
43.	What Lucretius wrote	249
44.	Oberon's potion	250
45.	Malvolio	251
46.	Let's briefly imagine	252
47.	Baladine Klossowska	253
48.	Rilke's grave monument	254
49.	Duino dialogue	255
50.	Hypothetical only	256

51.	Near Methymna's walls	257
52.	Orpheus dismembered	259

Part three: Passion. This Floating Shell — 261

Prologue — 263

1.	Before breakfast	265
2.	Pink silk dress	266
3.	Ecstasy itself	267

End to End — 269

1.	Dream Godiva	271
2.	You speak of Ovid	272
3.	Count Henri Marie Raymond	273
4.	Catullus 101	274
5.	Reading 'Epipsychidion'	275
6.	Fortunate foundling	277
7.	Goethe and you	278
8.	From Ovid to Goethe	279
9.	Bath and Trav	280
10.	Ovid on SMS	281
11.	Camille Claudel	282
12.	Before dawn	283
13.	Faustina and Rome	284
14.	D. H. Lawrence	285
15.	Delete the WAVs!?	287
16.	War of Shadows	288
17.	Sancerre et Renoir	289
18.	Genital hypertrophy	290
19.	Proust's muse and mine	291
20.	No drop wasted	292
21.	Never in my youth	293
22.	Charlotte Corday strikes	294
23.	BBHM	295
24.	Priapus in the garden	297
25.	No-one from nowhere	298
26.	This fleeting moment	299
27.	Cosmological optics	300
28.	Remi nepotes	301
29.	If I were Abelard	302
30.	The Three Graces	303
31.	Musée Rodin	304

32.	Leave your hat on	305
33.	Your Ovid	307
34.	Tall priestess	308
35.	Rommel of the heart	309
36.	These walls of Rome	310
37.	The bed of your voice	311
38.	Like and unlike	312
39.	It isn't easy	313
40.	Your languages	314
41.	Midnight in Paris	315
42.	Pharaoh's dreams	317
43.	Theseus ponders	318
44.	Dido and the knife	319
45.	Fucking to Wagner	320
46.	So nice to come home to	321
47.	Our labyrinths	322
48.	Oxyrhynchus fragments	323
49.	Kay Summersby	324
50.	After the tryst	325
51.	Aspasia	327
52.	Not wanting the day	328
53.	Summer's day	329
54.	Better than Christiane	330
55.	Catastrophe imagined	331
56.	Birthday bash in Bordeaux	332
57.	Dante and Petrarch	333
58.	Against the wall	334
59.	Philaenis and the saints	335
60.	All I need	337
61.	The true sex organ	338
62.	Were I Elon Musk	339
63.	I will, we will, he will	340
64.	OSINT and our privacies	341
65.	Emanuele Severino and nihilism	342
66.	We have little time	343
67.	Dichtung und Wahrheit	344

68.	All that you desire	345
69.	Our child is Voluptas	346

Epilogue   **347**

1.	Love of one	349
2.	Cupid, Psyche and the West Wind	350
3.	This floating shell	351

Endnotes   **353**

Acknowledgements   **379**

Index   **381**

This book and its genesis

This book includes three entirely separate and very different cycles of poetry. Each was written for a different muse and under very different circumstances. They might reasonably have been published as three distinct books. They have been published in one book because the contrasts between the three experiences seemed to me so illuminating that I wanted to offer them to others in a single volume. The sub-title of the book is a concise summation of the contrasts: companionship, discretion, passion were the dominant characteristics of the three experiences. There are, inevitably, certain common tropes. But the differences between the cycles are more striking than the similarities.

The book is dedicated to four women: the three muses of the poetry and a close friend of some years standing, with whom I was able to share and discuss the poetry as I wrote it. I shall, here, only refer to the muses (or graces) as Muse 1, Muse 2 and Muse 3. That sounds very abstract, but it is in order to protect the privacy of the women in question. The poems are in many cases intimate ones, especially those for Muse 3. To identify the women by name, therefore, would risk embarrassing them or exposing them to possible intrusion by others. The purpose in publishing the poetry is to offer aesthetic pleasure to readers, not to 'spill the beans' on the private lives of women I have loved and whose company I have kept. That would be autobiography. This is art.

With the exception of the first two components of Part I, almost all these poems were written between early 2019 and the first half of October this year (2021). Only in dialogue, in the spring of this year, with the woman to whom this book is primarily dedicated, did I realize that, beyond any design of my own, I had had such a beautiful trio of experiences one after another and that they actually formed a set. They complemented one another. The second built on the first, which, in an important sense, had made it possible. The third built on the second in a similar manner. Each was a radical new development based on experience and writing that preceded it.

I wrote poetry for many women when I was a younger man. Almost none of that poetry can bear comparison with what I have written in the last few years. Little of it has survived the culling of my archives in recent years. Perhaps the dividing line was laid down in part by the fact that for fifteen years, before 2019, I was besieged by life-threatening illness—aggressive melanoma that had me in and out of hospital. Love and meaning became existential issues in those years. Each in its own way, the three passions of the heart addressed here challenged me to see myself and my life afresh and to grow. They are not, however, by any means simply repetitions of the same experience. They are studies in very different romantic experiences.

The stories behind the cycles of poetry are personal and private. I will not divulge them here, beyond what is implicit in the poems themselves. They are already revealing enough. The reader will, I hope, feel free to both imagine fruitfully the kinds of experience to which the poems attest and bring to them personal memories, needs and longings, thus making the reading of these poems a meaningful experience transcending any immediate intention of the poet. That's what good and stimulating reading, whether of prose or poetry, is supposed to be like. A great many of my poems reflect on how I see myself in the light of the work of other poets and thinkers. I expect readers to automatically read my own work in the same way.

As I completed the final cycle of these poems and arranged for this book to be published, I was forcibly struck by the thought that all the experiences captured here have been fortunate ones for me. Not only because of the passions and poignant feelings involved, but because they came during what is, for so many people, the greying phase of life, when memories of youth are drawn upon to compensate for a sense of time and vitality ebbing relentlessly away. They led me to reflect upon the course my life had taken (in Part I), to imagine fresh possibilities (Part II) and then to begin to enact such possibilities (Part III).

I had barely been declared in complete remission from cancer when all this overtook me. I found poetry pouring out of me, as if it had been dammed up over a lifetime. In a strange sense, I think it had been. Muse 1 had been part of my life throughout those years and had urged me to embrace poetry as the key to my life. Muse 2 and Muse 3 only appeared in my life at the point of remission and after I had started to become prolific and liberated. The three utterly contrasting relationships excavated my heart, or psyche. They laid bare its foundations and inspired me to rebuild my life. And on those foundations I built this poetic structure. It now defines who I am, as none of my earlier poetry came close to doing.

As this book goes to press, I am vividly reminded of 'To the Fates' by the German Romantic poet Friedrich Hölderlin, which has haunted and inspired me since I first read it, almost half a century ago:

> *A single summer grant me, great powers, and*
> *A single autumn for fully ripened song,*
> *That, sated with the sweetness of my*
> *Singing, my heart may more willingly die.*

The soul that living did not attain its divine
Right cannot repose in the nether world;
But once what I am bent on, what is

Holy, my poetry, is accomplished:
Be welcome then, stillness of the shadows' world!
I shall be satisfied, though my lyre will not
Accompany me down there. Once I
Lived like the gods and more is not needed.

The creation of this book in the spring of an astonishing year of the heart, now feels to me as if the 'single summer' Hölderlin asked of the Fates will, for me, be this very summer. Here is my fully ripened song. I have, these past few years, traveling, loving, writing, coming alive again, truly lived like the gods—and more is not needed. Whether there will be more, as they say, is 'in the lap of the gods'.

Why poetry at all?

But why poetry at all? What is poetry? What is it for? Percy Shelley's long essay 'A Defence of Poetry', written in 1821 (exactly two hundred years ago) resonates with me not only on account of its eloquence and soaring vision, but because it articulates a powerful, if Romantic, case for poetry as important and even foundational to human experience and meaning. Poetry, in this vision of it, is the use of language not to register 'facts', but to express 'alterities'—dreams of what was, could have been, might yet be, reinterpreting and re-examining what has occurred, and articulating things hoped for or imagined—or lamented. This is human language at its most protean. It can give shape and meaning to otherwise dumb or bewildered states of mind. It is in this sense that Shelley claimed poets to be the 'unacknowledged legislators of mankind'.

Without writing at the same length here as Shelley did two centuries ago, or digressing to discuss his argument, I will posit—as a point of departure for the body of poetry within these covers—that there is no necessary clash between a scientific understanding of the world (which I hold) and a poetic experience of it. On the contrary, the scientific grasp of reality helps us to reshape our language, our vision and our self-expression. But it is poetry that bodies forth that vision and self-expression—in language. My poetic practice is one of bringing lucid understanding of reality together with deeply felt expressiveness and a vision of alterities. I am not an expressionist or symbolist poet. My poems are intended to make clear and, I hope, beautiful or at least poignant sense. Whether that makes me more or less of a poet I leave others to judge for themselves.

A number of the poems, in each of the cycles published here, draw upon the history and philosophy of science, on cosmology, physics, geology, evolutionary biology and cognitive science to situate my 21st century sensibility in its proper context. But that doesn't prevent me from appreciating and drawing upon the myths and tales of centuries and millennia ago and finding in them the clear echoes or anticipations of my own experiences. Bringing all this together has been the work of a lifetime. Having, in Part III, a muse conversant with so much literature and music has been a profound experience. She was so engaged with and responsive to the poetry that I often felt that *the* Muse—Robert Graves's 'White Goddess' herself had entered my life incarnate.

Along the way, I was able, also, to share the poetry with a small circle of other intimates, not least among them Pasiphae Seferis, to whom this book is dedicated, in thanks for her extraordinary role in the creative process. She might almost be called Muse 4, but she is at once more detached and closer than the others, in what might be called prosaic terms. She is also more 'European'. To say more would, perhaps be to intrude into her private life, which I won't do. But this I will say: she educated me in the many meanings of the ancient legend of Theseus and Ariadne, when I teased her about her name and how much 'bull' she must have suffered over the years on account of it. That was in Cancun, six years ago, when we met by chance and spent an unforgettable day at Chichen Itza.

Perhaps, in some ways, it was she who kick-started the revitalization that led to the writing of so much poetry since then. We had only a couple of days together in Yucatan before our ways parted. However, fascinated by both her beauty and her name, I wrote her a poem and gave it to her before we headed off on divergent trajectories. As this book was going to press, she begged me to include it in the Preface. It's one of two poems written for her during those two days. The other, 'Before breakfast', is included at the beginning of Part III of this book—a self-indulgence that I hope will be forgiven by Muse 3. It's called 'Bull of the Mound':

>*Daughter of Helios, Queen*
>*Of Gnossos and of ancient Gnosis,*
>*Mistress of Minoan mysteries,*
>*Quasi-divinity of the Double Axe,*
>*Woman of Linear B, enciphered,*
>
>*How have we met, other than*
>*On Crete, before the fabled Labrys?*
>*How can I have walked among*
>*Mayan temples, sacrificial altars*
>*With so legendary, so exotic a figure?*

But should I credit what they say:
That Daedalus artfully concealed you
So that you could copulate
With the bull of Poseidon –
The Bull of the Mound, you dubbed him?

I'll long remember your blonde laughter
At my ingenuous interrogation,
You Greco-German, polylingual
Polyamorous, golden-eyed muse:
'The goddess and the bull', you murmured

'The priestess and the incarnation
Of virile fertility take us back
To early Neolithic ritual,
Long before the Labyrinth at Gnossos!'
You laughed with joy at being Pasiphae.

Last night, then, after Chichen Itza,
You dared me play the fabled bull,
Under silken sheets in your Cancun rooms,
Passionate with ancient life you were.
What Minotaur might spring from this affair?

It's rather extraordinary reading that poem now, given all that has happened since 'Bull of the Mound' was written. My whole life has turned around and she has been a close interlocutor in that therapeutic process. Yet we met by chance and found there were elective affinities.

How I came to write poetry

But I digress. None of this came easily. It has taken much tenacity and painful experience. All three of the encounters reflected on in these poems involved varying degrees of painful experience—of separation, rejection, distance. But the poems rise above those things. Only now can I look back with a sense of what Friedrich Nietzsche called 'amor fati'—retrospective love of one's fate— over the nature of erotic defeat and futility, as well as the splendour of true companionship, honest romantic longing and intimate, mutual desire. When I was young— and for many years afterwards—I longed to live a 'poetic' life.[1] Yet I lacked even the most rudimentary theory as to what exactly this would mean or how to go about it. Had I had the resources of a Lord Byron, I might have known what to do. I did not.

---

1   See (or rather listen to) my hour long podcast interview with Nick Fabbri on this subject: https://www.nickfabbri.com/bloom/paulmonkonpoetry or on my own website: https://www.paulmonk.com.au/podcasts-1/onlivingapoeticlife

I would now say that *poiesis* (from the Greek for 'making') is what is at stake here. *Autopoiesis* or the making of a self is at the heart of it—as it is at the heart of life itself, from the primal, cellular level.[2] Lacking any mentoring of the sort needed to chart a clear course of the kind I intuitively wanted to pursue, I had to make it up as I went along. I had to seek out both the education and the experiences that might make me what I romantically longed to become. Readers of the present volume will judge for themselves whether or to what extent I have succeeded. Part I recounts something of that story, looking all the way back to my childhood and my delight in various children's books and romances.

In his book *Nietzsche: Life as Literature* (1985), Alexander Nehamas argued that (at least according to Nietzsche) we need to shape ourselves and our values with deliberate artistry and integrity, if we are to become fully realized human beings. That is the idea at the core of Nietzsche's famous and controversial concept of the *ubermensch* (overman, or 'superman'). In my own life, I have attempted that in several ways, but poetry has been at the heart of the project. Perhaps in this body of poetry it attains something close to realization. Certainly it does so at the personal level. How it will occur to others will vary appreciably, depending on their own courses in life and receptiveness to poetry as such.

I discovered Nietzsche's remarkable books, starting with *Thus Spoke Zarathustra*, shortly after leaving secondary school and they turned my Catholic world upside down. A passage in Zarathustra's Prologue (Section 6) has always been close to my heart throughout an almost fifty-year journey since then. It is that scene in the marketplace in which the tightrope walker loses his balance when his rival jumps over him. He falls and is fatally injured. Zarathustra ministers to him as he dies. He says to the broken tightrope walker, 'You have made danger your calling. There is nothing in that to despise. Now you perish through your calling: so I will bury you with my own hands.'

---

2   I know of no finer explanation of this or of its importance than that by Evan Thompson in his magisterial *Mind in Life: Biology, Phenomenology and the Sciences of Mind* (Belknap Press, Harvard University, 2007), notably in Part Two Chapter Five 'Autopoiesis: The Organization of the Living'. But in his own Preface, Thompson wrote:

> The self-producing or 'autopoietic' organization of biological life already implies cognition, and this incipient mind finds sentient expression in the self-organizing dynamics of action, perception and emotion, as well as in the self-moving flow of time-consciousness.

Thompson explained that the purpose of his book was 'to bring the experimental sciences of life and mind into a closer and more harmonious relationship with phenomenological investigations of experience and subjectivity.' My own autopoiesis is subjectively understood along these lines.

'Uncanny is human existence,' says Zarathustra, 'and still without meaning. A buffoon can be fatal to it.' He rebukes the philistines in the market square, the progressive bourgeoisie and modern socialists, who see themselves as the 'ultimate men' at the 'end of history'. 'What is love? What is creation? What is longing? What is a star? Thus asks the ultimate man and blinks. The Earth has become small and upon it hops the ultimate man, who makes everything small. His race is as inexterminable as the flea. The ultimate man lives longest.'

There is so much in Zarathustra's Prologue that means more to me now, in its fulfilment, than it could have meant when I read it as a young man tentatively starting to cross the tightrope strung over the market square. Passages such as the following now read, for me, less as challenges—as they did long ago—than as descriptions of how I have lived:

> *I love those who do not know how to live except their lives be a down-going, for they are those who are going across.*
>
> *I love him who lives for knowledge and who wants knowledge that one day the overman may live. And thus he wills his own downfall.*
>
> *I love him who is ashamed when the dice fall in his favour and who then asks: Am I then a cheat?—for he wants to perish.*
>
> *I love him whose soul is deep even in its ability to be wounded and whom even a little thing can destroy: thus he is glad to go over the bridge.*

But perhaps never before now, putting this seal on *The Three Graces*, have I felt so keenly and with such delight the resonance in me of Zarathustra's opening address to the Sun, when he emerges from his cave in the mountains, at the tender age of forty:

> *Great star! What would your happiness be if you had not those for whom you shine?*

I am a generation older now than Zarathustra was, when he decided that he wanted to descend into the valley and be as generous with his acquired wisdom as the Sun with its warmth and light. But it is in that mood that I am celebrating the creation of this book. By an extraordinary coincidence the woman to whom the book is dedicated is Greco-German. Her father is German, her mother Greek and she chose to take her mother's surname in adult life. She, in a long correspondence since Cancun, has coached all my natural and cultural longings towards an expressive rounding.

Nietzsche, notoriously, lacked women in his life, except for a sister and mother he didn't much care for and Lou Salome who appreciated his genius, but kept her distance from him. I have been far more fortunate than the author of *Thus Spoke Zarathustra* in terms of the company of women and I would like to think that the poetry gathered here demonstrates that. It also, of course, demonstrates a few other things. But those can be left to the reader to discern.

No-one taught me poetry at school in any serious way; to say nothing of coaching me in how to write poetry myself. By the time I was a young adult, I felt embarrassed and conflicted about my poetic impulses. They seemed to be an eccentricity, which had no place in the social milieu in which I had grown up, or the academic, to say nothing of the (later) bureaucratic world, in which I studied and worked. This induced a kind of depression and a self-consciousness in what poetry I did write that held me back for many years, both expressively and stylistically.

By the time I was a graduate student (almost forty years ago), I had come to the gloomy conclusion that I would never become a poet. Then, quite by accident, I began to write sonnets—Shakespearean ones. I was engaged in a massive PhD research program on counterinsurgency in the peasant societies of Southeast Asia and Central America, which was deeply absorbing and prosaic. But the English tutor at the student residential hall where I was bivouacked, took it upon himself to run a sonnet writing competition.

I was ambivalent about whether to even enter the little competition. However, the beautiful young woman I was then seeing urged me to do so. I demurred, declaring that I was 'a historian and political scientist, not a poet'. She countered that I was good with words and should try my hand. She was herself a student of French, Chinese, Arabic and Linguistics, so language was her thing. And she was very lovely. How could I decline?

So, I took Shakespeare's *Sonnets* off my bookshelf and read the lot, in order to get a handle on what a sonnet was: fourteen lines, five beats to a line, three quatrains and a concluding couplet. Having satisfied myself that I understood, I slept on the idea of what to write my sonnet about. Not surprisingly, it was about the young woman. I wrote a sonnet called 'Romeo and Rosaline', which implied that she was Juliet. The 'Rosaline' in question was a young woman of the same age with whom I had become besotted the previous year, in a different student hall.

I won the competition and was touched by the expressions of appreciation that a number of fellow students—as well as both 'Rosaline' and 'Juliet'—offered me afterwards. 'Rosaline', to whom I showed the sonnet, read it standing under a lamp in her dorm room, then declared, in her enchanting voice, 'I think it's beautiful. I think everyone should write poetry!' My heart turned over and I realized that the prize-winning sonnet itself had just been refuted. 'Rosaline' was my true 'Juliet'.

From that point, I had at least a little confidence that I could write sonnets. In fact, on fieldwork for my PhD a few months later, I wrote my first cycle of sonnets—for 'Rosaline-the-true-Juliet'. They didn't turn the trick. She unwisely married another, and we never met again. As with so much that passes through one's life, I later destroyed that set of sonnets, disillusioned with the apparent futility of the exercise. For about a decade after that first cycle, however, whenever I fell in love (never mind how many times) I would write (mostly) sonnets to give shape to my infatuations.

This ended up generating a cycle of some forty new sonnets for a particularly beautiful young woman in the mid-1990s. She declared to me, in response to them, that I seemed able to express my feelings about anything (something I certainly did not believe to be the case). She also declared, taking me a long hop beyond the earlier episode or any in between, that I must get the sonnets for her published. 'Whatever happens between the two of us', she exclaimed, 'I'll then be able to hold up your book and say, 'I inspired this!''

It took another decade before that happened. A selection of twelve of the better sonnets for her were published in my book *Sonnets to a Promiscuous Beauty*, some fifteen years ago. That book itself was a work of art, with superb etchings by the late Jorg Schmeisser and my own commentaries, explicating the story that unfolded within the sonnet cycle. For the first time, I felt that, at least to a modest extent, I had become a poet.

By pure coincidence, that book was being prepared for publication at just the point in my life when Muse 1, for whom the 173 poems in Part I of this book would later be written, entered my life. She would become my first real muse and she has remained a cherished companion. She calls me, these days, her 'best friend in the whole world' and her 'mentor'. My first poem for her, written within weeks of her first arriving in Melbourne, in 2004, from Mexico, where she had been lecturing in information analysis, and moving in as my guest (which she was to remain for three and a half years), was 'Ancient bridge'. It sits framed on my living room wall to this day. But by that time, I was in my late forties—a very late budding poet. I had become increasingly interested in the *theory* of poetry and actually read more 'criticism' and biographies of poets than poetry as such.

For years, Muse 1 urged me to start taking poetry more seriously and to diversify my offerings. She gave me a copy of the great Chilean poet Pablo Neruda's *Twenty Love Poems and a Song of Despair*. Her influence is deeply incised in the present book. She and I have remained good friends—or rather more than that—ever since. We have travelled widely together—as the poetry in Part I testifies. That was particularly so between 2016 and 2019, as I slowly recovered from the cancer. All the poems in *Lyrical Epigrams* were conceived and most of them written during those few years. The last of them were written in 2020.

Four key educators in my development as a poet

Over the years, four books had an especially strong influence on my thinking about poetry: Robert Graves's *The White Goddess: A Historical Grammar of Poetic Myth* (1948), Timothy Steele's *Missing Measures: Modern Poetry and the Revolt Against Meter* (1990), William Waters' *Poetry's Touch: On Lyric Address* (2003) and Helen Vendler's *Dickinson: Selected Poems and Commentaries* (2010). The first entrenched in my sensibility the idea of the Muse—the White Goddess of archaic Indo-European mythology, associated with the Moon. The second freed me up to experiment with forms of poetry other than sonnets and to wrestle with the question of *musicality* in language.

The third was decisive in shaping my sense of voice in poetry and the questions of introjection, projection, imaginary and extended discourse. Waters, more than any other critic, in his beautiful and unjustly neglected book, shifted my focus from *the* Muse to *my* muse, from the idea of Graves's Goddess to the intricacies of actual, simulated or hermetic dialogue with one's all-too-human muse. That would come into full play in the poems published here in all three Parts of the book. It's influence has been profound and ongoing.

Helen Vendler, an especially scrupulous and exquisite analyst of poetry—including that of Shakespeare[3]—schooled me in the intimacies and privacies that must attend poetry, written either to express one's very personal experiences or to address another person for whom one has intense and authentic feelings. This influence is explicitly acknowledged in my poem 'Emily Dickinson'. Steele, Waters and Vendler were, in short, my pre-eminent educators in writing the poetry brought together in this book.

I think now of sonnet writing as my own apprenticeship in writing poetry. There are, however, no sonnets in this book. There are a great many poems that might be regarded as quasi-sonnets: the 119 twelve-line poems that make up the bulk of Parts II and III. I don't have a name for this form. I invented it, in order to be able to capture a long series of experiences and reflections crisply and concisely, while eschewing the strict rhyme patterns of the Shakespearean sonnet and cutting the latter by two lines. Most, but not all, are written in pentameters (five beat lines) and blank (non-rhyming) verse—the most natural and conversational form of English prosody.

The longer, thirty-line poems that bookend both those cycles are, in turn, based on a form I improvised, when writing the first poems that became the very long (136 poems) cycle

---

3   Helen Vendler *The Art of Shakespeare's Sonnets* (Belknap Press, Harvard, 1997).

Lyrical Epigrams—all of which have thirty lines, though in widely varying internal structures. The first of them was written on a flight from Lisbon to Caracas in 2016, looking back some days to a brief sojourn in Jerusalem. It isn't, however, by any means placed first in the cycle—near the end, actually. The order of that cycle isn't chronological by composition, but to some extent by autobiography.

I found this long form, thirty-line verse structure congenial and stuck with it to the end of *Lyrical Epigrams*. I found it a delightful challenge, as with any strict or conventional form of prosody, to stick to the form rather than fall short or overrun its boundaries.[4] I like aesthetic symmetry. I am classical, even Aristotelian, in that regard. I rather like my poetry cycles to resemble Greek temples. It's no accident that the Proem to this book features a Greek temple, even if the poem itself is forty-five lines and stands on its own in that regard and was written for Muse 3.

Illness and the rebound into poetry

Despite the publication of the sonnets in 2006, two external factors constrained the development of my poetry for some years after that: I was working as a consultant in a company I had co-founded (while also doing a considerable amount of freelance journalism and essay-writing). I was, also, from 2004, chronically afflicted by melanoma (skin cancer). Between late 2004 and early 2018, I was in and out of hospital for endless checks, scans, surgical procedures (sixteen of those), drug infusions (every fortnight for about three years) and radiation therapies, especially after the cancer metastasized, in 2013. I had, finally, to give up my consulting work altogether while undergoing immunotherapy. It wasn't clear whether I would live much longer. There are poems in *Lyrical Epigrams* reflecting this sense that my days were numbered.

However, to the astonishment of my surgeons and specialists, I survived the challenge. I was declared in complete remission in March 2018 and began a whole new phase of my life. As early as 2015, I travelled again, though still seriously depleted and under drug treatment for the cancer. It was on that journey, to Yucatan, Jamaica and the Cayman Islands, that I first encountered the wonderful Pasiphae, in Cancun. On another journey, in 2016, via Israel and Malta to Venezuela and Brazil, I wrote the first six poems in what would become

---

4   My villanelle 'A poet's bell' in Part I was a deliberate exercise in trying my hand at this particularly demanding form and I confess I was delighted with the piece of work, not least because it was not only a strict form accomplished, but a complex thought of an intimate kind given expression. Similarly, the Sapphic ode 'Cleis Scamandros' was a playful experiment in form.

Lyrical Epigrams—all addressed to Muse 1, as part of our prolonged and enormously fruitful conversation about existential questions and partnership. We had been on a very long journey of life together by then, though we had not lived together since late 2007.

It is that conversation and journey which give Part I its title 'Companionship'. It comes to a rounding in the Epilogue to *Lyrical Epigrams*, written in early 2020. The sense of looming mortality is conspicuous, despite the fact that I had been declared in complete remission in early 2018. It was accentuated by the death, in early 2020, just before the cycle was completed, of her mother. That event is registered in my poem 'Blue velvet bag'. The concluding poems in that Epilogue, such as 'Listening to Chopin' and 'This book is Chauvet Cave', refer to my life more or less in the past tense, as something nearing its end. They close that cycle of poems as being a book I have left behind for Muse 1—or other future readers. I plainly had no idea of what was about to unfold.

Annus mirabilis

Two unexpected developments, both in 2021, would trigger the outpouring of poetry constituting Parts II and III. The reader will see, however, from the start of Part II, that the situation which suddenly developed in the late summer of 2020-21 was complicated. For reasons that the poems in Part II will make plain, the precise situation will go undescribed. The tone of address in the poetry changes dramatically from Part I to Part II. A wholly new and different encounter had occurred and had to be handled with some delicacy—poetically—with discretion.

No sooner had that been done (by April 2021), through the composition of a cycle I called *Delphic Deixis* (which constitutes Part II), than yet another situation unexpectedly developed (from July 2021). Muse 3 initiated contact from afar, as an admirer of my public writing and 'reputation' and so enchanted me that a totally unexpected romance has ensued. The challenge was twofold: she was in Paris and was the mistress of a powerful European businessman—himself married and with two young children. I refer to him in the poems as 'Douphol', based on Verdi's opera, *La Traviata*, in which there is a love triangle between Violetta Valery, Baron Douphol and the poet Alfredo Germont. Why had she contacted me? She longed for poetry and he, she explained, 'a man of large appetite' had 'no appreciation of poetry'. Thus it began.

This was as radically different from the second situation as from the first. In Part I there is a prolonged dialogue between two human beings who know each other well, have lived together, travelled widely together and have developed deep bonds of trust. In Part II, there is a solitary reflection about an abortive love in which the other party has rejected the poet. In Part

III, there is a very active dialogue and what becomes a deeply passionate romance, but between two people thousands of miles apart and one of them entangled in another relationship—itself adulterous.

This brought forth different poetry and a different mode of lyrical address than either Part I or Part II. Hence the title of Part III—Passion. Here, more than ever, the work of William Waters came to seem richly fruitful. I had re-read his book while writing both Parts I and II. I now turned to it once again, seeking to master the tonalities and subtleties of lyrical address. Half a dozen of the poems in *Delphic Deixis* evoke Rilke's poetry and Waters was my guide in finding a way to do this. Muse 3, however, was in passionate dialogue with me by text and phone and not simply inspiring but requesting and responding in detail to my poetry.

Through no design on my part, the set of contrasting personal experiences giving rise to all these poems followed a trajectory that led from conversation *about* poetry to deep immersion in the delicacies of *addressing* an absent, heedless muse who fled from me, to becoming the poet of a breathtaking and transcendently erotic, but physically distant muse simultaneously intimate with another man. It was this last development, in the winter of 2021, that led to the decision to publish all three cycles of poetry (as well as some three dozen poems written as far back as 2011) in the one volume. They have come to seem like an organic whole.

Muse 3 amazed and delighted me, in a manner that dissolved much of the debris left over from the days of my feckless poetic youth, including 'Rosaline', 'Juliet' and the sublime 'promiscuous beauty' of my book of sonnets—but also the antinomies and perplexities embedded in the experiences given expression in Parts I and II. It has been an intoxicating and liberating experience—and one that, as of this writing, is far from over. Just as this book was being edited into its present shape, she emailed me declaring, 'Each day for us, now, my poet, is an experiment in love'. I would like to think that Part III bears witness to that being, in fact, the case. It culminates in three longish poems celebrating her, while reflecting on the complexities of the situation we had placed ourselves in by declaring love for one another.

Muse 3 and the genesis of this book

As the sense deepened within me, while out walking one day in the early spring, that Muse 3 had become a unique and culminating experience, I improvised the following short poem for her, typing it straight into my phone and sending it to her, around the other side of the world, on the spot:

Romantic poets tend to die when young.
I could have done. I took my share of risks.
And, had I fallen, as I easily could,
Cut down by chance or my own hand,
I would have missed the time I've had with you,
Which, in its tangled splendour, has redeemed
The heartaches and the shattering defeats
Of youth and strife and standard aspirations.
And even recently there was rejection -
You have wept for it in Delphic ways -
Yet that rejection and its overcoming
Now seem like the mere theatrical
Prelude to your entering my life.
Or rather giving life, in such a way,
That poetry became the way I am.

She had loved the already complete cycle *Delphic Deixis*. Thinking that it had been written for her, she declared that it reduced her to tears. When she realized it had been written for another, she threw it in the bin in a fit of jealousy, only to retrieve it and confess 'You must know that this work in each and every part, is beautiful'. I laboured to persuade her that she was giving me a vastly richer experience than Muse 2 had done and was a dazzling muse herself. But I confessed to her that I was still worn down by illness and no longer young. 'I will breathe new life into you. I promise', she responded. Within the limits of the possible, she has truly done that.

Her love of poetry and languages (English, French, German and Latin), her vitality and her wonderful intelligence have made her a most extraordinary muse. I can't readily think of a poet who has had a better or more complete one—and I know the lives of the poets, going back millennia. Certainly neither Shakespeare nor Goethe had such a muse. And, as the poem 'Dante and Petrarch' spells out, I think I have been far more humanly fortunate with Muse 3 than those famous poets were with Beatrice or Laura. But for her appearance on the scene, the poetry for Muse 1 would have been published separately and that for Muse 2 perhaps not at all. It was the revolutionary impression on me made by Muse 3—and her own response to the poems written for Muse 2 but never shared with her—that gave me the idea for this book. Or, more precisely, it was Pasiphae who pointed out to me the possibility of such a book.

Neither Muse 3 nor I (nor Pasiphae, at first) had the faintest idea, last July or August, that her boldly reaching out to me, giving me the sound of her lovely voice out of the blue, would produce a cycle of 75 poems. After the first, tentative conversations, she asked could she see the cycle of 52 poems I'd only recently then written, which I had mentioned to her. She was deeply moved by them, to the point of tears, she confessed. From that point, there was no looking back. I became her poet, she my muse—to the growing annoyance of 'Douphol', as he slowly became aware of what was happening between us and how my poems, when she received them, would make her glow. That's the backstory to Part III.

This book as a whole is, however, a set of romances in poetry, not an autobiography. As they say in movies, what follows is 'based on a true story'. It is not, in itself, an account of that true story—or those three, very different true stories. Here all three stories are confined to poetry. The true story behind my 2006 book *Sonnets to a Promiscuous Beauty*—which took place in 1994-95, when I was working as an intelligence analyst—has never surfaced. The elements of it are buried in my personal journals and known only to a tiny number of intimate friends. So it shall be in this case, or these cases, given that there are three of them. That is not only because I intend to protect my personal privacy, but also because I respect that of the three women to whom these poems are addressed.

Poetry is, after all, the ornament and expression of a personal life; not the warts and all confession of the experiences that lie behind such ornamentation. They remain, in the nature of the case, obscure, not only because common decency and the privacy of my muses demands that this be so, but because one's own experience is ultimately unfathomable. The poems are essays in interpretation, where alternative or supplementary interpretations would always have been possible—not least by the women whom the poems address.

I know that the poems in Parts I and III have the explicit approval of Muses 1 and 3 and that both also admire the poems in Part II. Unfortunately, I have not been in a position to share Part II with Muse 2. She broke off communication without knowing they were being written and it would have been improper to send them to her in the circumstances. The poems, in each case, while open to interpretation and response, are intended to set a seal on things. Readers will, I hope, enjoy their surface and find their own depths in them. The private depths they have are intended to remain exactly that.

Paul Monk
Melbourne
30 October 2021

And you, oh my beloved songs, may you blossom and flourish,
Swaying in love's warm winds, rocked by their gentlest breath;
Chatter as those reeds did, and at last tell Rome all about us:
Tell of two lovers whose glad secret is secret no more.
–Goethe *Roman Elegies* XIII ll. 577-80 (1788)

A Poet is a nightingale who sits in darkness and sings to cheer its own solitude with sweet sounds; his auditors are as men entranced by the melody of an unseen musician, who feel that they are moved and softened, yet know not whence or why.
–Percy Bysshe Shelley 'A Defence of Poetry' (1821/1840)

The approach to death is an approach of the world to oneself, the encroaching of the world on the riddle of what it has meant, after all, to be someone—a question made urgent, perhaps made visible, only by the felt certainty of having to become no-one.
–William Waters *Poetry's Touch: On Lyric Address* (2003) p. 82.

Temple ritual

There was an ancient ritual, they say,
Belonging to the Cult of Aphrodite,
Whose practice takes us back to long before
Ascetic or self-flagellating sects
Slandered and suppressed the Queen of Hearts.

Devotees or adepts of the Cult,
According to the legends handed down,
If they desired to be initiated,
Had to bring an offering to the Temple:
Pork sausage, figs and fresh goat's milk.

Once within the Temple's sacred precinct,
The male initiand had to disrobe,
Then bring his gifts and lay them at the altar.
There the long-haired priestess would inspect
His proffered goods, while hailing Aphrodite.

Should his sausage, figs and milk pass muster,
The young initiand would then be guided,
To a perfumed pool for his ablutions,
Where nymphs would cleanse him for the Temple's use,
Anoint him and then lead him back to her.

Then he would, or so the legend tells,
Be taken by the priestess, at her pleasure:
A woman of extraordinary ilk,
With hair of gold, with eyes of emerald green,
Her skin like silk, her limbs both lithe and lean.

But should the adept's offering not find favour,
The supplicant was driven from the Temple,
Whipped and scorned by those same striking nymphs.

Then, crying 'Aphrodite!' in his pain.
Chastened, he'd reflect—and try again.

The priestess, on the opening day of spring,
Would, by custom, of the adepts choose
A fine, upstanding youth and, leading him
Within the inner confines of the Temple,
Bring him, at last, to her own secret room.

There, upon soft coverlets of wool,
She'd murmur to him Aphrodite's lore
And, when he thought he'd learned that lore in full,
Extend him, in the arts of love, some more:
The ecstasies and mysteries at the core

Of that eternal Cult, its source divine;
And, even as she did, would feed the youth
On Aphrodite's anchovies and wine,
That he would taste, not only hear, the truth,
Imbibing her deep wisdom, line by line.

Part one: Companionship

A: Darkness Over Love

We karyotes

How would life be?
Would it still be erotic,
Had it made you and me
Simply prokaryotic?[1]

Not very, I'd say—
Endless self-replication.
No cellular play
To exchange information

So, second my motion
As life bobs and floats
On the Archaean Ocean,
"We're eukaryotes!"

Will you carry oats,
If they come from me,
As we play wild motes
On a billion-year spree?

I'd love some from eu,
If eu sent them my way,
To refresh and renew
My own DNA.

Nutcracker man

Paranthropa went looking for Nutcracker Man,
Boisei, in the Oldowan Woods;[2]
She hadn't in mind a particular plan;
Just to get him to give her the goods.

Her Nutcracker man, a promising youth,
Sat gazing aloft at the Sun,
Delighted and even astonished, in truth,
On account of the thing he had done.

She found him, at last, by the Olduvai stream
She cooed to him sitting alone.
He turned to her slowly, as if in a dream,
And showed her a curious stone.

"I can see", Paranthropa then teasingly laughed,
"That I've caught you down here again knapping!
I admire, I suppose, your neat handicraft,
But you should be out hunting and trapping!"

Boisei was cut and, in some disbelief,
Exclaimed, "Oh, you're clueless, by Jimbo!
You'd be more impressed by my almond-shaped leaf
If you weren't such a Palaeobimbo!

I had thought that the genius of my chips and cuts
Would light up your mind and connect us;
But I see all you want is fresh meat and rich nuts.
Well, look here, I'm now *Homo erectus*!"

Fire and the wheel

I've loved you from the beginning,
With the simplest of gestures;
With inarticulate cries;
With unself-conscious mimicry.

I've loved you since the first fire-wielding,
When we yelled together at encircling beasts;
Feasted on fire-roasted insects and nuts;
Huddled round the flames in awe.[3]

Was that Eden, that long ago aeon;
As the hand formed and the inner eye,
The larynx and Broca's brain;
Before ever we sang to one another?

Or was Eden the time of hand-axes,
As all this came together,
In our hearths and hunting,
From old Andalusia to the Chinese rivers?

What years those were of wide exploring!
Eurasia was ours with new spears!
Exulting in our uncanny craft,
We wondered at what we were.

Our long days fell like forest leaves;
They endured like evergreens.
Our fire-circles lit the long nights;
Changing our dreams.

Were those shimmering years,
Those many hundred millennia
Before our love made music,
Truly our Golden Age?

Did you feel loved then,
As the wide seas rose and fell?
As the ice advanced and retreated?
As the giant forests shifted, again and again?

Or was it only later, only later,
That sentiment came and crooning;
Coaxed by oxytocin out of the flicker
Of long light under the waxing Moon?

Was I a caricature, to your mind,
Of all that was possible—possible—
For a singing hominid under the Sun?
Was I stone in need of shaping?

Ah! We buried each other many times,
Again and again with grief and ochre,
Over ages under the ageless stars,
From Jebel Qafzeh to Beringia.

Remember the times, sheltered from
The harsh climate shift in the north,
When we relished our little piece of Africa,
In Andalusia? Those idyllic coasts and caves?

But your love transformed me:
Your call for songs and stories;
Your playing to me on bone flutes;
Your vivid art of changing forms.

We shook the shackles of the ancient trees,
Hailed the Sky God with high hands;
We took to the open horizon;
Pitched bold camp on the stark steppe.

There, at last, you carved me into shape!
Your love cut antler into a figurine;
And I, deer hunter, roamed forth Gravettian,
Making long lasting legends on the plains.

You wove me a coat of wool,
Dyed in wondrous new colours,
Finer than any cured skin and
I revelled in your homespun beauty.

Even that was a long age of ardour,
Under the high wheeling stars;
Rich with rumour of far mountains,
With mammoth hunts and possibilities.

Then the revolution came at last: the wheel,
The mastery and mustering of horses,
The making of wains and war chariots,
The being of bright burnished bronze.

Ah, sky gods! The wheel and the horse
Brought an end to our long cycles!
Ah! My lover with golden hair,
The wheel set us rolling, riding, racing

In the chariot of the Sun, did it not?
Since then, everything has gone in a flash:
A riotous blur of songs and innovations;
A nightmare of blood and terror.

I've loved you from the beginning.
Let's not now go under the wheel.
All our myths are confused.
I long only for your beauty.

Circles in the dust

You went under the wheel, Archimedes;[4]
Pondering spheres and a theory of gravity;
Absorbed in the beauties of geometry;
Drawing fine circles in the dust.

Did you forget yourself, old man?
How could you think that a Latin sword,
Fired with rage at your machines
Would be withheld from your circles?

Or had you given up on the City,
Now swarming with the legions of Marcellus?
Had you given yourself over to pure thought—
Drawing those perfect circles in the dust?

You'd made mockery of Rome's big ships
And elaborately prepared siege engines:
With your artillery and hydraulic tricks,
You used its vessels to ladle the sea into your wine-cups.

You transcended the factions of Syracuse;
In the chaos of the Punic War;
Your mind was elsewhere, deep thinker;
Divining the workings of the real world.

Had you high hopes of Alexandria at that point:
Remembering conversations with Ctesibius,
Knowing the catalogues of Callimachus,
Reckoning with Aristarchus regarding the Sun?

You went under the wheel, Archimedes;
Pondering spheres and a theory of gravity;
Absorbed in the beauties of geometry;
Drawing fine circles in the dust.

Lucullus to Clodia[5]

I've built a house upon a hill—
The Pincian over Rome.
It's aspect's great and, if you will,
We'll make it our sweet home.

It's really quite a marvellous place,
With statues in the garden;
With trees and nymphs and lots of space
And patios and, pardon,

A library you'll not believe:
The finest books in Greek;
All catalogued. We can retrieve
Our choice and softly speak

Of any poet we desire
Within a leafy arbour.
'Til, stirred by an Aeolian lyre,
The longings that we harbour

Can issue in unbridled passion,
Upon the upper floors;
Where, in the most exotic fashion,
We'll recline behind closed doors.

I know you've other interests, lass,
Like gambolling and drinking;
But aren't these just a little crass?
Is it not time for thinking

Of all the subtler things in life
And all that we might share,
Were you to play my Pincian wife?
Come see. The house is there!

Cave and woman

Your tousled gold emotions,
White breasts and active thighs;
Your tongue's unfeigned devotions,
The fervor in your eyes,

Have summoned forth my darkened heart,
From deep within its cave,
Where it had painted ochre art,
Depicting it as brave.

It chanted long its lonely song
And dwelt beneath the ground,
Where ghosts of night and mourning throng
And hope cannot be found;

But somehow, down from unguessed light,
Your laughing passion thrown
Has cast to me a line of sight
To love that I might own.

So kiss me, kiss me, soft as breath,
Beside the ancient stream.
Withheld by you from senseless death,
I live once more and dream.

Aztec verses

He goes his way singing, offering flowers
And his words rain down
Like jade and quetzal plumes.
Is this what pleases the Giver of Life?
Is that the only truth on Earth?

From whence come the flowers that enrapture man;
The songs that intoxicate, the lovely songs?
Only from Ometeotl's home do they come,
From the innermost part of heaven.

Not forever on earth; only a little while here.
Be it jade, it shatters.
Be it gold, it breaks.
Be it a quetzal feather, it tears apart.
Not forever on earth, only a little while here.

Like a painting, we will be erased.
Like a flower, we will dry up, here on earth.
Like plumed vestments of the precious bird,
That precious bird with the agile neck,
We will come to an end.

Hymn to Ometeotl

Ometeotl, Cosmic King,
To you, Great God, these gifts we bring:
These hearts that beat with chalchihuatl,
Won for you in faithful battle.

Lord, who rules beyond the sky,
Accept them, on your altar high,
As offerings that will feed the Sun,
Lest light and order be undone.

Since time began, before the stars,
The strife between your sons that mars
The beauty of the truth you know
Has cast in tumult all below

As each, in turn, has quenched the light,
In reckless and remorseless fight,
With only intervals of peace,
In which one rules and warrings cease.

In Huitzilopochtli's strong domain,
We flourish, Lord, and will remain
The servants of the bright Fifth Sun
And nourish it, as must be done.

For sacred hearts in copal burned,
Sustain that Sun. Your priests have learned;
That this high ritual must not falter,
Here upon the highest altar.

Dance me on down from Toledo[6]

Come and dance with me down from Toledo,
By the light on the bridge we have made;
To a land with a non-Christian credo,
Where flamencos and tangos are played

Dance me speechless to high, snow-capped mountains
From which orchards and pastures are fed,
Then the cypresses, arches and fountains
Of Alhambra, the Isle of the Dead.

There the rich Andalusian muses
Sing softly to all who can hear,
Though a pallid, blue past still confuses
The mind and the heart and the ear.

For vengeful and dark Catholic violence,
Five centuries since, overthrew
And condemned to the grave or to silence
The voice of the Moor and the Jew.

But dance with me down from Toledo,
By the light on the bridge we have made;
To a land with a non-Christian credo,
Where flamencos and tangos are played.

Though golden al-Andalus perished,
Suppressed by the scepter and cross;
The ballads and songs Gypsies cherished
Plucked song lines from ruinous loss.

The spirit of Araby lingers,
In the genius of Spanish guitar;
In flamencos for feet and for fingers;
In Tarrega and in Falla.

Those flamencos and song lines in flower,
The soul of Granada reborn,
So offended the fascists in power
That they murdered poor Lorca at dawn.

Still, dance with me, down from Toledo,
By the light on the bridge we have made;
To a land with a non-Christian credo,
Where flamencos and tangos are played.

From there, let's dance on out of reason,
With our hearts full of Lorca's deep song;
Until beauty has come into season,
And we know that that's where we belong.

While we dance, let's sustain that illusion,
With whatever good faith we can find.
May our steps take us wide of confusion;
May our love keep us blissfully blind.

For to sing and to dance in our yearning,
To share our deep song face to face;
To glide into each twist and turning
Is to live with both freedom and grace.

And so, dance me on down from Toledo,
By the light on the bridge we have made;
To a land with a non-Christian credo,
Where flamencos and tangos are played.

Macondo mambo[7]

Melquiades, up and dance!
Come on, baby, take a chance.
Let's really go bananas!

Turn a trick, but watch the peel;
Show us, baby, how you feel;
And go, go, go bananas.

Hey, the Colonel's got the beat;
Amaranta's on her feet;
The cast has gone bananas.

Let the soldiers march and shoot;
It's Carnival, who gives a hoot?
It's time to go bananas.

Dance on down to Buenos Airs!
Coups and counter-coups, who cares?
The world has gone bananas.

Let it go in old Havana,
At the forties Tropicana,
With Prado's sweet bananas.

Or head to Franco's Barcelona,
Now the solitary owner
Of all your old bananas.

Roll those writer's saucy hips,
Let's hear mambo from your lips,
Til we all go bananas.

Melquiades, dance with me;
The country's heading out to sea.
It's time to go bananas.

The dream

Shadows, gloom, a red and white veined dark;
Muffled voices, murmurings, running, fear;
Horses gallop on a sunless plain; stark
Clash of angers; then—ah! ah!—the spear!

A wounded leg, a pallet and a chill;
Fevered tossing, winter heart and hut;
Lamed and lingering, flickering hope and will;
The limb and life-force fester quickly. Cut

To memories of a settled hearthside scene:
The eye, by fire, enlivening the hand
To carve from unknown bone a figurine—
A likeness hoped and longed for more than planned.

And then, above my fevered form, there swept
The kiss, the breast, the eyes—but—glassy stone;
Mute, I watched agape as those eyes wept,
For I was gone. The kiss stood there alone.

Thought, sharper than spear thrust; start—
Dream died and woke a succoured heart.

Lara[8]

Is it you who stands over the table of my years,
Flanked by masses of white lilac, cyclamen and cineraria?

Is it you who stands out for her casual beauty,
Among a crowd drawn dimly by my poetry and science?

Is it you whose presence fills the unceremonied silence,
In which only the flowers stand for singing and for psalms?

You are conversing with my brother, the watcher,
Learning of the long, coincidental meanings of our lives.

Ah! You exclaim in wonder at that late learning:
Is that really true? How astounding! How foreordained!

But have you guessed how my candle burned—
How my candle burned on the table of our winter's night?

Kiss me with that last kiss prescribed in the ritual!
Kiss me amid the white lilac, the cyclamen and cineraria!

Lean over me, shielding me with your whole being:
With your head, your breast, your heart, your loving hands.

Feel what a love ours was: how free, how pure,
How true to song and void of mere passionate necessity.

It transcended all around us in soaring scope:
Trees, clouds, sky, crowded streets—the wide world.

We made everything high and ravishing our own:
The open horizon, the myriad forms of beauty, the very Sun.

Cry freely now—abundantly—for the riddle of life,
The riddle of death, the beauty of genius, the winter of love.

But don't stand over me unable to live, in pitiful misery,
Thinking you can't go on, with your hair standing on end.

Above all, do not vanish somewhere, forgotten as
A nameless number on a list that has been mislaid.

This I want for you, after flowers and psalms:
A long life, rounded with the joy that I have been yours.

The poet's bell[9]

My love for you does not disperse
The virtues of myself or soul,
But rather the entire reverse:

It prompts me to express in verse,
My spirit's heartbeat, with the goal,
That thus my love will not disperse.

In doing so, I must rehearse
Both rhyme and metrical control,
Or bring about the mere reverse

Of music beauty and, what's worse,
Disordering the part or whole,
Imply my love could thus disperse.

In these brief stanzas, then, immerse
Yourself and play the critic's role;
Then turn—and play the charmed reverse.

This simple villanelle, though terse,
Might, like a poet's bell, then toll
Of love that, rather than disperse,
Regathers sound from each reverse.

You walk away[10]

You walk away—love's happiness and pain.
How shall I call you, call you back again?

My past, my life, my bliss, retreat behind that door.
I hear your footsteps slowly die away—
And fear that they will die for ever more.

You walk away—love's happiness and pain.
How shall I call you, call you back again?

I want to breathe you in as one breathes air,
Be absorbed and lose myself within
The beauty of your snow-white care

You walk away—love's happiness and pain
How shall I call you, call you back again?

I'm tortured by a sense of loss and cry
In anguish to the blank and heedless walls:
Always the question, why, why and why?

You walk away—love's happiness and pain.
How shall I call you, call you back again?

But then at night unearthly powers
Wake me to your presence in a dream—
Your presence from past days and vivid hours.

You walk with me, beloved, once again
And hark I call you 'Life'—and bitter pain.[11]

Your architect[12]

Your love is enough for my heart
And your wings for my freedom.

Your love has called to me,
From the Parthenon and Mount Athos.
It has had me hail tyrants
With visions of clearance.
It has built Ronchamp for the Sun.
It has drawn me through darkness.

Your wings have flown me to La Plata.
They have created a spectacular residence,
A jungle of courtyards and gardens,
Cantilevered roofs to shelter my longings,
Inspiring me to pitch my freedom
Outside the given ground

Your love is enough for my heart
And your wings for my freedom.

I yearned to rebuild Paris,
But your love took me elsewhere:
It had me hurl myself into New York;
It had me scorn the Ossete in his lair;
It had me leapfrog every setback
And take my exuberance to Chandigarh.

Your wings are our secret:
They free me to swim towards
The star we steer by;
Each stroke an act of worship,
Of light, of air, of sea—
And the hope of a right ending.

Your love is enough for my heart
And your wings for my freedom.

Proust and prolexia[13]

I suffer from prolexia—
An insidious disease:
When it comes to orthographic tasks,
My brain finds them a breeze.

This bothers me, as it may mean
That I am none too bright;
For Da Vinci, Einstein, Edison
Could barely read or write.

Dyslexic savants, it appears,
Prefer to think in pictures,
Leaving logocentric souls,
Like me, in mental strictures.

I learned all this, I hate to say—
Was it my loss or gain?—
By ploughing through (you guessed): a book
On reading and the brain.

It is a book you'll not forget,
It's called *Proust and the Squid*.
Its thesis may redraw me yet;
Revealing all that's hid.

Staying Seine

I've been at a table, not far from the Seine,
With Marcel and a bottle of wine.
I'd been there before, again and again,
But this evening he helped me refine

My take on old memories I cannot forget
And a doubt which insistently asks,
If your voice and your beauty are those of Odette,
Or if she's merely one of your masks.

I sat at a table at Les Deux Magots
And I glided like some kind of Swann
On the waters of memory (swiftly they flow):
The current that life moves upon.

With binocular vision,[14] I plucked from its banks
Red flowers one might call Odette-me-nots;
They're bright blooms of gratitude, perfumed with thanks;
Better far than mere fabled forget-me-nots.

They're for you, from this café on old Saint Germain,
Where I mused on Odette with Marcel;
On the poignant aromas of unassuaged pain;
And on pleasures one cannot foretell.

What fortunate hours of privileged repast,
A la recherché du temps perdu.
Now, cleansed and reordered, my psyche recast,
I can be far more present to you.

So that you will hear me[15]

So that you will hear me,
My words,
Like lithe chameleons,
Are changing shape and tone.

Before you touched them,
My words were murmured darkness
And cold stone;

But you soothed my psyche,
Persistently making murmurings light:
Lamps over the muttered.

Now I want my words
To say what I want
To say to you,
So that I will hear you say
That you want to hear me say them.

I want my words
To form a necklace of pearls
For your hidden self,
For your heart's throat.

Leaning into the long afternoons

Leaning into the long afternoons, I look seaward,
Full of memorious musing.

Out there, in the wide, turbulent currents,
My nefesh swims and dives;

It sights and brings high to the light to show you
Sparkling, many-colored things of beauty.

It revels and frolics, like a dolphin of the deep,
In the green and the blue of your regard.

And when the gulls circle closer to the stars,
It sighs with wonder and sings

Over the ancient, darkling sea, of its desire
To harvest you a necklace made of suns.

We have lost only a possible twilight

We have lost only a possible twilight.
No-one can see how our hands link at night,

Or how clear is the sky of our mutual longing,
Arcing over worlds and across all time.

We can see, through this window, a fiesta
Of possibilities, looming like mountains.

We have our piece of the Unconquered Sun:
It is the coin of our ancient realm.

I remember your laughter, catalyst of conquest;
Your musical capirote punishments.

You have urged me to song, beyond my horizons,
Ploughing up the Moon to make myths.

We are writing the book of time and meaning and
When I dream, it falls open at tantalizing pages.

Losing Neruda

I lost Neruda in the cold—
Misplaced him in the rain;
But look! I found a thing of gold—
No—better—think again:
I found the truth of things.

Is that claim simply far too bold?
Can any human brain
Think that and not be merely sold
A bill of goods in vain?
The truth of things?!

Yes, the ruth, sooth and tooth of things;
The root and the stem and the grain;
A sense of their seeds and their springs
And all that that brings in its train:
The simple truth of things.

They are, it's only we who ache,
Bewildered, to belong;
We who, for our longing's sake,
Make poetry and song.
That's the truth of things!

But ah! What plenitude is there,
For those with eyes to see,
With opened selves to build and care
And less to have than be!
Such is the truth of things.

Yes, the ruth, sooth and tooth of things;
The root and the stem and the grain;
A sense of their seeds and their springs
And all that that brings in its train:
The simple truth of things.

This came to me one winter's day,
When, hearing quite alone
Sinatra's 'If You Go Away',[16]
I saw that I had grown
Into the truth of things.

But, truly, it was not the song
That had me feel so true.
It was the sense that I belong,
Affirmed, through loving you,
In the truth of things.

Yes, the ruth, sooth and tooth of things;
The root and the stem and the grain;
A sense of their seeds and their springs
And all that that brings in its train:
The simple truth of things.

Manuela, my love[17]

Manuela, Manuela, Manuela, my love,
Remember our valley, the clear sky above.

I remember our autumn,
Our fall in the South;
The light in your eyes,
The love in your mouth;

But you asked, lovely bird,
What I could not deny,
'Let me wing on my way,
Give me freedom to fly!'

I was awed by your spirit,
In love with your wings;
And said in response:
'We are made for such things!

Your hopes must be fertile,
Your nefesh set free;
So go, with my blessing,
And fly far from me.'

In response, you delivered
An exquisite blow
That shaped down the grain
How the future might go:

You'd now be my muse.
I was struck to the bone!
You had shattered to sharpness
The starkness of stone

You opened a clearing
Beneath the bright sky,
Where I'll not knap alone,
To no point, 'til I die:

A clearing for planting
The hopes of the heart in;
Where new autumns loom
For us two to part in.

Manuela, Manuela, Manuela, my love,
Remember our valley, the clear sky above.

The bell and the choir[18]

There are hymns to be heard
On the Isle of the Dead,
Or such is the word
That is still being spread:

Neither brimstone nor fire,
As threatened of old;
But an angelic choir
With voices of gold.

The singing will start
With a high, ringing bell
And conclude with a chant
That will solemnly tell

Of salvation history,
Wonders made plain,
And of life's inner mystery,
Its glory and pain.

Our labors well done,
Past the portals of night,
We'll rejoice in the One
And repose in His sight.

Oh, if life would end so,
On that Isle in the West,
Under Evenstar's glow,
Then I'd go to my rest.

But we all should beware
Of the Sirens of death
And resist going there,
While still we have breath.

For in truth all the Muses
Of rest and delight
Demand that one chooses
The noon, not the night.

The bell and the choir,
The chanting of story,
To be heard all require
The world's 'passing glory'.

So, I'll not dream of songs
On the Isle of the Dead,
But proclaim what belongs
To the living instead.

For I am a being
Of flesh and of bone,
Not a soul that is fleeing
To star and to stone.

It is here, it is here
And not in the West,
That what touches the ear
Can make it feel blest.

It's through metaphors drawn
From our love of the world
That our souls are reborn
And our hopes are unfurled.

And so we conceive,
With extravagant eye,
An eternal reprieve
For all those who die.

Too often this tends
To a fervid belief
That the visionary bends
To delusion and grief.

So, though we must die,
Let us love while we may,
The light in the sky,
The sensations of day.

Let life be renewed
By the joys that we find,
In what saints have construed
As the 'world' of our kind.

Our religion should nourish
The flowers and trees;
The creatures that flourish
In the skies and the seas.

Our solemnest vow
Of our purpose and worth
Should centre on how
We have sprung from the Earth.

Nor should we yet long
To flee from this green,
With the thought we belong
In places unseen.

For indeed we do not,
But have gardens to tend,
On our aqueous plot
At the Milky Way's end

Let's cherish, then, all
Of the gifts of the Muses
No longer in thrall
To the One who refuses

To grant us surcease
From predation and strife,
Except through release
From the pleasures of life;

And with Orphic intent,
With sublime orchestration,
Spend all we've been lent
In the brilliant creation

Of a culture profound,
With its halls full of song,
In which will resound
The cry, 'We belong!'

Ah, that is an Isle,
Of cypresses high,
Where I'd live well awhile,
Then peacefully die.

Thanks for the thread, Ariadne[19]

Thanks for the thread, Ariadne
Ariadne, O thanks for the thread
Without you, I'd be dead, Ariadne;
So, thanks, O thanks for the thread.

I was sent on a boat to old Knossos,
Like many a poor youth before.
The elders had decided to toss us
Into Minos's cavernous maw.

I was feckless and dumb, like the others;
And would, therefore, have gone to my grave;
But you urged me to think of my druthers,
Think quickly, be cunning and brave.

You had no time yourself for King Minos;
Did not like your old man at all;
So, you gave me the eye to align us,
Then slipped me gold thread in a ball.

Ah! Thanks for the thread, Ariadne.
Ariadne, O thanks for the thread.
Without you, I'd be dead, Ariadne;
So, thanks, O thanks for the thread.

You knew—I did not—Ariadne,
Of the dark in the Minotaur's maze.
Unassisted, the brute would have had me
And gnawed on my entrails for days.

But I laid the gold thread that you gave me,
As I stole through the cavernous black;
Then, knowing the trail laid would save me,
Slew the monster and found my way back.

Ariadne, O Ariadne,
Ariadne O,
Thanks, thanks so much for the thread.
Ariadne, O Ariadne,
It's not me, but the bull that is dead.

Thanks for the thread, Ariadne.
Ariadne, O thanks for the thread.
Without you, I'd be dead, Ariadne;
So, thanks, O thanks for the thread.

That Minotaur won't kill again,
I hit the horned beast to the max.
I broke his skull and spilled his brain,
With a handy old ritual axe.

Let's make our escape, Ariadne;
Run off to some balmy Greek island;
Then, after we've laughed and you've had me,
Come back to Athens, to my land.

Thanks for the thread, Ariadne.
Ariadne, O thanks for the thread.
Without you, I'd be dead, Ariadne;
So, thanks, O thanks for the thread.

Ariadne, O Ariadne,
Ariadne O,
Thanks, thanks so much for the thread.
Ariadne, O Ariadne,
It's not me, but the bull that is dead.

Lullaby for Junius[20]

Little Lumpkin Junius
Sit lala on my knee
And I will sing a song to you
Of how to human be

Little Lumpkin Junius,
Oh apple of my eye,
You'll need to transform everything,
Then bid it all bye-bye.

You see, my dandled darling one,
To sing the thing quite plain,
The loving world I've placed you in's
Completely in the brain.

Your papa's conjured up a world
Of memories, hopes and dreams
To play with Little Lumpkin in,
But little's what it seems.

You'll find, as you reach out for it,
That much of it recedes;
You'll have to make it all again,
Consistent with your needs.

But sing lala with Papa now
And grin and clap your hands;
There's time enough, when you grow big,
For making future plans.

Little Lumpkin Junius,
Sit lala on my knee
And I will sing a song to you
Of how to human be.

Little Lumpkin Junius,
Oh apple of my eye,
You'll need to transform everything,
Then bid it all bye-bye.

Fusion[21]

Hold me now, as Astor would,
His sweet bandoneon
And let us dance as if we could
Just tango on and on.

Dance with me as Frida did,
With Tina—Ashley Judd,
As if we're both in Mexico,
With tango in our blood.

Press yourself right into me,
With fire in your eyes.
Set every vital passion free,
As Gardel's voice denies

That we will ever be apart,
Or subject to confusion;
But will be blended heart with heart,
Achieving deathless fusion.

I'll dance upon Jean Jaures street,
Tu Buenos Aires Querido.
And then we'll fly, with winged feet,
To Granada, from Toledo.

Kiss me, kiss me, long and deep,
For life and dance are flying.
The time will come when we must keep
Appointments, each, with dying.

Oh hold me, then, as Astor would,
His sweet bandoneon;
And dance with me as if we could,
In fusion, tango on.

Ovid's metamorphoses[22]

Everyone, it's safe to say
Is clear where fabled Rome is;
But few in our—or Ovid's—day
Could tell you much of Tomis

'Twas on the Euxine.
Who-xine?
Puke-scene!
A place of little promise

But there it was that Ovid went,
Punished for an error;
Well, went is not quite right—was sent
But Augustus, the Emp-error.

He was sent to the Euxine!
Who-xine?
Puke-scene!
A place of cold and terror

The pretext was *The Art of Love*
A book that Ovid wrote,
Which was declared, from high above,
To be pernicious smut.

So, off to the Euxine!
Who-xine?
Puke-scene!
For the Boss had had a gut

Full of Ovid's frivolity,
Obscenity, jollity;
Toying with morals,
For poetic laurels.

Off, off to the Euxine!
Who-xine?
Puke-scene!
It's the Boss that wins such quarrels.

When the Boss man and poet
Tangle in quiet,
It's over, you know it—
The promiscuous riot

The poet is off to the Euxine!
Who-xine?
Puke-scene!
On a very much simpler diet

But there Ovid, alone, in a place very strange,
Cut off and deprived of his pleasures,
Reflected and learned and started to change
And harvested poetic treasures

On the Euxine!
Who-xine?
Puke-scene!
In hexameters—Homeric measures!

Yes, though out in the dreary Euxinian cold,
The poet refused to stop writing.
He compressed what he felt in elegiac mould,
Letting beauty do all of his fighting.

From the Euxine!
Who-xine?
Puke-scene!
And the beauty is lastingly biting!

He wrote the *Metamorphoses*,
Or rendered it complete;
And sang, with fabled Orphoses,
In face of love's defeat.

On the Euxine!
Who-xine?
Puke-scene!
This the Boss could not delete!

And so we read our Ovid still
To conjure transformation;
We love him for his magic quill
And exiled lucubration.

Upon the Euxine—
Who-xine?
Puke-scene!—
He achieved transfiguration.

Orpheus among the stones

Clear the dark and let the green emerge!
And be that there is Orpheus.

Upon the carven space of sunlit green,
Then pluck the lyre of ages.

And so recite the litany of trees.
Until they form a temple.

Summon into it the flocks of birds
To form a winged chorus

That, circling round, will rouse the very stones
And so the Earth enliven.

Then sing a song in tune with all that is
Within that hallowed place;

Until it be for Orpheus and his spouse
A clearing for the sacred act of love.

Sappho and Alcaeus[23]

Ah! Sappho, Sappho, glancing back at me,
You know I know, your eye and posture tell;
That, though you drink from Anactoria's well,
It's only I who understands; that we

Sibling seedlings, sprung from Orpheus' head,
Uniquely draw from Heliconian springs;
That only I, when all your girls are fled,
Will share with you an ecstasy of strings;

Of summoned forms, of new, exquisite sounds,
Aeolian moods exhaled upon the lyre;
Mixolydian passions without bounds
That, come a thousand years, will still inspire

Every light-filled mind that knows the Muses;
That longs to touch the trembling hand and face
Of absent loves; which contemplates and chooses
Evocative recall, by Arion's grace.

Here, upon Terpander's music isle,
We've lived and loved and, see what songs we've made!
But—ah, your gaze!—I'd linger yet a while,
Before the light and longing falter, fade.

Cleis Scamandros[24]

Dark Cleis sat across the room from me.
She shared her table with some learned Greeks.
My eye was caught by flowers in her hair—
And then I caught her eye

That night we dined and spoke of Sappho's verse.
She led me deep within the labyrinth.
She told me that the Popes burned Sappho's books,
And saying so she sighed.

"Come to Mytilene", she then breathed
"You can join me on a boat, if you so choose.
I'm going to research the ancient songs
Of the only mortal Muse."

We climbed through cypress groves, up from the port,
To where they staged the comedies of old,
And sat beneath the trees with Lesbian wine,
At noon in flowering spring.

She murmured, then, 'Eressos' in my ear;
And, once there, told of Lilley's play,
Of Sappho's silence, Phaon's spotless vow.
She urged I learn these lines.

The evening was beguiled in her soft lounge,
Where, after drinks, she put some music on:
An opera: 'Gounod's *Sappho*', she announced,
And asked me of my loves.

I lost myself, in wine-enchanted talk,
Of all the great Dembowskis of my life:
Their beauty, their intelligence, my loss.
She lay and urged me on.

Tell me more, she breathed, of your desire;
Of why these long-haired lovelies turned you down,
And whether they have quite put out your fire.
Oh tell me everything!

I told her of the greatest of my loves:
Of Catriona, Nathalie, and Weili Wu,
And then I spoke of Buenos Aires and you—
While she removed her clothes.

In retrospect, she'd played me like a lyre
And how could mortal man resist such hands?
The conversation turned to her desire
To sate my pent-up needs.

Her long hair tossing, wild and open mouthed,
She told me that she thirsted for my seed,
And fell on me with reckless, ardent kisses.
My manhood stood up well.

For all my recent weariness in Austin,
For all my chaste and funerary vows,
I could not flee like Phaon from her snare.
We coupled then till dawn.

Those hours on Lesbos will not quickly fade.
The taste of Cleis lingers on my tongue.
But when, at last, the Sun had risen high,
She washed and bade me leave.

Be quick, she urged, your craft will leave at noon.
White flower petals rain upon my heart.
I've swallowed all your loss and grief and fear,
But now you must depart

And so I left bright Sappho on the coast,
Of bitten mouth, of shouts and twining limbs,
Of copulation fraught with life and force—
And took to sea again.

Part one: Companionship

B: The Seven Songs of Queen Nefesh[25]

Song of friendship

O Seshat, whose mysteries form characters,
O Thoth, whose stone this is,
Sing, through me, and move my hand to make
An ode, an ode of Naqada,
A song of the companionship
Between the divine Horus, your servant Raneb,
He of the red crown and of the white,
And his consort Nefesh,
She who is breath and life.
An ode, an ode of Naqada.
An ode to the two companions,
In the valley of the great river,
Where they walk, O Seshat, under the eye,
Under the outspread wings, O goddess,
Of the falcon; the wings of the falcon.

Song of joy

Rejoice, rejoice, my beloved,
In this day of days;
For the harvest is ours and the garden of life,
Even in Memphis; Memphis of the kings,
In the Halls of the North,
In the days of our youth and our love.
Dance for me in the high room.
O dance for me to my heart's delight,
Beloved of my years.
Rejoice, rejoice, my beloved,
In this day of days;
When Raneb, your hunter, has returned,
Like an arrow leaping from the bow,
Out of the lands above the cataracts,
To the place of our youth and our love.

Song of comfort

Lord Ptah, creator, master of those who make;
Lord Ptah, high god of Memphis;
O Ptah, spouse of Sekhmet,
She of the fearful ravages,
She, the lioness of the hunted day,
Intercede with your beloved, O master,
That she will spare our blood and our seed.
O send us the priests of Sekhmet,
Healers of the cankered flesh;
The priests of Sekhmet, your beloved:
She, the lioness of the hunted day,
She of the fearful ravages,
O Ptah, spouse of Sekhmet,
Lord Ptah, high god of Memphis,
Lord Ptah, creator, master of those who make.

Song of knowledge

Sing, Thoth, sage of the night sky.
Sing of number and form.
Sing of Atum, spirit of the pre-existent,
Afloat in Nun, the primal sea.
Sing of Neith of the seeded ocean.
Sing of Ra and the coming of day.
Sing, O Thoth, sage of the night sky,
You, Thoth, keeper of the Hermetica, sing.
Tell of Geb and the parting of waters.
Tell of Nut and the wideness of the world.
Tell, O Thoth, of those who are aloft,
Over the formed and founded Earth.
Tell of the Sia, the thought of Ra.
Tell of Ma-at, the order of Pharaoh.
Sing, Thoth, sage of the night sky.

Song of religion

Behold, Nebra, called Lord of the Sun,
Does homage to the great god Ra.
Raneb bows to the Sia of Ra,
Bows to the wide horizon of his light.
Let the temples ring with a new song.
Let the cult of the bull,
The cult of Apis, the bull god,
Give way to the worship of Ra;
The cult of Apis give way.
Let blood give way to the great light.
Let there be obeisance to Ra the Creator.
Bow to Him who rises out of the Atum.
Bow, all, before the Sia of Ra.
Do homage to the great god Ra,
In the name of Raneb, servant of Ra.

Song of love

Arise, my beautiful one, my lord Min.
Arise as Horus, the falcon.
Arise as Ra out of the sea.
For I am Neith, goddess of the primal waters.
Arise and come into me, my lord Min.
Arise, swift falcon, on wings of urgency;
As the Sia of Ra, come unto me,
For I am the companion of your heart,
Who walked with you even over the ash,
Even over the first lands.
Who came up with you out of the south,
In the day before days.
In me is the salt and water of life,
In me is the fullness of your desire.
Arise, O my beautiful one, my lord Min.

Song of healing

I have healed you with my breath.
With my hands and those of my sister Nepthys
Have I brought you back from the House of Death.
For you are my beloved.
You are my beloved, even from the womb;
The womb of our mother the Sky,
Seeded by our father the Earth.
Therefore are you remembered.
From the sarcophagus of Set,
From the pillar in a pagan palace,
From the shattering of your limbs,
I have brought you back, with my hands
Isis has brought you back
With the perfume of her breath,
For you are her beloved.

Part one: Companionship

C: Lyrical Epigrams

Prologue

How to use our tongues

There is a passage in *The Odyssey*,
In which the beauties of Icmalius' chair
Are brought before our eyes;
Almost so that we, in wonderment,
Like it's fabled footrest,
Find ourselves mortised in the frame,
Draped with a heavy fleece
And listening, as Penelope
Instructs her house help, Eurynome,
To seat the guest for story.

Imagine that fine Icmalian craft
And conjure, in your mind, the scene in which
Penelope, in her own voice declares
'I wish our guest to tell his story whole
And patiently to hear me out, as well,
As I'll be full of questions, point by point.
I want him, seated in our polished chair,
To tell me of his travels, in good time.
For this stranger, who has come into our halls,
May know somewhat of Odysseus himself.'

All poetry is such an Icmalian chair:
Its music mortised into practiced frames;
Mellifluous rhyme and artful assonance
Cast over it, like Homer's softened fleece.
Through aeons, both these crafts have been refined,
Since earlier than Gilgamesh or Ur;
And they have fitly shaped the conversation,
From Pindar's odes to Martial's epigrams,
Of all that we call prosody or verse—
And taught us better how to use our tongues.

Hamlet and then some

Have you ever, like the Prince of Elsinore,
Held a human skull before your eyes
And had not morbid thoughts, but something more;
Not clichés fixed on how a person dies,
But dwelling on what human skulls are for?

My favoured treatise on this weighty theme,
The Evolution of the Human Head,
Utterly eclipses Shakespeare's meme.
It's not the kind of book you'd take to bed,
But page by page, it's scholarship's a dream.

It grounds our grasp of what we have in hand,
Exquisitely, in natural selection,
Enabling us to gradually understand,
Through reading and re-reading and reflection,
That skulls are tinkered things—evolved, not planned.

The human skull's unique, in crucial ways,
Our brains five times as large, by body size,
As mammals of our own or other days.
We've foreheads and no snout; unusual eyes;
An external nose projecting from our face.

The wonderment that we should properly feel,
In contemplating all this book contains—
A century of researches, which reveal
The long formation of our skulls and brains—
Pivots on the way it makes us real.

When you and I behold each other's features,
Or mutually caress each other's faces,
We ought to see and feel our past as creatures:
The hominin marvels, the vestigial traces
Of ancient pasts that only science reaches.

The long summer

We live, beloved, at the complex height
Of what the scholar Brian Fagan dubbed
The Holocene Long Summer, since the Ice.

The implications of all this are stunning—
For religion, for our histories and for science.
Yet few, among our fellow human beings,

Have as yet acquired the flimsiest knowledge
Of the revolution that has taken place
In geo-science, just within our lifetimes.

Today, for instance, we can say it's known
That there have been at least nine glacial eras,
Broken, every hundred thousand years,

By relative respites, called inter-glacials;
Which last, on average, just ten thousand years;
But ours has lasted half as long again.

The Vostok ice core, from Antarctica,
Allows us to infer that we have flourished
Chiefly in that half as long again.

Yet now we learn that that mere flourishing
Has itself brought quite disturbing change;
Which, we're informed, could bring us all undone.

What are we to make of this new finding,
Even as alarums ring world-wide,
Of global over-warming, caused by wealth?

Before the onset of the said long summer,
No humans lived in lasting settlements,
Or cultivated fields, or tended kine;

But the summer caused our numbers to explode:
Our technologies, our factories and our yields;
And now we must learn fast, before the fall.

Emily Dickinson

You've said you really don't much care
For the stitched up, private verse
Of Emily Dickinson, quiet recluse;
Or, to be strictly fair,
It's her lot for which you have no use.

What leaps to mind, from this refusal—
Or so it's always seemed to me—
Is more the fear of her seclusions
Than critical recoil, upon perusal,
From her epigrams or stark conclusions.

Terence Davies' film, *A Quiet Passion*,
And Helen Vendler's detailed commentaries[26]
Have captured her, in all her fraught concision—
Her loneliness, her wit and her precision—
What you reject is just the first of these.

Consider, though, the way in which she chose
To read, to think, to craft, until—knows,
With Shakespeare and the Bible as her foils,
She miraculously wrung essential oils
From all her griefs—the perfume from the rose.

She lacked all other outlets—that's agreed—
And which of us, with wider choice, would choose
To suffer what she did and take her lead?
Yet lead she did, devising subtle screws;
And so, secured the murmurings of her Muse.

Dickinson accomplished, Vendler shows,
What each of us should, properly speaking, will:
To be able to conceive and to compose,
By moonlight to creatively distil
The poignancies that heart and mind disclose.

Extrafloral nectars

There was, a century since, a botanist,
Whose work has been neglected and forgotten,
Who corresponded, quite extensively,
With the master naturalist, Charles Darwin,
On what to make of extrafloral nectars;
But their views were diametrically opposed.

Now, why would I, my extra floral love,
Given our extensive correspondence,
Raise this subject here, in poetry;
Dig up Federico Delpino,
As if he held allure for you or me;
As if his memory promised pollination?

Well, Delpino, don't you know, advanced a theory—
Neatly published in a monograph—
About the lure of myrmecophilous plants
(Three thousand species being listed),
Which use their honied extrafloral nectars
To entice, addict and subjugate the ants.

Ants, of course, are drawn to floral nectars,
Since nothing attracts insects more than sugar;
But many other subtle chemicals
Within these nectars, such as alkaloids,
Manipulate the guileless myrmeces
And render them the servants of the plants.

Your extrafloral nectar, sweetest love,
Like the decoctions of Acacia plants,
Those master myrmecophilous ant-seducers,
Drew me to you; but your alkaloids,
Your subtler charms, are what addict me
To generating verse—as your Delpino.

Before they cleaned you up

Just weeks before you emerged,
In the usual helpless manner—
Before they cleaned you of blood and fluid
And cut your umbilical chord
And placed you at your mother's breast—
I was taking summer holidays and reading
Of the Great Terror and the killing
Of countless thousands—tens, hundreds—
In the name of 'revolution';
Fascinated by the great purge trials
The Georgian monster concocted—
Framing up his 'Trotskyite clique'
Of traitors and conspirators
That riddled the raddled Party and its organs;
Peering, leering, squinting,
(From behind his judicious curtain)
As the broken fools confessed
And the craven judges shouted,
Again and again, as if it set free
Some avenging god from the,
Let's say 'the dark side of the force':
'Shoot the mad dogs!'
That was my summer holiday;
My initiation at twelve into...
Shall we say 'reality'—starkness.
Only weeks before you sucked
The milk of life in innocence
And opened your little eyes
To gaze upon unhappiness and love—
In preparation for our meeting.

Treasure magazines

My mother gave me many magazines;
Most notably the newly published *Treasure*,
Whose vivid pictures helped me take the measure,
From childhood until my early teens,
Of the history of—well, the motherland.

Should she have told me of some other land?
Of this continent, perhaps, of droughts and rains;
Its ancient peoples and their searing pains;
Being colonized and laid low by disease,
As waves of our lot swept in—from the motherland?

Another magazine was *Look and Learn*,
But *Treasure* was my well-beloved island;
And, most of all, the tales of all the waves
Of those who swept across the northern seas
To the smaller, greener—other—motherland.

I looked upon the Stone Henge as it rose
And Bronze Age culture beautifully emerging.
I marvelled at the Celts and Romans warring
And how old Vortigern naively chose
To call the Saxons in, at someone's urging.

I watched, intrigued, as Arthur tried restoring
Some vestige of Romano-Celtic times;
How Alfred fought the fierce invading Danes
And Harold, with his fated Saxon thanes,
Succumbed to Norman conquest, rule and crimes.

The history of this childhood motherland
Extended down to Cromwell's parliament.
The coloured pictures made me understand
That thrones and fated kingdoms came and went—
Over there—while, on Australia's strand...

Uncanny gift

How does a boy of eleven years,
Not yet out of elementary school,
Still in short trousers,
With voice unbroken, chin unbearded,
Find himself irresistibly drawn
To books like Deutscher's *Stalin*?

Yet I was and look back now in wonder
At the very copy gifted at my own
Request, no less, by young parents:
Yes, signed over, in all innocence,
This dark weight—'Happy birthday,
Love from Mummy and Daddy'.

From Mummy and Daddy with love,
On a famous Trotskyist rendering
Of that tyrant's monstrous life?
What possessed the boy to ask;
His parents to so lightly give,
A gift of this portentous nature?

It wasn't a whim on the child's part;
That's clear, since he—my junior self—
Had autonomously reached out already
And bought himself the life of Mao,
And Werth's De Gaulle, into the bargain—
And Moses Finley on the ancient Greeks!

That was uncanny enough in a child,
One has to say, pondering such purchases now;
But the giving—with 'love'—of *Stalin*?
That quite takes an old man's breath away!
That's why I've always kept the battered book,
Long superseded, in awe and wry wonderment.

Section one

A Pageant of History

The truth is that the said 'uncanny gift'
Had had, three years before, its premonition:
A history book whose lavishness would shift
My gaze, my dreams, my schoolboy's disposition;
Making me quite pert.

Pert in that I peered, you understand,
From tale to tale with ever keener eyes,
Absorbing from the etchings that I scanned
What it might take to grow up worldly-wise,
Making me ex-pert.

The scope of this red book was truly stunning;
Vastly more than that put out by Mao:
Two thousand years of British wit and cunning
In more than sixty essays, showing how
The modern world was shaped:

From Caesar's rise right up to World War Two,
With pieces on the Bible and St Paul,
With Dante, Shakespeare, Clive and Winston, too
With Britain's many monarchs, one and all,
And so much more besides.

The photos, etchings, maps, were black and white,
Unlike the vivid ones in primary colours
In earlier books, they challenged my insight
By sombrely portraying history's dolours:
It's oceans, storms and tides.

> Its longest essay diagrammed the story,
> From witans and from moots to modern acts
> And laid before my mind the sober glory
> Of how we got a parliament—the facts:
> Why liberty abides.

The taste for books

You and I succumbed, from early childhood,
To the affliction that the droll Virginia Woolf
So mordantly suggests must have infected
The colourful Orlando in his cradle,
Wafted out of Greece and Italy
In the floating spoor of asphodel;
The bane of knightly vigour and ambition,
Of pedigree and masterful volition,
Enfeebling hand and eye and noble tongue,
Sapping vital instincts in the young.

The love of literature is a disease,
Slyly quoth that Woolf in writer's clothing,
Which, of its fatal nature, substitutes
A phantom for reality, such that
The likes of the young baronet Orlando
Lose any sense of their inheritance
And so neglect their pleasures and their duties,
Besotted by the squiggles on a page,
That the lordship and the fortune they've been gifted
Dissolve, among their books, into a mist.

Yet it has been quite otherwise with us,
Who, lacking lordship of Orlando's kind,
And granted strong immunities from birth
To those conceits that addle noble brains,
Absorbed into our blood the potent spoor
And turned the fateful germ of asphodel,
Which so depletes the force of feudal houses,
Into the stuff of our transcendent dreams:
Of well-informed and boldly free opinions—
A greater wealth than manors or dominions.

Report card

For years I kept a simple envelope,
In which were filed, for some posterity,
My school reports from Prep until Year Twelve.

They all, of course, record an easy passage—
No hint of failure, or scholastic stumbles.
Quite the contrary, at every little step.

You arrived some thirty years on
And didn't need such records to infer
That then and ever after I'd excelled.

And yet, unbidden angel from above,
Alighting, beyond any expectation,
In my sad, resistant shadowlands;

It was you who brightly lauded my achievement
As fantastic, in a way I couldn't see—
In awe of all my hoarded shells and pearls:

The classics and deep studies, old and new,
Which, as one old acquaintance once exclaimed,
Dealt with every subject known to man;

And which I, with proud disconsolation,
Called the remnant Alexandrian
Museum of my earthly aspirations.

Only now, in mellow retrospect,
Has it occurred to me that one report—
My teacher's summing up of my Year Three—

Provides a clue, in simple gravitas,
To the disconsolation you discovered:
The boy, she wrote, has the ability

To do quite well, provided that he learns
To focus on the subject that's in hand.
Not this idiot savant! Understand?

Little Marco

The picture books of Lawrence Peach—
John Kenney's pictures chiefly—
Filled my childish mind with coloured dreams
Of exotic countries and far off times—
Beginning with Marco Polo.

Travelling much, in intervening years,
I've marvelled, more than ever, as an elder,
At his images of Caesar and of Alfred;
Of Harry at Agincourt, Nelson at Trafalgar—
But, not least, of little Marco Polo.

The very opening pages show the boy,
Crouching nimbly on the Venetian docks,
At the age I was when gaping first at him;
Looking with round-eyed wonder
At Chinese characters on a bale of silk.

'Little Marco Polo,' Peach intoned,
'Whose father was a merchant, often stared
At the queer Chinese or Arabic writing',
Pondering, as did I, from whence
These bales of wonder had derived.

Niccolo, his father, brought the bales
From the rim of the Euxine Sea,
Which Jason crossed, in fables, long ago;
But they'd come from farther, Peach related:
On the longest road from the farthest Eastern lands.

The ancient Silk Road led to Xanadu,
To the awesome Mongol courts of Kublai Khan;
And there, Peach showed, the youthful Marco went,
While I, all eyes, went with him on his journey
And, aye, have done, on all my travels since.

Beyond the borders

I think my path was laid when I was ten:
When I first heard 'The Shadow of the Past',
Which awed my ears, with things beyond my ken;
And, from that time, has held my childmind fast—
Recurring ever in my dreams again.

Beyond the River bordering the Shire
There called the Wild, outside its homely edges;
The lure of mountains high and ever higher
And Elvish books that made me solemn pledges
Of knowing the tale of Middle-earth entire.

Frodo looked at maps and so did I,
Fascinated by their empty spaces;
For Shire maps intrigued the curious eye,
Displaying mostly white in foreign places;
Provoking a young hobbit's mind to pry.

But ventures out beyond were long delayed;
The interim spent in questioning dwarves and elves,
Or other strangers who had haply strayed
Within the Shire's bounds—to salve themselves
Against the Dark that on white spaces preyed.

Those refugees told many a direful tale
That Frodo pondered at his Bag End hearth.
They spoke of things to make a hero quail:
Of lengthening shadows over Middle-earth
And fears that soon, at last, the West would fail.

Little of this, of course, had reached the ears,
Of ordinary hobbits in the Shire;
Much less the Ring, the sum of Gandalf's fears,
Or Frodo's need to find the Mount of Fire.
But these things shaped my mind in after years.

Christina Hardyment's novel houses

Christina Hardyment writes curious books;
She started years ago with *Dream Babies*,
On childcare from Locke to Doctor Spock.
She then wrote ones on common household work,
Domestic comforts, British eating habits;
Thereafter, one on valorous Malory,
Composer of the epic of King Arthur;
As well as an official guide to Oxford,
A recent one on pleasures of the table
And one on how to write about the Thames.

But now she's written one called *Novel Houses*,
Which really is a connoisseur's delight.
Published by the splendid Bodleian Library,
It's one I've journeyed through in bed at night.
From Horace Walpole's *Castle of Otranto*
To the Hogwarts School in Rowling's *Harry Potter*,
Via *Mansfield Park* and *Waverley*,
Through Bronte's, Dickens', Stowe's and James' fables
And Hawthorne's haunted house of seven gables,
She guides us through imagined habitations:

The bachelor pad, where Arthur Conan Doyle
Lodges his detective, Sherlock Holmes;
Galsworthy's Robin Hill, in which he set
The Forsyte Saga, centering on Soames;
E. M. Forster's nook, in *Howard's End*,
The quite grotesque West Egg of Scott Fitzgerald
And Manderley, or the vast Palladian hollow
Of Evelyn Waugh's romantic conjuring.
But Woolf's *Orlando* and Peake's *Gormenghast*
Alike made the impressions that will last.

Enchanted by Tinuviel

A Tolkien poem that nothing mars
Lit beauty for me, under stars.
It brought before my dreamy eyes,
Canopied by Doriath's skies,
The figure of Tinuviel.

Quite as struck as Beren I was,
Though far more haplessly, because
I could not be there at the green
Where music, from a pipe unseen,
Enchanted fair Tinuviel.

I saw her dancing in the glade,
But he it was who swiftly made
A hero's bid to win her heart,
While I, alas, could play no part
In wooing sweet Tinuviel.

He called her by her Elvish name;
She halted, spellbound, and he came
And took the princess in his arms,
Enraptured by the matchless charms
Of Gondolin's Tinuviel.

Ah! Long ago they went their way,
Through fearsome dark to fabled day:
To Morgoth's and to Mandos' halls—
An epic quest that still enthrals
My memory of Tinuviel.

But I was left in waste and wood
To find another, if I could,
With whom to plunder Morgoth's crown
And face life's mortal furies down:
My very own Tinuviel.

Book bindings

I took possession of some fraying family books
And, on a loving whim, rebound them in new covers:
Dark blue for the history tales of childhood,
Vividly remembered, in all my waking dreams,
For the pictures of venturers and heroes:
Like little Marco, previously evoked;
But, long before him, henge-builders and hunters,
Boadicea and the Roman legions at war,
Alfred and the settlement of Angleterre,
William called the Bastard and the Conquest;
And on and on, as far as Nightingale—
All graced together now and with a golden ribbon,
Moveable between prose tales and drawn dreams;
Just as, in the tawny-covered volume,
Which lay, a lifetime since, within my father's hands.

The many coloured maps in that old book,
When I was still a child, enthralled my roving eyes.
Now a scarlet ribbon, red with history's blood,
Moves from the dissolution of the Roman Empire—
(As the venerable title still proclaims)—
Down to 'the present time', which meant,
Through each edition, up to my father's schooling,
The era of the Great War and then of Hitler's rise.
But in burgundy rest the finely printed works
Of Shakespeare, dated nineteen ten and signed
Robert FitzGerald, Springhurst, a century ago;
While, in a stately black, with golden reader's guide,
Sits the poetry of Tennyson, and written just inside
Springhurst, again, and the words 'Presented to
Katie FitzGerald' and the date: 21. 3. 11.

Book of revelation

We grew up, we two, in Christian homes;
Bathed, for all we little knew,
In the aura of the apocalypse:
That diffuse cultural notion,
Shards and shimmers of which,
With elements of Catholic ritual,
Fragmentary scenes from the odd Gospel
And dimly apprehended lines from Paul,
Glued together, like a colloid,
Our patchwork of quite confused beliefs.

Is that not so, or was it not just so?
Yet what, then, did 'apocalypse' denote?
When did we ever have explained,
By one who may have known their many meanings,
What sainted John of Patmos might have meant
With his Alpha and Omega and Amen?
Innocent, of course, of what the saint deplored
In the patient tribulation—so he wrote—
Of all the seven churches then in Asia;
What should we have thought?

Yet, looking back to that cacophony
Of late first century mystical imaginings;
And, steeped now in many sound sciences,
I discover, in his fiery flow of images,
Borrowings from both Daniel and the Stoics.
I see Nero as the shadow of the Beast
And contemplate world-ending cataclysms,
In terms of the later sack of Rome,
Or fears for our blue Earth in human hands.
Do you so read the Book of Revelation?

The Wind in the Willows

Did you ever read, as I did, Kenneth Grahame's
Little classic about Toad and all the crew:
Ratty, Mole and Badger—and the Weasels—
Messing around in boats,
Taking to the road,
Getting into strife,
Until gentrified decorum was restored?

I'm referring to his only lasting book;
A charmingly eccentric masterpiece,
Which he thought was not a children's book at all—
Nor did his publisher;
Nor was it an animal story:
The animals were simply chaps;
Nor were there many willows in it, actually;

But quite apart from all that kind of thing,
I have to say how much I loved the tale,
When I was still a child and not a chap.
I never did become a chap,
Or mess around in boats
Or hit the open road,
In any but the most serious kind of ways.

I loved the picnic had by Rat and Mole,
I loved the nature of their conversation;
I found the Piper at the Gates of Dawn
Mystically evocative;
Played Toad on stage myself,
Most exuberantly;
Then staged my own rebellion, as a youth.

Kenneth Grahame was an Edwardian banker
Who identified, it seems, with Mole and Toad,
From boredom at the banker's tedious round.
He did go boating
To seek a wider world;
Then did, at last, hit the open road:
His life being overtaken by his impish art

Not only did he leave the Bank of England,
But his name was then expunged, in some disgrace.

The river banker

I cannot leave the story there, now, can I?
Did you ever read the book yourself?
More's the point, did you ever wonder
Who Kenneth Grahame was?
Or why he wrote of Ratty and the rest?

His literary agent, Curtis Brown,
Once described the man who gave us Toad
As tall and broad; a lean and handsome chap
Who really looked as though
He should have been in fact

The Secretary of the Bank of England
With just a hobby interest in letters;
Which is, of course, exactly what he was:
Well-off in many ways—
Descended from the Bruce.

He made a name quite early, writing stories:
Wry, sardonic, witty little ones,
Directed more at adults than at children,
But then his father absconded
And he had to get a job.

That's when he approached the Bank of England
And made another mark of some distinction;
When, for the Bank's demanding entrance test,
He got the perfect score—
Never equalled since.

He rose up through the ranks, but naturally was bored,
As any man of taste must be in banks;
And he wrote assays for varied cultured journals.
Went boating with the chaps
Then, somehow, just cut loose.

The piper at the gates of dawn

Whatever I have said of Kenneth Grahame,
By way of wry or frivolous aspersions,
His fable was most beautifully written.

The phrasing is Edwardian and elegant,
The sentiment restrained and civilized,
The worldview most aesthetically refined.

I wrote that I experienced as mystical
The evocation, in his seventh chapter,
Of the piper at the gates of dawn.

The vital passage covers just six pages:
Beginning with 'a bird piped suddenly';
Concluding with young Portly's 'joyous squeak'.

I'd read it to you, if you were at hand;
But here I am reduced to paraphrase,
Extolling Rat's great reverence, in the boat:

'O, Mole! The beauty of it,' he exclaims—
The clear and happy call of distant piping—
Such music as he'd never dreamed could be.

'O, row on, Mole. Keep rowing, while you can,
For this music and this call must be for us!'
Then it quite transfixed the breathless Mole.

The piping broke upon him like a wave;
Caught him up, possessed him utterly—
Intoxicating, in the light of dawn.

And then both Rat and Mole beheld Great Pan,
His pipes just fallen from his parted lips.
They crouched to earth and bowed their heads in worship.

And then the vision passed, as if a dream—
As did the Edwardian world, a few years later,
When Pandemonium hurled it into war.

Thomas Hardy, April 1914

Why was it that my youthful teachers
So failed in their appointed task
That I was never taught the features
Of common prosody?
Why do I ask?

It puzzles me that what's so strong
In all we call our old tradition,
Which should instil where we belong,
Was wilfully neglected.
Why this omission?

Yet suddenly, in English class,
When I'd become a sophomore,
Some feckless tutor played a farce
By calling for critique
Of 'Channel Firing'.

We weren't told Hardy was the poet,
Nor what he might expect of us;
Nor, sight unseen, how we would know it.
I never did find out
And stopped inquiring.

In nineteen ninety-one, at last,
I bought a book of Hardy's verse.
A decade of disruption passed,
Before I chanced to read it,
While rewiring.

It struck me then he'd presaged war:
The omens of a red revenge,
Composed the fateful spring before
Tuchman's guns of August
Shook Stonehenge.

Elspeth and Constance

Now, perhaps it won't surprise you if I write
That Kenneth Grahame had two great female friends?

Elspeth Thomson was the one he married;
Constance Smedley then became a muse.

And, get this, they are said to have inspired
The banker, bored, to write his famous book.

When Toad—I'm sorry, Kenneth—first met Elspeth
He was a bachelor boy of forty-three.

Like you, when I was all of forty-eight,
She brought a great deal to their wedding party:

An heiress of some means, she hosted soirees
With the likes of Swinburne, Wilde and Browning.

Fluent in French and Flemish and a painter,
She wrote verse, too, and nom-de-plumed a novel.

She corresponded with old Thomas Hardy
And whimsically, with Toad, in baby talk.

Constance Smedley, on the other hand,
Founded Lyceum clubs for women writers.

She also wrote a string of plays and novels;
Most notably one called *An April Princess*.

Kenneth and Elspeth had a son called Mouse,
For whom his father made up bedtime stories:

Featuring a mole and water rat
And nursery tales concerning Mister Toad;

Or that's the story told by Constance Smedley:
The adventures of some charming little animals,

Whose genteel frolics and respectable concerns
Were adapted from the banker's social life:

It's boats and caravans and twee conventions,
With Hardwick House, on Thames, the first Toad Hall.

James Cook, voyager

Peach's little tale of Captain Cook
Was one of those that, like his Marco Polo,
Fed into my cognitive fruition,
Planting seeds from which my ventures grew,
Conferring innocence on global navigation.

Three voyages he made, of epic scope,
To chart the vast, primordial Pacific,
From the Antarctic to the islands of Alaska,
Which lodged themselves in colour in my mind,
Long before I grasped what all this meant.

Yet, looking back, I'd guess that my intent,
My longing to explore the wider world,
May have its root in Kenney's water colours
Of Cook's *Endeavour* circumnavigating
That wild and little charted ocean world.

His second voyage, in the *Resolution*,
Involved repeated probes of the Antarctic,
Establishing with reasoned certitude
That no Great Southland lay in the Pacific,
Save only what he'd found on his first voyage.

The description of Antarctic's 'Isles of Ice'
In the pages of the *Resolution*'s journal,
As calling for the pencil of a painter,
From the beauty and the terror they inspired,
Speaks, even now, to me of Kenney's drawings.

But Cook's third voyage, still in *Resolution*,
Via Tenerife to the Outer Ocean,
Thence northward to the Aleutians and beyond,
Abruptly, in Hawaii, brought his death:
A risk that we all face who venture out.

Render unto Caesar?

The cruelties and crimes of ages past
Are a moral education of a kind.
In Tacitus, for instance, one can find
A wildly varied and appalling cast
Of characters that quite expand one's mind.

He wrote his *Annals* of the imperial court
At pretty much the time, it would appear,
When John of Patmos passionately sought
To instil, in equal measure, hope and fear—
With the vision of apocalypse he taught.

But never mind the trumpets of St John,
Or all his talk of angels, lambs and seals;
Just sit and read and meditate upon
The sombre things with which the historian deals—
And how the clear-eyed Stoic thinks and feels.

He clinically vivisects the Roman scene:
The endless rounds of murder and intrigue,
Of flatterers, informers, torturers in league;
Of beauty raped and all that long had been
Held in honour treated with disdain.

'Render unto Caesar,' Jesus said—
A famous coinage, parsing 'church' and 'state'—
But not long after this the man was dead;
Crucifixion was his brutal fate:
The Romans flogged and nailed him and he bled.

That's the world of which the *Annals* tell:
Harsh and unforgiving to the core.
Octavia perished, Seneca as well;
And rebels, slaves and quietists galore.
Nor were there angels when the Empire fell.

The merest waste of time

I wished, at seventeen, to study Latin;
I and I alone among my peers.
I was a Catholic, after all, and longed
To find in it the roots of ancient Rome;
But I was told, in no uncertain terms,
That Latin was the merest waste of time.

The one who so advised me, long ago,
Taught maths and physics and, for all I know,
Taught them well and had been quite sincere
In advising me to carelessly steer clear
Of the language of the Church, the law and science;
And who was I to set him at defiance?

But let us just suppose, upon a whim,
That I'd have had the wit to challenge him;
That I'd then known what I might have learned,
The depth and access that I could have earned:
The roots of all that holds our culture fast:
A grounding in the rich, imperial past.

It doesn't seem impossible to dream
That, tutored by Orbilius, I'd have found
Like Horace, a secure and fertile ground
And, thus, have come to be, not merely seem,
A master of all kinds of prosody;
But this I missed, as I suppose did—he.

When Horace, at the age of forty-two,
Published, in three books, his polished odes,
We know, from his concluding lines, he knew
That he'd remastered all the lyric modes.
I might have learned from him, while still at school—
Had it not been for one uncultured fool.

My private 4th of July

July the fourth, it's true, is claimed by others:
A feast day of a well-known public kind.
I honour it with our American brothers—
On liberty we're—mostly—still aligned.

But privately, in fact, I celebrate
A rebellion that was mine and mine alone
And which occurred, by chance, on that same date:
When I quit Law and struck out on my own.

Upon a sombre winter's afternoon,
While brooding over some unfinished paper
That had to be submitted pretty soon,
I decided I'd have done with that whole caper.

What the paper was I can't recall,
Only that a mood took hold of me
That made my basic legal studies pall:
A cocktail of ennui and anomie.

Who was I that they'd urged to study Law?
Where, in fact, did I most long to go?
Restlessly, I hungered to do more
And so, I started dreaming like Rimbaud.

I'm out of here, I recklessly decided,
There are other things I badly need to know;
Abruptly I then vowed that I'd be guided
By an improvised, inspired manifesto:

I'll read and think and travel round the world;
I'll learn to love and plumb my true desire;
I'll study only once my flag's unfurled,
Then master things that truly light my fire.

With that, I left the paper where it lay—
And set the course I've held until this day.

Tokyo blond, 1985

My encounter with Ms Rand was existential:
She was blond and statuesque and twenty-four,
Fluent in Chinese and very bright;
And, as we strolled the streets of Tokyo,
Where she, of course, was looked at, goggle-eyed,
By many avid, stressed out little men;
And after we had danced through Ueno Park
And lunched with Hunter and Christine in Habaraku—
He an engineer and she an artist—
Urged that just we two run off together.

Let's go, she said, to Hamamatsu-cho
To a coffee shop she knew and talk of dreams;
Of Jung, especially, and of my Anima.
How could I decline, on any count;
Especially as she plainly seemed to think
That, as Christine had said, I was a genius—
Imagine how surprised I felt at that!
And what young genius, fresh in Tokyo,
Could conceivably turn down a striking blond,
Who proposed a blend of dreams and coffee beans?

Politeness strangely held me by the toes:
We spoke in caffeinated animation
Of archetypes and of my tangled loves;
She dug my dreams and made good sense of them.
Enchanted, it was plain, by my persona,
She said to me, with flagrant sexual candour,
That I shouldn't feel confined to just one muse.
Even now, when I'm no longer young,
My memories of her shy, seductive words
Tantalize my still ingenuous tongue.

Gaius Petronius Arbiter

I'm drawn, as if to a fatal flame,
By the wine cup of Petronius,
Cut at vast expense from deep green stone
And treasured, through an opulent life,
As arbiter of taste at Nero's court.

We know so little of this daring man,
Who seems to have written the *Satyricon*.
We would have lost the tale entire,
Deleted by delators and by time,
If not for snippets in two classic books.

Tacitus it was who wrote a brief obituary,
In mordant praise of this voluptuary;
Noting both the wit and style
Of how Petronius briefly lived
And, even more, the manner of his death.

Betrayed, by jealous Tigellinus, to his doom
And seized at Cumae, close to Nero's court,
He passed his final hours reciting verse;
But sent his savage master, with despatch,
A jewelled dagger of a document—under seal.

Recounted therein, by the literate spy,
Were all the debaucheries of the master's weal:
The secret truth of its depravity.
He thrust this truth into the murderer's eye—
Then broke his signet ring to seal the deal.

The wine-cup tale we owe to learned Pliny,
Who tells us that the dying man of taste,
In a final act, defiant of the monster,
Took his cup of deep green fluorspar—
And smashed the thing to pieces on the floor.

Lord Byron's travels

Lord Byron's travels took him far afield,
(Though not as far I have been with you);
But, more important, we still have the yield,
Of what 'Childe Harold' saw—and gave its due:
From Lisbon east—in Cantos One and Two.

His countless observations sparkle still,
Attributed to fictive Harold's eyes;
His learning and imagination fill
The mutest landscapes with such rich surmise
That hidden meanings constantly arise.

Thus, stanza thirty-nine, in Canto Two,
Hails Lover's Leap, where Sappho took her leave,
On Cape Leucadia, as Byron knew;
And he, a poet, still saw fit to grieve,
In gliding past the Lesbian's ancient grave.

The later, longer Cantos, Three and Four,
Take Byron down the full length of the Rhine,
Past relics of the tyrannies of yore,
Through Switzerland, then to the Palatine;
With Venetian interludes—and Florentine.

At one point, as he skirted Rhenish towers,
The traveller paused to praise the deep blue eyes
Of peasant girls, who brought him lily flowers.
He called their simple world a paradise—
In all except the absence of his lass.

Quite late, in Canto Four, he came to Rome,
(As we shall, now—two centuries since his time).
He hailed the mighty Ruin as Europe's home,
Lamented its prolonged decay in rhyme—
And so completed his Romantic climb.

Pantheon

We reached the fabled Pantheon at dusk,
Meandering down from the Borghese Gardens,
Where we'd lingered on the Pincio,
Discoursing on the villa of Lucullus,
As the sun declined above the Vatican.

We made our way past Trinita dei Monti
And through the crowds upon the Spanish Steps,
With passing thoughts of dying Keats and Shelley;
We cast our coins into the Trevi Fountain,
Then came, at last, to the Sanctissimum.

Remember Nietzsche's madman sagely asking,
When hauled out from a church for having chanted
His requiem for the eternal God,
'What are these buildings now, if not the tombs
And sepulchres of what we thought divine?'

In just that spirit, surely, Hadrian,
The Empire's ruler at its apogee,
Reconceived what M. Agrippa built;
Bequeathing us a truly stunning shrine
To all the seven planetary gods.

But, as with other monuments that day,
What most impressed itself upon my mind
Was less the awesome structure in itself,
Than your naively beautiful response
To all the layered meanings of that space.

And how, in Catholic pews beneath the dome,
That Michelangelo himself described
As the work of nothing less than angels,
We sat by candlelight and spoke in earnest
Of all our deepest thoughts and future plans.

Notitiae

Our fleeting hours in Rome,
You now remind me,
Were animated time:
What being, properly speaking,
Seeks to gather, lest it dissipate:
Love and deeply shared experience;
The accentuated sense of feeling
Recognized and cherished by another,
In a landscape of the highest, haunted
Architecture time has adumbrated;
So that it chants to passers by
Of what it means to be human
And more conscious than the they of how
Singularly uncanny and how poignant
Our condition is.

If only, in our flying time together,
I could have shared with you
The unparalleled, wondrous catalogue
Of all that lay around, beneath, behind us;
First fabulously assembled,
By those long mute and nameless,
With dazzling skills of mind and hand.
If only I could build or craft
Into our most vivid common sense
Lanciani's stunning reconstruction
Of what Rome was, before its long destruction:
Colonades, basilicas, temples, theatres, baths—
Or even be with you in Trajan's Forum,
Before, like all the rest, it was dismantled;
Leaving just Romantic dreamers' ruins.

Being in Rome

If they document our lives at any point,
That day in Rome will surely have to feature;
Although, in fact, the 'they' don't do such things,
Neglectful both of being and of time.
Will even we agree on what took place,
Between Testaccio and the Arch of Constantine?

Here's my take, beloved, for the record:
After croissants at the Café Barberini,
We set off past the ruined Gate of Paul;
I gestured at the mass of Aurelian's Wall
And spoke of where the Gothic camps had been,
But led you on across the Aventine.

How much did I relate of that Hill's tale,
Conscious of our evanescent parsing?
I mentioned Roman mansions, I recall
And their looting, on the City's fall—
My mind aflame with histories that I knew,
But what do all such histories mean to you?

Beyond that one of seven fabled Hills,
We came, as we had purposed, to the Baths;
And there, as I had hoped, your awe awoke.
For there the soaring arches that remain,
The hints and hollowed haunts of ancient marbles,
Sighed 'ROME!' to you, with all that that implies.

I've written of the Baths of Caracalla
And been immersed in their imagined glories;
I've dreamed for years of concerts in their gardens;
Of Shelley's sojourn there and other stories;
But your gratitude and shining, chestnut hair
Have quite transformed my sense of being there.

The City falls

Before we venture to the Colosseum,
Linger with me in the ruined Baths
And listen while I discourse on the fall;
While I tell at least a little, if not all,
Of why and how the great barbarian king,
Alaric of the Goths, wrought violence here.

Heed the tale, for it's more complex than tradition,
Which romanticizes, somewhat, Rome's perdition:
For Alaric, warring chieftain, loved the West,
At least as far as Gothic kings might do;
And simply asked the Emperor to invest
In him command of Rome's most potent forces.

Short of that, the Gothic king declared,
Give me Noricum, Dalmatia and Venetia
As a fastness at the cross-roads, West and East
And from this stronghold, while you idly feast,
I'll keep the feral Franks and Huns at bay;
Preserving your broad realm in its decay.

Olympius, a counsellor for the ages,
Deflected, through intrigue, the Goth's request;
Whereupon, having been insulted,
Alaric marched on Rome and all the rest—
The epic sack and mayhem that resulted—
Is related best in Gibbon's famous pages.

The Goths, admitted by rebellious slaves,
Burst into Rome through the Salarian Gate
And, venting on the City's choice enclaves
The lust and fury conquerors will sate,
Raping, burning, seizing what they find,
Signalled Rome's demise to all mankind.

Colosseum

'Come with me to the Palatine,' I said
'And there I'll show you all that now remains
Of the palaces that housed the lords of violence,
From Augustus, prince of princes,
To Theodoric, the Gothic king of Rome.'

But we had all too little time to linger
In the houses of Augustus or of Livia,
In the sombre ruins of the Aula Regia,
The Septizonium that Lanciani pondered,
Or the hollows of Domitian's hippodrome.

You wished, you said, to see instead
The famed, forever ominous Colosseum—
To the right, beyond the Arch of Constantine;
The most notorious symbol still extant
Of Roman games and Christian persecution.

Titus, it is said, inaugurated
This signal amphitheatre of his house,
With lavish, week-long, violent spectacles;
In which five thousand animals were killed,
While gladiators by the hundred died.

We both, it seemed to me, on entering
The precincts of that classic slaughterhouse,
Could well have been among its countless victims,
Had we lived in Rome in classic times:
Disloyal Stoics, vocal in dissent.

I watched, in quiet awe, for some two hours,
As you, my dove of peace and clearer thinking,
Contemplated all those blood-drenched stones,
The stands where brutal crowds had yelled and cheered;
And gently reconfirmed your great commitments.

If, at Babi Yar

When I contemplate the hecatombs of violence
Done by human beings to one another,
Going all the way back to our collective
Invasion of the hominin worlds beyond
The Africa of our long genesis;

When I contemplate, in sharper focus,
The atrocities of just our scientific century,
From the Belgian Congo via the Somme
To the Cultural Revolution and Rwanda,
My fear and nausea become personal.

No abstract principle or religious icon
Enters the picture. No, it's you:
The dread thought of such brutality
Being visited upon your singular beauty—
And my being helpless to avert it.

If, at Babi Yar, the Einsatzgruppen
Gunned down thirty thousand helpless Jews
Into a forest ravine, within two days;
What is that, among the tens of millions?
Only fearful empathy stirs one's horror.

Such empathy arises, like a bloody mist,
When I imagine us among the thirty thousand,
Shepherded out of Kiev by the SS,
Dread misgivings growing as we're marched
Into the Wald on a fell morning.

You I want to shelter with my body.
You I'd shield by any means at all.
Your slaughter is the inexpiable crime;
Mine the inextinguishable lament—
If, at Babi Yar, I cannot save you.

Gordion knots

In the second book of Arrian,[27] it's related
That young King Alexander, bent on conquest,
Paused at fabled Gordion, where Midas
Had, in legend, turned all things to gold;
Drawn by the tale of the wagon yoke
Whose knot, if one could just unravel it,
Would yield, to he who did so, all of Asia.

Desire seized Alexander, Arrian wrote,
To climb to where the fated wagon stood,
In Gordion's citadel and see the knot.
Once gazing on it, he could not resist
The chance to try his wit and strength upon it.
He must have pondered omens, should he fail,
And, vowing not to, cut the thing instead.

Arrian demurs on what occurred,
Allowing that there were two different stories;
As to which was true, he was uncertain.
Yet all of Asia, meaning Persia, fell
To Alexander's swiftly wielded sword;
And so, of course, folk memory would tell
That cut he had, as Asia's destined lord.

I've known the folksy version of this tale
Since reading it when I was still a child
And wondering how one came to be as wild
As youthful Alexander, whom they hail
As conqueror of the ancient, cultured East;
But as I grew beyond his span of years,
I sought to conquer worlds by other means:

I chose not to cut, but to unravel
Gordion knots—by study, thought and travel.

Abel, my little brother[28]

In my fieldwork journal, volume one,
Dating back to nineteen eighty-four,
There's a brief account, a paragraph
No more, telling of an encounter I had
With a little beggar being, a child of strife,
Who approached me as I left the troubled Isthmus.

I was queueing to depart the strife-torn
Little country of El Salvador:
I had a ticket out and work to do,
A scholarship and studies to pursue.
I'd purposely conducted interviews
And taken notes and many photographs.

But here, as I was lining up to leave
Forever and quite physically unscathed,
A child's hand gently touched my own
And, with the meekest and most diffident of voices,
This waif of civil war and deep injustice
Inquired could I spare just four colones.

I asked his name. He said that it was Abel.
'Donde es tu padre?', I then asked.
'No tengo' was the simple, quiet answer.
'Y tu madre?', I then asked, like a padron.
'Ella es muy pobre', he replied and I believed him.
'Y porque cuatro colones?' I inquired:

Why just four—a single US dollar?
'Para comer', the little one responded:
Simply to obtain the merest portion
Of the nourishment that we all need to live.
I had precisely four left in my wallet.
And, moved and startled, gave them to my brother.

Salvadoran oligarch

Through the US Embassy in Salvador,
I was put in touch with one Eduardo Llach.

His family was among the old elite
Of whose history I had just begun to read.

This was the barest, tentative engagement
With a drama dating from the Conquest.

Alfaro, Regalado, Palomo,
Dueñas, Orellana, Escalon,

Prado, Menendez, Hill and Alvarez,
D'Aglio, De Sola, Goldtree-Liebes,

Deininger, Sol Millet, D'Aubuisson—
These were the oligarchic families.

Eduardo was a scion of these clans,
Who'd ground the country's peasants into coffee.

Ana asked me later what I thought
Of this landed gentleman, educated

At the Wharton School of Finance;
Articulate, well-groomed, self-assured.

Well, we'd spoken for two hours—over coffee—
In the Zazumal Garden at the Sheraton.

He'd told me that Roberto D'Aubuisson
Had had no hand in death squad operations.

That, he'd claimed, was left-wing propaganda.
I'd known this was untrue, but held my tongue.

The country's overpopulated, Llach had said,
The peasants kill each other randomly.

Of course, he added, the Army kill some, too,
But that is what the Army's plainly for.

Had I believed Eduardo? Not at all.
I questioned him and noted what he said.

Section two

Ana Gloria Hirleman

Twenty pages in my fieldwork journal
Record my visit to El Salvador;

Yet even these exiguous materials,
When read at several decades' distance now,

Brim with tales of what I'd been immersed in:
A little world like Conrad's in its violence;

Of stark discrepancies in wealth and power—
My visits to the US Embassy;

My letters written back to Honolulu,
To a woman who had wept when I departed;

The days I spent with Ana Hirleman,
Interpreter and Christian Democrat,

Who took me to my interviews in Spanish,
Who bridged the flow and helped me cross the River

Into a country studied first in English;
Into the minds of Salvador's officials.

We'd sit, between such outings, in the coffee
Lounge inside the Sheraton Hotel;

In which, as I knew well, there had been killings,
By death squads, of the leading land reformers.

We worked superbly, as a research team,
In lengthy interviews at MAR and ISTA.

Never mind the acronyms for now;
The point is that we gleaned an awful lot.

But privately she told me many things:
Of loves she'd shared with murdered oligarchs.

We lunched upon San Salvador volcano:
Panoptic views and sombre conversation.

'Of all the foreigners I've met here', she averred,
'You are, by far, the most honest and informed.'

Childhood awe

Hannibal of Carthage was an early hero,
Stumbled upon in *A Pageant of History*:
An omen, Rome's enemy, a mystery

The tale told there was very incomplete,
But memory retains its salient features:
His generalship and the giant creatures,

Great elephants from out of Africa,
That he led from Celtiberian Spain
To Italy and victory, but never back again.

He hammered Rome's all-conquering legions,
Yet Rome, for me, already was quite fabled
As the fount of arms and laws that had enabled

The rise of that most awe-inspiring realm,
Which humbled every foe, both near and far,
Beneath the banner bold: SPQR.

Livy's book, *The War With Hannibal*,
Enlarged the canvas of the Punic War,
Allowing me to learn a great deal more

About how this indomitable man,
Son of Carthage, scion of the Barcae,
Had challenged not just Rome, but all the Parcae.

Two things made the deepest of impressions:
Maharbal's words, on victory at Cannae,
And how the cornered general chose to die.

'Let me ride at once,' Maharbal said,
'With the Senate and the City in a daze;
And you will conquer Rome within five days!'

But his master bade the bold Maharbal stay.
Fate turned. The long defeat would finally bring
Great Hannibal to bite his poisoned ring.

Juvenal's spite

It was less Livy, let's reflect, whose lines,
Regarding Hannibal's exile and undoing,
Etched themselves into my memory,
Than those of Juvenal, in his *Satires*.
Do you know them?

Juvenal lived centuries later, of course,
But got some schooling in his native tongue
And, waspish with a rentier's disappointments,
Vented his quite copious wit and spleen
Composing barbed verse.

Satire X (we'll call it Satire Ten,
To render it less liable to perplex),
Was where he had a shot at Hannibal,
In lines as famous as the hero's victories—
Well, perhaps not quite.

'Put Hannibal in the scales,' quoth he
'How many pounds will that peerless
General mark up today?' Good question!
'A fit subject for caricature,' he dubbed him—
Scribbling in a garret.

'Alas, alas for glory! What an end was here!',
The satirist sneered at Hannibal's downfall:
No sword, no spear, but a poisoned ring
Wiped out one who'd 'wrecked a world'—
Thus, he mocked the man.

'On, on, you madman, drive
Over your savage Alps to thrill
Young schoolboys and supply
A theme for speech-day recitations'—
Thus is Juvenal recited.

Synesius

Before we fly from Rome to Marrakesh,
Sweet courtier of reason,
Let me tell you, briefly, of Synesius,
A man of sage opinions,
Who delivered a most eloquent oration—
Around the year four hundred,
To the court of young Arcadius—
On sound imperial rule.
Observe the futile measures he proposed
And note the court's response.

I'm drawing, once again, on Gibbon's lines,
In summing up *De Regno*,
Where Synesius urged the Emperor to revive
The courage of his subjects:
Extolling manly virtue in the camp,
Quelling luxury,
Replacing barbarous mercenaries with men
Committed to their laws,
Their properties and common civil rights,
Then leading them in wars.

Guess how young Arcadius responded?
He indulged Synesius' zeal,
Applauded the orator's eloquence,
Neglected his advice.
Gibbon, with his wonted irony,
Reflected that, perhaps,
Synesius hadn't thought to offer up
A practicable scheme
For turning round a secular decay—
Nor was there one to hand.

The last of the Romans

Do you know the name of Stilicho?
He was near the last of Roman generals,
Excepting Gluck's romantic Ezio,
Who fought, with long and valiant effect,
To save the foundering Empire in the West,
From both its craven rulers and from ruin.

Half Vandal, but a Roman of conviction,
Flavius Stilicho rose up through the ranks
Of late imperial arms, the favoured servant
Of Theodosius, last of serious Emperors,
Who, ruling all from Constantinople,
Raised this Vandal up, as his lieutenant.

As Master of Arms, he fought the Emperor's wars,
Securing all the West from sundry foes,
Repairing even Hadrian's crumbling Wall;
Held the Rhine and quelled revolt in Africa;
Deftly dealt with Alaric of the Goths;
And was made regent, at the Emperor's death.

But genius couldn't save him from intrigues
And even genius must needs have resources.
He stripped the Gallic limes of their legions,
To stem the tide in northern Italy;
Whereat the Germans poured across the Rhine,
While Britain fell to the rebel Constantine.

As will happen, when a hero falters,
The circling, vengeful foes of Stilicho
Closed in upon his person in Ravenna
And slew the only master of their forces;
Which left not just Britannia and Gaul,
But Rome itself exposed—and ripe to fall.

Trapped on the Aventine

We knew the Gothic siege was on
But thought the walls would stand,
Since, after all, no foreign enemy,
Not Hannibal himself, in ancient times,
Had passed the walls of Rome;
Not in eight hundred years, we said,
In the salon of the good Praefectus Urbi,
Among our fellow Aventine grandees;
And so we fanned away the summer heat,
Until the heralds came, with dire alarms.

Damned slaves, we learned, had opened wide
The Salarian Gate to the horde of brutal foes;
Goths were loose in Sallust's ancient gardens,
Looting and burning on the Quirinal;
Nothing strong now stood or could
Between the raging torrent and this Hill
Of palaces, where we were domiciled;
Nor was there sanctuary to be found
Or any that we knew would be respected:
We caught each other's eyes in disbelief.

One thought and one alone then took possession
Of my psyche and prompted urgent action:
To save you from the rampant tide of death
By fleeing to the only place I knew
Where, hot for gold and other precious things,
The rapists of the City would not go:
A lofty room I knew within the Baths,
Where we could shelter from the coming storm;
Returning to the ashes of our lives—
As we duly did—when it had passed.

Love among the ruins[29]

How did we survive those days of chaos?
How the unhinged panic of so many?
How the trauma of the fires and fears,
Upon the Aventine and Caelian Hills?
It wasn't just good fortune.

Three days the sack went on and fires burned
And so much went to ash that we had cherished.
Our residence we found, when we returned,
Had been despoiled and many friends had perished.
This was Nemesis.

We found a box of coins that we had buried
And hid them further, while we made new plans
My books lay slashed and seared, but some we ferried
To a new abode; spared by chance.
Treasured fragments these.

Our beauteous Aventine and all it housed
Had drawn upon itself, of all the City,
The worst assault of Gothic lusts aroused
And suffered ravishment devoid of pity.
So very much was burned.

Splendid manors, centuries in age,
That had belonged to ministers of state;
Libraries, frescoes, gardens felt the rage
Of bearded, savage men who desecrate
All that's good and fine.

Although assailed by smoke and desolation,
We wept, but breathing still beyond our grief,
Conferred and kissed, electing transmigration,
Remembering where we could find relief:
Our farm in Africa.

On some lines from Kulikowski[30]

They say that I read Gibbon in the womb,
Such was my precocious predilection
For imbibing, like the nutriments of life,
Not at the breast, but intra-uterine
The epic tale of Rome's decline and fall
And nostalgia for the forts along the Rhine.

In any case, from very early youth,
Immersed in the accounts of Caesar's wars,
His exploits, dreams of glory and despatches,
Awake, as well, to Alexander's fame,
I swept along the Danube and Euphrates;
I flew from Babylon to Hadrian's Wall.

I studied Roman history, then, at school
And, once again, at university;
I wrote, at last, quite thoughtfully on Gibbon,
As on Mommsen and the Russian Rostovtzeff;
Forming, thus, my sense of how Rome fell,
As well as why and what it means for us.

But recently I chanced upon a book
By Michael Kulikowski, whom I knew,
As the analyst of all Rome's Gothic wars.
It seized my rapt attention in the browsing,
Because he claims, in his first paragraph,
That pundits draw quite false analogies

Between the fall of Rome and our fraught time;
Their vehemence quite inverse to discernment.
For history does not repeat itself,
Nor, contrary to convention, does it rhyme.
What tantalizing words! How bold, how free!
They hooked the wry contrarian in me.

The life I live

Consider ethically how I now live:
A frankly Epicurean, aging writer.
I cultivate, as Voltaire said one should,
My garden, or to be precise, my leisure—
Gardens I admire, but don't possess.

Leisure is a problematic thing,
From a Christian or a bourgeois point of view;
But let that rest; for me it's *otium*—
That ease advised by all the classic thinkers,
To be devoted chiefly to reflection.

That's well known of me; I won't deny it:
Learning, to the point of eccentricity,
Aversion to the pull of church or tribe,
Decided preferences in terms of company
And chiefly that of all Mnemosyne's Muses.

But other than devotion to the Good
It's long been known how much I like my food:
Just look at what I brought back from the Market
(To entertain good friends, not eat alone)—
Then put aside, with quite sage-like restraint:

Dried figs, quince paste, Saint Agur Blue;
Salmon fillets, prawns and flathead tails;
Fresh cherries, olive bread and peppers;
Tomatoes, eggplant, broccoli and carrots;
Rose water cubes of Turkey's famed delight.

But why am I confessing this to you,
As you move from town to town in Venezuela,
Seeking to ignite the flame of thought
Across a country wracked by wretched failure?
There's the root of what I mean by ethics.

Our Ringstrasse moment[31]

That was quite a pitch you put to me—
Walking north in sunlight, years ago.
It's graven still, upon my memory—
In words at once so colourful and bold
That even now they win my wonderment:

'There's something that I have to say to you
And that is this,' you suddenly announced.
'That I am Alma Mahler and I know
A genius when I see one. You are set
To do things of which I want to be a part.'

Or words to that effect—without a stammer—
Fully formed and confident, as if
You'd meditated long upon the thought;
As we strolled, so freely, through that southern spring,
Our own Ringstrasse and surrounding streets.

'Alma?' I almost burst out with a laugh.
'Are you for real? As in Tom Lehrer's song?'
Am I, then, Mahler, Gropius or Werfel?
Or someone else in your sublime beguine?
Alma?! Ah! You took my breath away!

We've had, since then, of course, our replica
Of Alma's life with Mahler in Vienna:
Two girls and many compositions, right?
A love that struggled long to find its way
Then rose, at last, above their tragic fate.

For you've been less the Alma of Vienna
Than the Muse I'd longed for—more than for a wife—
My Anima, my soul, the gift of life,
Who, since she would or could not simply stay,
Has raised me up to dream and fly away.

Proust's way

You, my love, and no-one else,
Unless, perhaps, it was Roger Shattuck,[32]
A year or so before you first arrived;
Introduced me to the world of Proust.

You used to claim, to my bewilderment,
'I am Odette de Crecy'—with a smile.
But, strange as it now seems, all the while,
I thought you said, 'Odette the Crazy'.

You, my love, and no-one else,
Not Shattuck, much less de Botton,
Must have been, therefore, the very first
To murmur Proustian nothings in my presence.

You, however, did become Odette—
Hence some poems I wrote you years ago,
About lost time and feeling I was Swann,
Conversing with Marcel beside the Seine.

You were long gone when I actually read
The whole six volumes of the master work,
While ill and all but corked, like Proust;
Dwelling on remembrance of things past.

You, if no-one else, will understand
How passages from each volume now inform
The Proustian reworkings of my life
The autopoiesis I'm embarked upon.

When, in *Swann's Way*, Proust wrote of floating flowers
Or in the pages of *Within a Budding Grove*
Compared bewildered love with lack of causal science,
Or when in *Sodom and Gomorrah* he described
The Luxor obelisk as pink nougat, the Moon a bitten orange,
He wrote for me—and you—and no-one else.

The ink pot and the quill

There's a really funny passage in *Orlando*,
Concerning how the book-besotted brain
Descends by fevered steps accelerando,
Compulsively into a world of pain:
The inky Stygian realm of pot and quill,
Where Sirens sing of beauty and of fame,
Of authorship and how its glories will
Immortalize one's thoughts and very name.
Oh! To write, the voices chant, to sub-create,
Transcends the mortal stuff of blood or state!

To write one little book and make a name
Among the poets and tragedians of old,
Shall be, beguiled Orlando vowed, my aim;
But found, alas, not Drake's Peruvian gold,
Nor all the Kentish holdings of his house,
Not all the labours he expended to refine
His mastery of prosody or prose
Could purchase from his pen a well-turned line.
And so, at last, in dark exasperation,
He cast his drafts into a conflagration.

What wry delight Virginia must have felt,
As reader and as author in this scene;
Watching her own demons quake and melt;
Venting, through Orlando, her own spleen.
Not least because she had, in fact, done well,
If not in verse then certainly in prose,
Even in the eyes of Julian Bell
And all the Bloomsbury set, one must suppose;
Including Duncan Grant and Maynard Keynes.
She's gone, of course. But ah, her work remains!

Percy Bysshe Shelley[33]

Shelley died when he was half my age
And left behind a monument of verse.
He perished reckless, as he'd lived:
Heedless of rede or storm warning;
But passionate he was in prosody.

Sprung of the Sussex squirearchy,
He learned his Latin and was gifted Greek
From childhood at fabled Field Place.
Fabled, I write, since it was Tudor,
Save for its belated Georgian wing.

It harboured many mysteries and attics,
As well as arbored gardens full of life,
Where boisterous Bysshe adventured;
Returning thence with wild imaginings
Confabulated for the ever-eager ears

Of his young, adoring sisters;
As, in like manner, he affected Alchemy,
Plunged his febrile brain among strange books
And annotated them with horned sprites.
He was fey and broke with his staid father—

Not least on account of a brutal schooling,
That instilled in him a turbulent character:
At once a leveller and violent in disdain
Of all that might advise, accost or thwart him.
His liberty he loved and roamed abroad.

Described, in his most memorable verses,
Are the fall of Ozymandias, King of Kings
And Prometheus Unbound, defiant hero.
He revelled in Caracalla's ruined Baths;
Then, tempting fate at thirty, died at sea.

Are we tempting fate?[34]

Are we tempting fate, to dream like this?
Descrying things that no-one else can see?
What substance, what reality inheres
In all the claims I make for what we have?
Oh, little enough: mere possibility.

Have we not tempted fate at every turn?
Your coming here from Mexico began
What those who loved you thought was nothing less
Than flying to the Moon in search of—what?
Your intuition said 'There's something there!'

Who'd have thought that something, then, was me?
Yet things occurred the day you first arrived
That spoke of fate and choice to both of us:
The Frida and Diego tale was ours;
And Nietzsche and Zhivago in our youth.

We were not young, of course, and that has helped;
For had we been, the scope was great for failure.
No, each of us had lived some sobering years
And had the strength of other, broken loves
To temper and to deepen our resolve.

We've needed that to find our wended way,
Through all that we have faced and overcome;
But we have met now in so many places
And beaten paths where most would go astray,
That the power to dream is etched into our faces.

And this is not the least of why our love
Is fuller now than ever it was before:
That you have spoken always of your dream
And mastered things that daunt all lesser persons,
Provoking emulation thus in me.

Evelyn Waugh's Oxford

We've not yet been to Oxford;
Perhaps we'll not get there;

But I headed there last year,
Before we met in Paris.

To walk among the Colleges
And rendezvous with friends:

The polymath you know
With his good-natured wife;

Then a woman I had courted
When both of us were young.

Naturally, I revisited
Museums, yards and bookshops

And so it was I chanced
To find, in blessed Blackwell's,

A book I never thought
To put back on the shelf:

Evelyn Waugh's Oxford,
With lovely illustrations.

With altogether unapologetic
Bibliophile's delight

I read it, most absorbed,
At the Hilton Garden Inn

At Heathrow, pre-departure—
The perfect gloss to being

Where Waugh, back in the day,
Had studied badly, drunk,

Debauched and wallowing
In disillusioned dreams;

Then left to write his tale—
Of Flyte and deliquescence.

For you I wrote a villanelle

For you, my love, I wrote a villanelle.
Did I write it well?

I composed it on the cusp of my recovery
From the loss of you.

I felt in it less my grieving or bewilderment
Than acceptance of your freedom

The illness out of which it sprang
Was itself a symptom

Of my years of grim resistance
To losses in the past

You were not those losses, but an offering
An angelic bell

That bell was a summons to my psyche:
'Now is the time!'

It was—you are—an existential summons:
'Choose to live—or die!'

The toll, of course, had sapped my sense of choice
The poet in me was moribund

But you were having none of my demise.
I was in your clear eyes

In need of poetry and you thrust at me
Neruda's book of love

Ah! Yes! Neruda was the bell you rang
A call to tongues, to vividness

You climbed the tower; called out for poetry
And then it came to me:

With every tolling of the bell within that tower,
With every passing hour,

You longed for me to live and to live well—
Whence 'A poet's bell'.

My Apricot

We've come quite a distance, haven't we;
Since you left a note for me,
Which I've always kept and always will,
That commences 'Dearest Frodo'—
Un nom d'amour that's tacitly explained,
Of course, within these lyric pages—
And which concludes, 'A Kiss, Your APRICOT'?
That, all on its own, is testimony
To the freshness of the love you bore me then.
It's moved me, every which way, ever since.

But down the lapse of time and from afar,
You've indicated that, by invitation,
You gave a talk at an Opus Dei villa
On the highest and most abstract of all themes:
'Thinking and Being', in a cocktail lounge.
Ah! That's my wondrous muse!
My first thoughts were of Heidegger,
But then the Bec-de-Gaz came back to mind:
Simone de Beauvoir's colourful account
Of Sartre, Aron and herself discussing
Phenomenology in that Parisian bar.

And here an apricot came into the picture:
'You see', young Raymond Aron said to Sartre,
Indicating, Beauvoir claimed, in *Prime of Life*,[35]
An apricot cocktail sitting on the table,
'If you are a phenomenologist,
You can make philosophy of actual things like this.'
Sartre turned pale with emotion, Beauvoir wrote,
'For here was just the thing he'd longed to do.'
And here we are, beloved APRICOT,
With just such work now being done by YOU!

Erotic autonomy[36]

When I engage in innocent self-pleasuring;
As, pardon me, I do from time to time,
Should I accept the well-known modern charge
That all such acts are, in themselves, depraved?
Should I, in awe of solemn declarations,
Recoil from my own pleasure, racked by guilt
And not explore the ecstasies of freedom?
Am I required, by any natural law,
To set aside my will, in supine deference
To alien maxims foisted on my person
By obscure and minatory hierarchs?
Must I confine my quest for mere relief
Within the narrow bounds of sad tradition,
Fearful of a reprobate condition
And bowing to irrational belief?

Or should I, rather, claim the liberty,
The care of self that hand and brain confer,
To exercise both freedom and self-love;
To set at nought both Rousseau and the Pope
(As well as Sigmund Freud, let it be said)
And entertain the milder, reasoned hope
That all their harsh injunctions will be fed
Into the maw of my own higher learning;
Ingested, then, and broken down by enzymes
Within that gut we're often told to trust;
While other thinkers, poets most of all,
Not least the inner poets of my memories,
Provide the richer nourishment I need—
That it may fuel my flickering desire
To be myself and, being so, love you?

Margaret Island, Budapest[37]

You should have been with me in Budapest—
My journal makes it clear I'd wished you were—
To walk with me, across Szechenyi Bridge,
To gaze from Castle Hill across the Danube,
Stroll along Andrassy Avenue
And enter, in some awe, Saint Stephen's Square.

But I was passing through, en route to Washington,
To run some workshops for the CIA;
And so, as I explored the ancient city,
(Well, not so ancient, just a thousand years)
And breathed among its monuments and beauties,
I vowed I'd bring you back with me one day.

The Danubian Grand Hotel, on Margaret Island,
The geographic heart, they say, of Europe,
I noted, as the perfect place to stay
'With just my muse, as writer and as poet'—
In the charming, old Franciscan convent there—
Long since made a house for just such uses.

Did you know that all the Isle is filled with roses:
Two hundred kinds, in odoriferous gardens—
Beautifully kept, among plane groves?
And that the convent's founding abbess, Margaret,
Is celebrated annually, on her birthday,
With holy mass, held in the open air?

Conscious of the picture Lukacs painted
Of the city, as it was, when in its prime;
And Frigyesi's book on Bartok's Budapest,
I sat beside the Danube lost in time—
As poets and historians will do—
Absorbing what I longed to share with you.

El Prado

Someone should have painted us together,
Across from Puerto de Alcala,
Taking coffee, planning our next steps;
Talking of the layout of Madrid;
Of the histories of the Spanish Civil War;
And, of course, of Vargas Llosa's novels.

It was revolutionary of me
To rendezvous with you, my foreign muse,
In Madrid, of all potential places,
Given our protracted civil war;
And then arrange to see Francisco Goya
Y los otros pintors grandes, at the Prado.

It was I who, seeking peace, had booked us,
At Only You Atocha, near the Station.
It wasn't just the name that shaped my choice
For the hotel's near Retiro Park,
Thus, to Puerto de Alcala beyond
And an easy stroll from Paseo del Prado.

We're both, of course, inveterate partisans;
Whose commitments never did allow
Capitulation or negotiated peace;
And so we've both been in the hills,
Where artfulness alone has kept us free—
To circle one another at a distance.

But there we circled all the classic art,
Inquiring of each other 'What most draws
Your innermost and lingering attention?'
For you, as I recall, it was the Bosch;
But I was drawn to Rubens' epic canvas
Of Seneca, expiring in his bath.

Charon on the Styx

El Museo del Prado—what a visit!
And in its bicentennial year!
We must, when time allows, go there again.

But, having read my 'Prado', you've informed me
That in it I had failed to mention, by default,
Your most vivid, valued memory of the place.

Not Bosch, as I quite wrongly recollected;
But Patinir's remarkable depiction
Of Charon rowing down the River Styx.

How did I forget our conversation
Concerning Patinir's art and Charon's work,
Given that it meant so much to you?

You say you've quoted things I said
In many workshops since, in Venezuela
As well as Panama and Medellin.

Apparently, I claimed that Charon's gaze,
With the angels all behind him on one side,
The Gates of Hell looming just ahead,

Exhibits a decided lack of leadership,
Or grasp of other options than sheer Hell;
That the boatman would surely have done well

To look around and heed the angels' voices;
To still his oar and not go rowing on,
But stay a while, considering his choices.

Yet, given what we know of Charon's job,
He didn't have the grace to turn around,
Or take dead souls to any other place.

Happily, the same's not true of you.
Pay Charon's obol for what served you well,
Then justly send him down the Styx to Hell.

Museum in Taipei[38]

Peng Mingmin, when we met in Taipei,
Gave to me a copy of his book
And spoke of what he'd been through in his life,
Between the killings under martial law
And his return, from exile in the West.

That book makes sombre reading, even now,
Not least because Beijing might once again
Inflict upon the people of Taiwan
The kind of things of which the old man spoke:
Killing, torture, mass incarceration.

Troop ships, he recalled, had come from China
And landed, firing guns, at Keelung port
And at Kaohsiung; then swiftly set about
A round-up and a sweeping, bloody purge
Of all those who'd stood up to gross abuses.

Editors and teachers, doctors, lawyers,
Students who'd naively signed their names
On liberal petitions to Chen Yi,
Were rounded up and summarily shot,
Or drowned in burlap bags in Keelung harbour.

The Peace Park and Museum in Taipei,
To which I led you on our visit there,
Impressed itself so deeply on your mind,
By reason of its sombre photographs,
That you've spoken of the visit often since.

You asked me to present you, as a gift,
A copy of the memoirs of old Peng,
Which I was glad to give; but less to share
What's lucidly recorded in its pages
Than from awe at your devotion to their meaning.

A Taste of Freedom

Before we met, Taiwan was on my beat
I'd known of it, vaguely, since my childhood,
But got there first in 1994:
That was five years after Tiananmen—
Shorthand for all PRC repression.

After that, but when I'd freed myself
From defeat by DFAT of my aspirations,
I revisited the island for myself,
Meeting many major figures in its politics
And, by their grace, exploring so much more.

I sat and spoke at length with Lee Tenghui,
With Jason Hu, Ambassador Yang and Tsai Ingwen;
I visited the Cold War fortress on Kinmen
And, through an eyeglass, viewed the Fujian coast—
The sites of so much tension in the '50s.

Then, after that, I visited Green Island
Which, long a prison, had by then become
A memorial to the many tens of thousands
Incarcerated there by the Guomindang,
Across the many years of martial law.

Better yet, I met with Peng Mingmin
Whose book, *A Taste of Freedom*, tells the tale
Of his and of the island's long resistance,
From the massacre of 1947
To the founding of the native DPP.

Then, five years on, I took you there, my love;
And, best of all, observed your deep absorption
In the Peace Park and Museum that enshrine,
With exhibits of so many of the slain,
How Chinese rule was forced upon Taiwan.

The trial of Wei Jingsheng[39]

When you were just a boisterous ten-year-old,
The little modern master of all China
Cast into prison, put on Chinese trial,
An authentic hero and free spirit;
A man just shy of thirty: Wei Jingsheng.

By those inclined to view the PRC
As governed by a wise post-Mao elite,
As led by a legitimate people's party,
As recovering from long humiliation;
This is seen as just the Wei things go.

'What does it matter', asks our ex-PM,
Who always was both bluff and overweening,
'If dissidents in China lack due process,
When the Party's lifted half a billion souls
Out of wretched (Maoist) poverty?'

Well, Wei grew up in just such poverty
And called, when little Deng had taken power,
For real reforms and actual rule of law.
He wrote big character posters on all this
And was promptly lifted out of liberty.

Remember both these journals from his time:
Exploration, April Fifth Forum—got it?
Both were extolled on the Democracy Wall
And, when the tiny master shut it down,
Defiant Wei was arrested within days.

He was slim and twenty-nine when put on trial,
But confuted all the charges brought against him.
He ridiculed the court's repressive stance,
Dismissing Deng's approach to law as quackery—
And so, of course, they gave him fourteen years.

In praise of Liu Xiaobo[40]

Liu Xiaobo was a poet;
For that, if nothing else, I honour him.

There is, however, so much more;
Not least the Charter 08 agenda for reform.

His signature, his open-hearted stance,
Among 303 fine citizens of China,

Merits the celebrated status
He has been accorded as a visionary—

Except, you understand, by the Party—
And by despots and useful idiots everywhere.

The Politburo read the landmark Charter
As a British bullet fired at its head: a .303.

This was Western spiritual pollution.
These reactionary, counter-revolutionary ideas,

The Charter's talk of human rights,
Were a Smith and Wesson—aimed at Hu and Wen.

The kind that Dirty Harry used,
On thugs and punks: a .44 Magnum, a revolver.

Such was their guilt-ridden hysteria;
These mandarin heirs of Mao and Deng, in China.

The Charter's spirit put them in a spin.
Revolver? Well, then, spin for spin, they lied.

The state, the people's freedom, they asserted,
Would be subverted by this kind of agitation.

They moved at once to put Liu in his place;
In lieu of all reforms: imprisonment, repression.

But Liu was lauded—Nobel laureated,
Which haughty Zhongnanhai called an obscenity.

At Stockholm, in his place, an empty chair
Was the symbol of his courage, life—and fate.

Martin Bodmer's books

We've lived through books
And in them all our lives.
Some, let us confess to one another,
We love more dearly than
We love our closest relatives.

You loved me for my books
And gave them bright new lives—
As I have long confessed to you—
Through the forthright fervour
You bestowed on my collection.

So, it was altogether fated
That, once I'd been enchanted,
By your passionate insistence
I must become the writer,
The poet, the story-maker that I am;

Yes, it was surely written in the stars,
That we would find our way—
Even if serendipity played a part, admittedly—
To the precious books that Martin Bodmer
Had assembled, as an act of love.

Yet nothing quite prepared the pair of us
For the wonders now so beautifully curated,
Having all been summoned from afar,
In his edifice spirituelle in Geneva:
The Foundation, with its lamps and fine displays.

I'm certain I'd have revelled, if alone,
In the manuscripts—from ancient papyri
To Gutenbergs and classic works of Goethe—
But it awed and overwhelmed me, Apricot,
To be with you in gazing on such things.

At the restaurant Casanova

We were seated in the Restaurant Casanova,
With a panoramic view across the Lake;
And so, at intervals, as we conversed,
Could gaze upon Mont Blanc's iconic heights,
With all their fabled pasts of poetries,
With all their connotations of prestige:
From Wordsworth's meditations to the climbs
By Mallaby, rehearsing Everest.
But we were there to scale our own Mont Blanc
And both envisaged Himalayan exploits.

That's what's always made your love enticing:
Your bold insistence that we both think big,
Not regarding merely basic things—
Like money, or a villa in Provence—
But heights requiring real imagination
Like political reform in Venezuela,
Or the composition of a classic book.
It was because we spoke of things like these—
And the implications of the *Panama Papers*—
That Mont Blanc itself remained a mise en scene.

But afterwards, returning to our lodgings,
You quite astonished me when, in our cab,
You sang 'If you're going to San Francisco'—
Having asked, quite whimsically, that it be played;
And sang it with your wonted innocence,
So that all the conversation we had had
Was wafted off to when young Scott McKenzie
Had imagined, back in nineteen sixty-seven,
That promiscuous sex and wreaths of flowers
Would bring about the fall of earthly powers.

Considered as artists[41]

Camus defined the way I see my role
As a thinker, as an artist, as a man.
Do I envy him the terrors of the war?
No more than I envy him his French.
Words translate and stances resonate.
His do so especially well for me.

As an artist, must you be a witness?
Witness, he retorted, as to what?
The tyrannies of our time do not allow
Our silence or neutrality, he said.
One has to take a stand and, doing so,
Refuse their judgements and pretensions.

This was not directed just as Nazis.
It was aimed at the pretensions of the Left.
Camus, Camus, the anarchist in you
Declared for art as moral realism
Against illogical and deadly ideologies
That justify oppression with their cant.

All executioners, you drily told the Marxists,
Are of one family; all oppress;
And so, if we'd rebel against injustice,
We must, if we're considered just as artists,
Or if we'd be astringent existentialists,
Defy the obscurantists and the killers.

As artists, we must have an eye for beauty;
As men, commitment to the better cause.
Extolling, still, a Tolstoy or a Melville,
As artists, we must see it as our duty
To cultivate our gifts without a pause,
Without obeisance to the general will.

Return to Tipasa

My teacher read us excerpts from *The Plague*—
A notorious fellow, suspected by his peers,
Or so I'd learn in later years,
Of corrupting the youth (our class)—
But let that pass.

Like many a young fellow in his care,
I caught the bug from this Socratic
Reader of Camus, this luminous heretic,
And that summer, out of school,
Read *The Plague* myself.

But not just that! Oh no! For I was Plato—
Brightest, most inspired of the youth
Corrupted by this Socrates; this good Rieux,
Doctoring in our own little Oran;
And I, too, set to work.

I purchased all the Camus I could find
And ever so much else, and read it all;
Not least his *Notebooks* and *The Rebel*,
The Myth of Sisyphus and *The Stranger*;
Becoming an outsider.

That summer's heat still glows on all those books
Read forty summers since and even more,
By Plato in his youth, his mind on fire.
But when I now return to Camus' works,
They're my Tipasa.

After war and Holocaust, he'd gone there,
Seeking to recapture, he would write,
A summer freedom he could not forget
Of starry nights when he had felt alive.
Ah, Albert! I still live!

Anna Politkovskaya[42]

You'll forgive me if I liken you to Anna,
While hoping that you never share her fate:
A woman shot and killed for being honest,
For writing things that didn't please Vlad Putin.

That was now some fourteen years ago:
October 7—mark that bloody date—
When she was in her prime, at forty-eight
And famous for her lucid bravery.

Born in New York, of Russian diplomats,
Her maiden name was Anna S. Mazepa;
That was back in nineteen fifty-eight,
When Khrushchev's thaw had brought some hope to Moscow.

Her studies at the School of Journalism
At Moscow State University,
Culminated in a striking thesis
On the verse of M. Tsvetaeva.

And then she made a life as a reporter,
First at *Izvestia* until ninety-three,
Of accidents and sundry social problems;
Which set her up for the Putinschina.

Like you, she loved her country and insisted
That freedom, truth and dignity prevail,
But Putin's rule knew nothing of all that
And sentenced this good woman to travail.

Chechnya was the cockpit of the violence
Reporting on which put her in their sights.
They tried mock execution and then poison,
Then sent a brute assassin in the dark.

You, my beauty, have her kind of temper
And so, I dread what thugs may do to you.

Section three

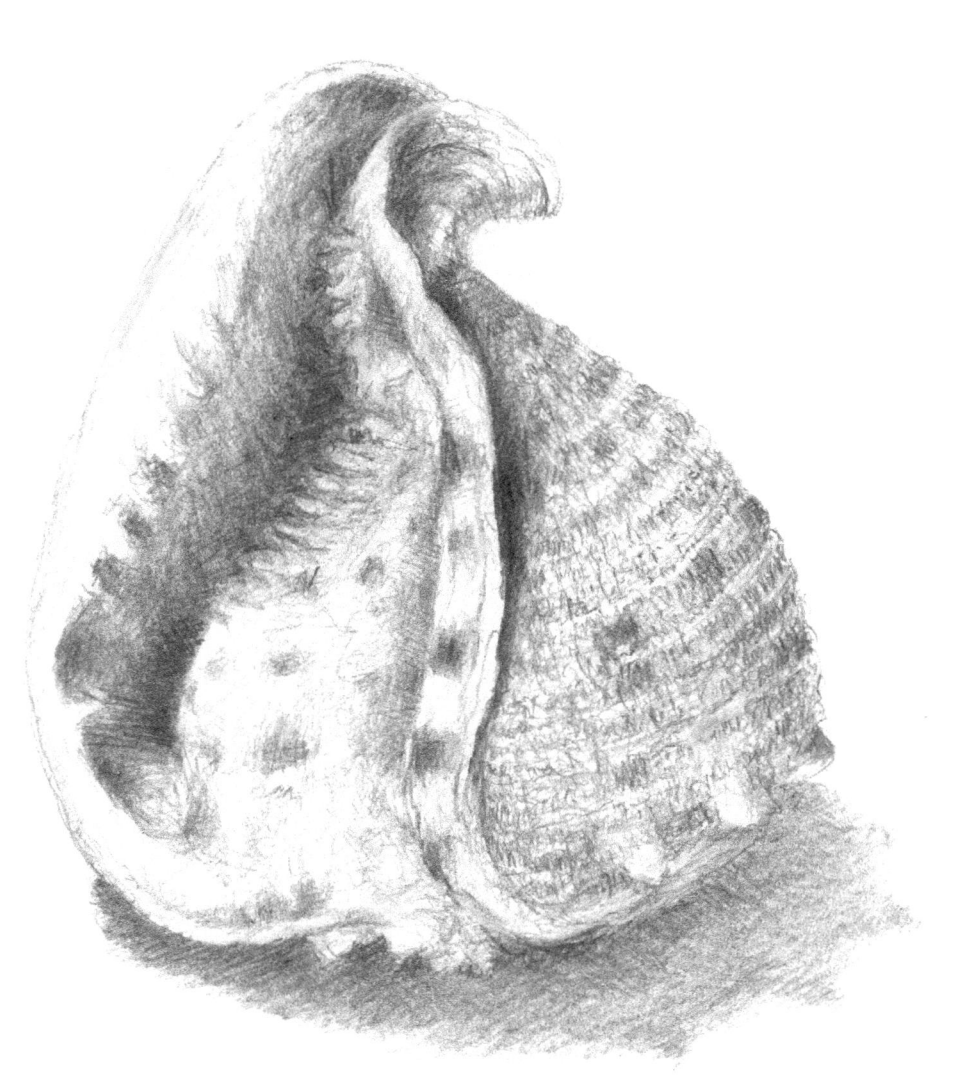

Lead and Polonium 210

I scream within when I recall
Those four shots in the elevator—
The elevator, mind, the means for rising—
With which a Putinesca killer
Snuffed beloved Anna.

I scream within, for her death stands,
Or rather falls with a crimson crash,
Over all promptings to despair
That gnaw my bleeding heart
Like Moscow slum rats.

That woman was good and principled,
Asking in her Russian diary, now in print,
What hope was there for change,
For a new narrative, a source of hope,
When state authorities live for greed alone?

Just days before he met his end
Defector Litvinenko said he knew
That one man only in all Russia
Could kill a journalist of Anna's standing
'And that is Putin, no-one else'.

Remember how that witness was killed off:
Polonium 210 in a cup of tea—
Trace elements of a soft and silvery metal
Ingested in the company of 'friends'—
Just like Roman Tsepov's, in St Petersburg.

I scream within, therefore, when I recall
Those four shots in the elevator,
That lethal tea at the Mayfair Millennium Pine Bar,
Thinking of you, the Tree House with its lift—
And your narrative for a tortured Venezuela.

If they come for you

If they come for you, my dearest love,
As well they might, being narco-thugs,
Being among the more remorseless bandits
Of Bolivarian abuse of power,
How will my unwinged spirit save you?

I know whereof I speak, regarding them:
I've studied their atrocities for millennia;
I've sweated blood in my Gethsemane,
Been crucified by pity and by horror,
More cruelly than the worshipped Son of Man.

How can I spell out what they might do:
Knowing too much of Assyrian tortures,
Roman savageries and modern GULAGs;
Being steeped in countless tragic tales
Of the vilest inhumations of the just?

Is it even permitted me to say
That, should they come for you, I will be there:
To breathe with you, in dignified defiance;
To speak with you, in uttering the truth;
To shame them for their brute banalities?

What haunts me is the prospect of their violence
My knowledge of the gross extremities
That torturers in prisons can inflict:
Will they pull your fingernails out,
Break your limbs or burn or rape you?

Let me kiss your fingers, hands and feet;
Let me salve your skin with tenderness;
Let me be within you, filled with passion;
To hold your psyche sane through all abuse
And have you know you're loved, beyond the end.

No water on Avila, Hugo[43]

'Chavez vive!' cry your posters in the streets;
And from the sides of buildings daubed
By artful Cuban propagandists, where
Your vulgar signature is scrawled;
Your narrow eyes peer unblinkingly
Down upon the criminal scene
Of rank impunity and shameless agitprop,
Lengthening queues and smart bachaqueros,
Bartering in nearly worthless Bolivares
For the country you've made insolvent.

There is no water on Avila, Hugo!
Sign off on that, high upon the sides
Of futures looming beyond your ken.
Boast of this Bolivarian achievement,
You paragon of demotic braggadocio!
Neither bottled nor running water—
In a nationalized park overlooking
The very mausoleum of your stolen hero;
Overlooking Chacao, where your crony,
Aristobulo, took his gated mansion.

No water on Avila, you stupid bungler!
Brown-outs and breakdowns on all sides,
Shortages of medicine, soap and oil;
And now a loony-tune bus driver
Calls out 'Chavez vive', as he runs
Venezuela over a social precipice.
This, you blockhead, is 'revolution'?
This is the price of Bolivarian socialism!
But your lot are clueless about prices:
Of water, oil, foodstuffs, justice, anything…

Doomsday machine[44]

Daniel Ellsberg, more than any other,
Was the mentor of my doctoral dissertation:
His *Papers on the War* and his dissent

From the bellowing, Cyclopean blundering
Of America's prolonged Vietnam War,
In which the VC played astute Ulysses;

Directed me, in that and other cases,
To seek for explanations outside cliché:
In the cognitive machinery of the state.

But, quite apart from bloodied Indochina,
Young Ellsberg, working for the Pentagon
And at RAND, on nuclear strategy,

Had learned some other terrifying things
That put Dick Nixon's bombing of Hanoi
And the use of Agent Orange in the shade.

War Plan Trojan, written in the fifties,
Showed him, in the spring of sixty-one,
The doomsday planning of the Pentagon.

In a memo, on a single sheet of paper,
The likes of which he never saw again,
Stamped 'Top Secret Sensitive:

For the President's Eyes Only',
An answer from the mighty Chiefs of Staff
To a question put by fated JFK:

'If your plans for general nuclear war
Are carried out, how many will be killed
Across the Soviet Bloc, including China?'

The total death toll was six hundred million:
A hundred Holocausts, Ellsberg computed.
This, he vowed, must simply never happen.

No irony Keegan

Young Dan Ellsberg had the coolest job:
Codeword clearances of which you never heard,
Access to the generals in the SAC;
Access to the arc of Pac Rim bases;
Access to the Agency's intelligence;
And all before he reached the age of thirty.

His task was tinkering with decision:
Risk, uncertainty, the calculus of deterrence;
Which required, to a first approximation,
He know the size of both sides' nuclear arsenals—
Throw-weights, second strike, casualties—
And here he butted heads with Thomas Power;

The boss at SAC itself, you understand—
Strategic Air Command—whose famous motto,
'Peace is our Profession', Power belied,
Planning a pre-emptive nuclear strike
That would, he soberly informed the White House,
Wipe out the Reds and leave the Yanks half-scathed.

This was several years before Buck Turgidson,
In Kubrick's *Doctor Strangelove*, tumbled out:
'Mr. President, I'm not saying we won't get our hair mussed.
But I do say no more than ten to twenty million killed, tops!'
Dealing with such chaps was Ellsberg's job,
The film, he'd later say, was documentary.

One day at SAC, he met George Keegan Junior
Chief of Air Force Estimates, SAC Intelligence,
Who asked him, steely eyed, without irony,
When Ellsberg challenged him on missile numbers,
Which SAC was prone to greatly overstate,
'Would you have us fudge our estimates?'

Sergei and Zinaida[45]

I wouldn't want to be Sergei Yesenin.
Sure, he had a gift from early youth;
Sure, his Russian verse brought him acclaim;
Sure, he had the love of many women.
But his fate? Not for any money.

What is it with the Russians and their poets?
They seem to want them drunk or suicidal.
Though, of course, they're not alone in that.
Besides, Russia always offered plenty
To drive one to drink or death.

But Yesenin's particular misfortune
Was collision with the Bolshevik Revolution
And the wreckage that it made of pastoral.
He was just a waif at the Stray Dog
Barking at the Symbolist Moon.

Think of those he mingled with, back then:
Akhmatova, Mandelstam, Blok and Mayakovsky,
Tsvetaeva, Gumilev, Klyuev and Khlebnikov,
All of them ill-fated, like himself,
Culled or muted by the Party state.

But none of this is what my heart rejects.
I honour them among the many fallen.
The tragedy of Yesenin was in love:
Betrayal of his beloved muse, Zinaida
And the downward spiral that involved him in.

Zinaida Raikh was beautiful and bold,
But Sergei, insecure, played fast and loose.
She left him for director Meyerhold;
The broken Sergei opted for the noose;
And Stalin's thugs destroyed the other two.

All we can retrieve

There's part of me that does not want to live;
Though it hasn't had recourse to gruesome violence,
It longs much less to take my life than give
A gift to an unyielding world: my silence.
It comes from weariness.

'To be or not to be?' bright Hamlet asked,
Soliloquizing in a deep despond.
His ghostly father having grimly tasked
The prince with vengeance, how should he respond?
He flailed in weariness.

'To die, to sleep' he famously reflected
And so be rid of all life's grief and pain
Was devoutly to be wished, but then again,
Suppose one dreamed? With that he was deflected
And sank in weariness.

Who'd grunt and sweat beneath a weary life,
But for dread of something after death;
Who'd not seize upon a bodkin (knife),
Cut to the quick, expelling his last breath
And, with it, weariness?

Well, I am not deterred by such a thought.
To die, I deem, would bring a dreamless sleep.
Quite contrary to all that we've been taught,
My pains would vanish, forty fathoms deep
And, with them, weariness.

Yet, older far than Hamlet, still I bear
The kind of fardels he could scarce conceive;
And, why? I vow because I truly care
For you, our love and all we can retrieve
From deathly weariness.

The secret key

Life takes its toll and wounds appear
Where most we're worn
And, if the toll's severe,
Rents are torn, or tumours born,
Or wrought within the fabric of our being.

So it's been with me for many years
And so, as you well know, the good physicians
Have excised from my plagued body, many times,
The feral cells that bid to overwhelm me;
Or fed me wondrous chemistries, instead.

All this, no doubt, has saved me from demise;
Allowing me to write my recent books;
Permitting me to travel far and wide—
At intervals between or grappling with
Lamenesses and months of sheer exhaustion.

But pneuma may have been the secret key
That's opened up the door to longer life
And had my surgeons wonder at the ways
I've long defied their worst prognostications—
Despite the odds in population data.

Quite why this has been so, it isn't clear,
Which leads to Hippocratic conversations;
Such as those with my good doctor, in Brazil,
Of how he'd love to bottle or to clone
My immune-defiance of the said disease.

Yet, could they reproduce the biochemistry
That's held the line in limb and lymph and groin,
I doubt they'd find the subtleties they sought;
For they perhaps derive from pneuma's arts—
Whose wondrous workings YOU have catalysed.

Sils Maria

We've been to Sils Maria:
Beneath blue sky,
We've strolled by Nietzsche's lake—
Just you and I.

It's Zarathustra country
Where we've been—
His refuge, in the Upper
Engadine.

We sought the Surlej Boulder,
Where, they say,
The seer found inspiration
One bright day.

We found the Nietzsche House,
But it was closed;
For Sils itself was not,
As we'd supposed,

Open into May,
Between the seasons
Skiers or hikers stay
For active reasons.

We were pilgrims, though,
In that terrain
And, Nietzsche readers, vowed
We'd come again.

His aphorisms glinted
In the air,
For many had been minted,
Even where

We nimbly trod, remembering our youth,
When Zarathustra changed our sense of truth.

The pact we've formed

Six years ago, in Kirchner's Buenos Aires,
You turned to me and said, in a quiet tone,
'Look carefully at all you see around,
Since this, as cities go, in all the Cone,
Is the finest and the grandest that you'll see.
It's all downhill in quality from here.'

But how, in saying such a scathing thing,
Could you have failed to take into account
Great Rio, with its beach and circling hills?
For, once one's breathed the air of Ipanema
And heard Brazilian music in the streets,
I have to say, one takes a different view.

I drove in from Jobim by private cab
And revelled in the pulsing sense of place.
Confessing to imprisonment in English,
I told my man, in halting Spanish phrases,
That all the world finds Rio fascinating;
As much, in truth, as any city known.

He answered me in swishing Portuguese,
With warmth that showed he'd plainly understood
The root and sense of all I'd tried to say.
He pointed, then, to Corcovado Hill,
Upon which stands the giant, sculptured form
Of Cristo the Redeemer, as he's called.

But it was not the sculpted, looming Christ
That made me feel redeemed on Rio's strand.
It was, instead, Atlantic Avenue:
The beauteous sweep of Copacabana Beach;
It's contrast with the grimness of Caracas—
And the pact we've formed for bravely thinking big.

Our hermeneutics in Zurich

Zurich was a rite of passage, wasn't it?
You'd always said that I could write—
Leaping from the many-storied heights
Of what you saw as my accomplishments—
Something quite fantastically creative.

'You could write a beautiful novel!'
These murmured words, uttered with such fervour;
More than ever, after Zurich, glowing
In the I-am-your-Muse dancing flames
Of your New Andalusian gaze, hold me.

We travelled via Paris, where we'd met,
When you alighted from Caracas, to be greeted
By me and a composer friend who's putting music
To some sonnets that I wrote for someone else;
And we Eiffel-toured the town, with Sils in mind.

But let's not get distracted here from Zurich!
In many ways, your vision brought us there:
To look for Herman Yutick and his house,
To ponder his translation of the priceless
Memoirs of the Falcon I was writing.

Then, as we roamed the streets of Herman's city,
I stumbled, in a bookshop, on a miracle:
The memoirs of a Mormon girl who'd written
Of her road to freedom: *Educated*.
'This,' you said to me, 'I want to read'.

You've read that book; I'm working on the novel;
And, lately, as I read some Aristotle—
On education, in his *Politics*, Book Eight—
Both you and Zurich leapt out from his lines;
Both Herman and the Mormon came to mind.

Gormenghast and my past

When I sit and read of Gormenghast,
That brooding and disturbing psychic shambles,
Through the halls of which, both dim and vast,
Its author moved and now the reader rambles,
I'm struck alike by Steerpike's vicious crimes
And the horrors Mervyn Peake himself had seen,
In the monstrous war that marred his life and times;
The widest and most brutal there has been.
His vulnerable and most artistic soul
Was traumatized by rituals lacking sense,
But far more by the things that he beheld:
Whole cities blasted, cruel experiments
Perpetrated by the Nazis at Belsen;
Barbarities defying human ken;
A house of horrors anchored in the past.

Within the tale, I'm drawn to Sepulchrave,
Driven mad by Steerpike's destruction,
By covert means as sinister and searing
As those the Hitler Youth used in the Operplatz—
Fire and suffocating Goebbelsmoke—
Of the library that all the Earls of Groan
Had laboured a millennium to acquire,
The loss of which deranged the aged Lord
And cut the heart from Titus—his inheritance.
There and in those scenes I'm somehow captured,
Riveted, confounded and enraptured,
Since that library of millennial proportions,
Like the shambled state in which it burns,
Pictures to me how I've spent my life:
In Gormenghast, as Titus, quite alone.

Carneades, critical thinker

Two little, green-covered books
Published as Loeb Classics
By Harvard University Press,
In Cambridge, where we've been, no less,
Offer us the barest summaries—
In what were, at first, ten scrolls—
Of the lives and thoughtful works
Of eighty-two notable philosophers,
Recounted, as the Empire cracked in crisis,
By an Epicurean—Diogenes Laertius.[46]

Here's a test of hoary erudition:
How many of these noted eighty-two
Whose works and wisdom vanished long ago,
With just a handful of exceptions,
Such as Plato and, by indirection, Epicurus—
Save for scattered scholarly citations
Here and there, in other half-lost works—
Would be remembered now, but for the labours
Of Diogenes, in his cribbed and crowded digest—
Which few now read, in our time, anyway?

One such case, to which he gave three pages,
Is Carneades, scourge of Chrysippus,
Whose industry, he says, was quite unparalleled.
Whose dominance in philosophical schools,
As lecturer and controversialist,
Was legendary, from Athens to Cyrene;
Who died by his own hand, when eighty-five,
At the fag-end of the Hellenistic era.
I doubt you've ever heard of Carneades;
But have you even heard of Chrysippus?

Volcanic texts

'Will my books endure?' I've come to wonder,
In thinking of the scrolls of Philodemus;
Recovered, so the scholars have informed us,
From the ruins of Herculaneum:
His many hundred damaged papyri.

Clearly, what I mean is, books can vanish;
As had all the books of Epicurus,
All the works of great Democritus
And the scholarchs of the Epicurean Garden,
Even of the famed Apollodorus.

But let's allow a subtler view of things,
Reflecting on the scrolls that were recovered:
The way that the less damaged, inner parts
Of his and of his sources' treatises,
Have been retrieved, to our enlightenment.

Isn't that what all interpretation,
All close reading, all true comprehension,
What we call hermeneutics, aims to do,
With any book in whole or treasured part?
Don't texts, if they endure, require such art?

So it would be with any work of mine:
It might remain on silent library shelves,
Unread, neglected, dust-begrimed, forgotten;
And, if so, would be like the pumiced scrolls
Long immured at Herculaneum.

But, should a curious soul, by any chance,
Stumble on an archived tome of mine,
It's inner core and endings would require
Quite as careful hermeneutic treatment
As the long-forgotten works of Philodemus.

Philodemus and I

There's a library that was found at Herculaneum.
It belonged, once, to a sage called Philodemus
Of Gadara—but no devilish swine—
And when I think of all his books, I think of mine,
Because of his interests.

He was a philosopher of Epicurean leanings;
Epicurean, that is, in the uncaricatured sense
Of serious atomism and its many implications,
Though more in terms of ethics than of physics:
The science of mens sana.

He studied for a while in Alexandria,
Where he made friends, then moved to Sicily.
But his atomism there caused some offence,
And so he settled on the Bay of Naples,
Beneath Vesuvius.

There, in a splendid Roman villa,
His collection of the works of Epicurus
And learned treatises regarding all the schools
Of classic Grecian thought, in countless scrolls,
Long outlasted him.

Until the famed Vesuvius erupted
And all his books were buried deep in pumice;
But, in our time, much has been recovered.
It's learned range and quality are striking—
As with my collection.

What most arrests my scholarly attention
Is that these ancient books were found at all,
Not lost like many others, in Rome's fall,
Four centuries after the eruption.
Will mine endure?

Chartwell with and without you

You got there first, you keen Churchillian;
And wrote to me 'We must come here together!'

I was lost in wonder at your wonder;
Its aesthetic sense, its deeper moral roots.

Twice, since then, I've tried to make that happen:
A pilgrimage to Chartwell, just with you:

To contemplate the politics and painting,
The lifestyle and the writings of the man

We associate with victory over Hitler;
With radio speeches of inspiring tilt;

With the Saxon roots of English liberty
And the glow of Empire's more heroic tales.

You admire the man and what he stood for,
Though your roots, unlike mine, are Spanish.

The link, I guess, is Simon Bolivar:
The dream of liberalism in the zone,

Where Spanish rule had long ago implanted
A reactionary lineage, unlike Churchill's.

At any rate, I went there quite alone,
But conjuring your presence at each step.

What struck me chiefly were two things:
His paintings and a life to live with you.

Imagine us with such a kitchen garden,
Or taking breakfast in the Dining Room;

Imagine I had such a writing desk
And wrote as copiously as Churchill did;

While you, my one and only Clementine,
Devoted days to troubled Venezuela.

So, I mused, as I strolled there alone,
Surveying all the two of them had done.

Festival of promise

You are so supremely full of life—
It's evident in all you do and say—
While I incline to fatalistic gloom;
Defying odds, to die another day.

But given that we both love Zarathustra,
Let's reflect, in passing, on his claim
That each of us should seek the kind of death
That's less an accident than choice and aim.

This doctrine still sounds strange, the prophet said:
That one die neither early nor too late,
But seek, instead, to hallow what one's lived for,
Rather than accept some random fate.

A festival of promise to survivors,
Is how he'd have us think of our demise:
An artful end; a dignified conclusion,
Consistent with one's life in others' eyes.

The doctrine's quite astringent, let's agree,
Zarathustra scornfully allows:
The passive and superfluous recoil
From the kind of death free spirits should espouse.

'All too many live and all too long!
Would that storms would shake them from the tree!'
A ripe and timely death is for the strong—
The self-possessed, the purposeful and free.

Give all you have, in homage to the Earth;
Bestow on it the honey of your soul;
Throw yourself towards your chosen end
And go down with the Sun, fulfilled and whole.

I think that almost all of this rings true—
But stumble over what it means for you.

Virginia and sex

Virginia Woolf and Vita Sackville West,
Literary lionesses both,
Were privileged to live life at its best.
Even if disrupted by the War,
Their Edwardian idylls lingered
Into the roaring twenties or,
More precisely, their roaring forties—
Well, Virginia's roaring forties,
With young Vita in her thirties
And less roaring, anyway, than soaring.

They first met in nineteen twenty-two,
And shortly got to know each other well.
Each was given to the Bloomsbury view,
Adhered to by their genial host, Clive Bell,
That saw in Sapphism and sodomy
The embodiment of a higher form of being.
But Vita was the freer of the pair:
Of dazzling gifts and unpretentious beauty,
With a nonchalant and aristocratic air,
Committed more to reverie than duty.

Their decade long affair was full of letters:
Literary, flirtatious and lubricious,
But Virginia's quite fragile disposition,
Her nervousness about the acts of sex,
Her sense of self as less a lesbian
Than a eunuch who recoiled from what she found—
The call to Vita activa in bed—
Had her pull the shade of coyness over
What she saw as sex's daunting 'fury'
And pour her pent-up ardour into books.

Mansion and mind

Have you ever heard or read of Knole?
If not, you haven't read your Sackville-West.
For, as Hardyment has shown us, on the whole,
Vita, all her life, was quite obsessed
By all it was: its scale, its age, its soul.

The scale of Knole quite beggars all belief:
A calendar of bedrooms (one each day),
Seven courts, twelve entrances, in brief,
A hundred chimneys, baked from Kentish clay;
A thousand verdant acres in its day.

When Vita met Virginia, she'd just written
A heartfelt family history of Knole;
And, ever after, filled with deep nostalgia,
She dreamed and wrote of what it meant to her;
Having been, from childhood there, quite smitten.

She wrote *The Land*, about the Weald of Kent:
The Wold, the wealth, the world once wooded,
Where Knole had stood sublime for generations;
And then wrote *The Edwardians*, a novel,
A romance of the privileged youth she'd spent.

Of course, her life there hadn't been all idyll,
Though she had roamed its many rooms and gardens,
Read avidly in her father's sumptuous library
And written plays and novels of her dreams.
Her ties to Knole became for her a riddle.

Her riddling gave Virginia increase:
She took in Vita's probings and conceived
How rich and dusky was her lover's mind—
The subject for a romance in itself:
Orlando, her erotic masterpiece.

Shrovetide

How did your emotional tenacity
Ride out the chronic unhappiness
Of living with my sexless gloom?

That's years ago, of course—another life;
But tears and anger came, back then—
For you felt trapped: an unloved wife.

'We're just like two old people', you declared
Once, mournfully, 'who've lost interest
In one another.' To which I simply gloomed.

I knew not how to love; or, rather
To desire with love and innocence;
Having been too often burned;

While you, starved, you thought alone,
Of mother-love, hungered so intensely
For unalloyed, demonstrative affection.

What tangled psychic knots
Bound our being then, withholding us
From both simplicity and joy.

Still, most knots have been loosed or cut
By years of existential therapy, in which
I suffered keenly your remembered pain.

Could I rewind the closely ravelled rope,
Gathering in the past for better binding,
I'd gently spare you all those inner chafings;

I'd weep for both our knotted pasts
And, letting fall the hair of grief,
Baptise our psyches in the purest love.

But we've been shriven by the passing years:
Your vivacity won out and my pure thought
Has salved our psyches, dissolving all our fears.

Finding the clearing

I couldn't give you happiness,
But only abstract thought;
And so our ancient married life
Quite quickly turned out fraught.
Yet you'll agree, in hindsight now,
That each of us was caught
At unawares, by complexes
Which neither could unravel:
Moods and fears and traumas past
That bound us up and dimly cast
Our fates on roads to travel,
Whose course nor ends could be foreseen
In any determinate time or fashion;
So that, faring them or finding them
Baffled foresight, imposing indeterminacy

Yet each of us held to subtle things
To which we were inclined to cling,
As lodestones of our fumbled intimacy:
Memories of bright sayings past;
Moments that shone or ached;
Perceptions of profounder possibilities;
Glimpsed through the prisms or lenses
That mediated our mutually tortured gaze,
Out of the thickets of love long lacked;
For what each of us somehow still conceived
Might yet arise along the shadowed roads;
Might yet break out into a bright clearing;
Might, after all, enfold our psyches' fates
In the very dance of awakened being
That we now, so improbably, enjoy.

We are not reasonable

We might reasonably despair, we twain,
Of the apparent lack
In our ostensive futures
Of that bank and shoal of time
The sweet and famous swan
Assigned to Antony and his—
Well, his triple-turned whore—
Now, there's despair!
We might vow to skip, if it was ours,
The apprehended lightness of—
Ah! The fabled life to come:
For a chance at that clichéd ardour
Green youth and soft porn magazines
In common swear by,
Even in the supposed ripeness of the time.

But we are far from being
Reasonable in quite that sense:
We are not green;
We are not feckless in our love;
We lack the poor naïveté
Of all those star struck striplings
Who take their raw arousal
For some unsullied originality.
No! I am a veritable prune;
While you, robbed of the merest eggs,
Can now bring to parturition
Only meanings and exquisite acts.
Not for us, therefore, the common cycle
Of reproductive and domestic fate;
But—wait—the accomplished ceremony of life.

Kafka and Brod

Did you know that Kafka, dying—
Forty years young, felled by consumption—
Instructed Max Brod, his literary executor,
To commit to the annihilating flame
Most all the books that later lent him fame?

I say 'books', but they were manuscripts—
The drafts of both *The Castle* and *The Trial*;
As well as notebooks, letters, other tales.
Consign it all, he urged his loving friend,
To ashes now, for I've come to my end.

Brod, of course, did nothing of the kind;
He carefully collected Kafka's papers;
Collated and curated them and went to work
Completing both *The Castle* and *The Trial*;
A patient bit of work that took a while.

Those are the books that Kafka's famous for;
As well as stories such as 'Metamorphosis',
'The Great Wall of China' and the like.
This, chiefly, for the existential view
That human life is puzzling, through and through.

Franz predeceased his sisters, but all three—
Gabriele, Valerie and Ottilie were their names—
Perished in the Holocaust, at Chelmno or at Auschwitz.
He had died in nineteen twenty-four
And hardly guessed what horrors lay in store.

A Zionist, Brod fled to Palestine,
Getting out of Prague before the Shoah;
And, having made that most judicious move,
Flourished as a writer without preaching,
Including books on Kafka's thought and teaching.

Archaic Earth[47]

In the prehistory of our present intimacy,
Casting about for how to leap the void,
Opened at my feet by your flight,
I conceived our love as all of life on Earth
And fancied I was some Silurian Nureyev.

Of course, I couldn't dance. I was a cripple
In almost every sense and, not least, sexually.
Dance? With my flat feet and shattered heart?
Nureyev? My antinomy! My shadow!
But Silurian? Ah! That's the secret clue!

You'd come to me from another continent,
Challenged me to see my own anew;
Then changed your mind. So, up and off you flew.
But our continental shelves, our inner worlds,
Had collided like two vast tectonic plates.

That is where 'Silurian' leapt to mind,
Out of Deep Time and all that is the case.
And Nureyev, my counter-self, my avatar,
My lithe persona, fleeing from the Bolshoi,
Danced across the Panthalassic Ocean.

He danced me back four hundred million years—
Stravinsky's *Rite of Spring* upon Gondwana—
When life was just emerging first on land
And our two present continents were fused
And you were Life and I was not confused.

There you pointed to the mystic scene
And took my hippocampus to its shores.
Where sea gods called out 'Dance for all the world!
Dance, emergent one, for all you're worth,
On nascent limbs, on the archaic Earth!'

Andromeda

Andromeda is something to behold:
The most fabled and wondrous of nebulae;
Object of long gazing and speculation.
'Minor cloud or regal constellation?'
The brilliant Kant conjectured,
But lacked the instruments to probe
The astral mystery, or compute the distances;
And show Andromeda was, indeed, a galaxy
Beyond the supra-Copernican vastness
Of our long-fabled Milky Way.

Four hundred billion stars, astronomers say;
Or roughly twice the calculated number
Scattered in our multi-stranded spiral,
Over distances that merely mathless brains
Simply can't begin to cogitate:
One hundred thousand light years, end-to-end.
Yet after Hubble's red-shift observations,
All cant and cavil of Andromeda
Concluded with the awestruck, firm admission
That it is separate from our swirl of stars.

It's radiance comes to us over gulfs
Of space-time numbing in their scale:
Two and a half million light years,
Which is to say nine and a half trillion
By that two and a half million, in kilometres;
And yet our instruments—get this—
Have found at Andromeda's great heart
Two black holes dancing tango with each other.
More stunning still, that it and our own galaxy
Are on a multi-billion-year collision course.

Tractatus Logico-Poeticus

Now, honestly, who would turn to Wittgenstein
To world his love for you poetically?
Given he made plain, in his *Tractatus*,
What can be said at all can be said clearly,
That the world is all that is the case
And sense consists in pointing, more than words?

His dictum, at the end of the *Tractatus*—
That of which we cannot speak,
We must pass over in silence—
Proclaims a pristine world of solid fact,
To which poetic speech does violence
Of its nature, in the vocal act.

He did, it must be said, make one concession.
It's numbered six dot five two two
And states there are, in fact, some things,
That, though they can't find meaningful expression,
Make themselves to us quite manifest
And are the things that we call mystical.

But where does this leave us, my mystic love;
Since, Wittgenstein or no, we're language beings?
For worlded love consists less of the facts
Than of the dreams we bring forth out of them,
The metaphors by which we recombine
What is the case with what we will to be.

Let me read this riddle, as a poet:
Ludwig's labours were elucidations;
Who comprehends them uses them to climb
A ladder of astringent comprehension,
Ascending which one sees the world aright—
And there the doves of poetry alight.

Boltzmann and Nietzsche

Ludwig Boltzmann, born in eighteen forty-four,
The same year as Friedrich Nietzsche,
Outlived him, as fate took him, by six years;
But both died younger than I already am
And both died badly, mentally collapsing.

Both loved music and learned to play piano;
Nietzsche, famously, fell for Richard Wagner,
Longing to find in opera his great solace
For the consequences of the death of God.
Boltzmann learned, instead, from Anton Bruckner.

But whereas Nietzsche studied Greek and Latin,
Boltzmann's guiding passion was for physics
And, while still young, he grasped its cutting edge.
He spent himself on entropy and gases,
Til drawn, like Nietzsche, to philosophy.

In awe of Darwin, as of James Clerk Maxwell,
He wanted to dispense with metaphysics;
But, as with Nietzsche, so with Boltzmann,
The riddles of existence haunted him,
Recurring without surcease in his dreams.

If all those questions don't admit of answers,
Why can't we dispense with them for good?
If they are only cognitive illusions,
Why, he pondered, don't they disappear?
Instead the daemons robbed him of his sleep.

As Nietzsche turned to his friend, Jakob Burckhardt,
Boltzmann turned to gentle Franz Brentano;
But neither Stoic friend could save his genius.
Boltzmann suicided at Duino,
Nietzsche died of pity in Turin.

Jefferson's library

Somewhere, I mislaid my notes;
Or somehow never made them,
Of our brief visit to the Jefferson collection
In the Library of Congress. Strangely,
My meticulous journal fails to record it.

Yet I have this photograph,
Among a dozen that I took in the collection,
Of your intent features, from a distance,
Unwaveringly focused on a tour guide's words
Concerning Thomas Jefferson and his books.

All I've known of you, in all these years,
Is captured in that snapped image.
There's the woman who, twenty years before,
Adoring Humboldt, prompted by Machado,
Had flown to Mexico to go beyond.

Cognitive development, analysis of information,
A Master's course in Mexico City,
Lecturing in Monterrey, attending Armando's soirees,
Reading Descartes while Gabi drew her;
Then the plunge, the bold Moon-landing,

Being Frida, being Alma, wooing
And winning a double scholarship
For still another Master's—in Philosophy;
Returning to the Earth on Orinoco;
Building a national praxis, step by step.

That was the persona—now in Washington,
In the footsteps of her hero, Alexander;
Listening, with minute attention, to Jefferson's legend,
In awe of the curated, glassed collection,
Who caught my eye—and drew my lens to her.

Wine at the Tree House

She calls you 'The Squirrel', doesn't she?'
Having taken you into what she calls,
Given its elevation and leafy outlook,
'The Tree House'—high above the street—
Doubtless on account of your energy;
That animation so central to your charm.

It's small, the Tree House, neat and cosy;
Expressive of its owner's personality:
Chaste, with a sommelier's refinement.
We consumed cassava flakes and cheese,
Toasted bread and Venezuelan wine—
And talked for hours of love and poetry.

That small repast was fiercely expensive
In dollarized, inflation-wracked Caracas;
Yet neither of you, there in your abode,
Would hear of my contributing to costs.
Moreover, rosy with generosity, she gifted me
A volume of Montejo's sombre verse.

I read Montejo's lyric melancholy
A week later, alone at Tantalo's.
But around the blessed Tree House coffee table,
Our three-way conversation turned to teaching:
Your qualities as a vibrant educator,
The fact that students now just won't read books.

When I look back upon that afternoon,
Inscribed now in the Book of Life,
It glows as quietly as Montejo's lines;
And has me call that place the Trio House.
There Rembrandt might have painted us together—
Three souls sipping wine in roseate peace.

McGurk's lament

Syria now must choose between bad options:
Erdogan's encroachments from the north
Sprung of Ottomania and Lausanne;
The Iranian aim to reach the Lebanon,
In a history going back to Gilgamesh,
Fuelled not only by Shia rage,
But by imperial dreams as old as Cyrus;
Hammered ISIS, dragon spawn of chaos;
Assad, the mass-murderer, in Damascus;
Putin coveting ports and Trump withdrawing.

Pity the poor millions, the civilians,
The Kurds in the northeast, the SDF,
Caught between these merciless, warring powers;
Merciless, that is, save Trump the Careless.
Now Brett McGurk, the erstwhile US envoy,
Coalition's guide, a soldier-diplomat,
Who'd laboured for three years to snuff out ISIS,
Is confronted by the Donald's witless call
For all the US forces to withdraw;
Thus, jeopardizing what McGurk's achieved.

But why do I write all of this to you,
Caught in quite another bugger's muddle—
In the midst of brute Maduro's rank defiance
And insolent, quite criminal alliance
With Russia, and with Cuba and Iran,
Ruined by a Weimar-style inflation,
While working on your country's re-invention?
Quite simply, it's because McGurk's lost labours
Parallel your own much humbler ones:
A study in how virtue works for order.

Section four

Gimme shelter

There are moments in the Stones' Havana Moon[48]
At which the Cuban crowd, in ecstasies,
Dancing, chanting to the rolling songs,
Seems cupped in Jagger's Dionysian hands,
While, upon the stage, the god of rock
Embodies what it means to be alive.

Never more than singing 'Gimme shelter'—
Anthem of a world in revolution;
Its lust for love, its chronic fear of war—
With Sasha Allen, hair down to her hips,
A classic Aphrodite to the core,
Her sultry mood, her eyes, her perfect lips.

How many times I've listened to them sing,
Accompanied by haunting ululations,
By Charlie's drums, Keith Richards on his strings;
And mused that this performance, in itself,
Epitomizes what we really are:
Beings of dancing passion and of song.

Seized by thoughts like that, I feel conflicted,
For Jagger doesn't deal in reasonings;
He doesn't move such crowds to understand,
But weaves some Gestalt magic with their moods,
Governing them with minor chords and beat,
Overlaid with spare but vibrant words.

Sasha Allen's beauty, Keith's guitar,
Demotic words of fire and love and war,
So stir the mass in that Havana square,
One longs to stage such scenes with one's own love;
To so project one's dreamings on the world—
And have it move in one's extended hands.

Coffee with the old historian

I'd heard you speak of the historian
With awe at his many writings,
Long before we met him in Caracas.

Herman Carrera Damas, sage and author,
Octogenarian, veteran diplomat, visionary,
Analyst of democratic possibilities.

He greeted us, on our arrival—
You and I and Gaston, your compadre—
And took us to a window, in his study.

There, at a small table, for two hours,
In English, since neither my French nor my Spanish
Was competent for the discourse,

Surrounded by his library, over coffee,
We spoke of Venezuela's deep travail
And Herman's work on Universal History.

He spoke of spells in Moscow, Prague and Paris,
Deflected the idea of writing memoirs,
Spoke with quiet hope about the future.

His love for you, in glowing evidence,
Was void of tell-tale signs of mere libido.
He finds you charismatic and compelling.

He knows that you are not just a disciple.
He respects the keen-edged temper of your mind.
He loves your reverent passion for your country.

You and I, of course, in conversations,
Have puzzled at his sere serenity,
Amid the mess the crook Maduro's made.

He and I might never meet again,
But those few hours have lodged him in my mind,
As mentor to my love—one of a kind.

Fermi's paradox[49]

Among the books on cosmology
In the personal library which,
As you know, I like to think of as
A fragment of the Museum at Alexandria,
Updated for now, of course, and all,
Barring a little Latin, French and Spanish—
And, of course, the whole of Shakespeare,
So almost all, in modern English
And, thus, not Greek to me—
Is a splendid tome just titled GALAXY.

Now, what's your mental map, beloved,
Of what is out there—if not 'God'?
Never mind the Cosmos as a whole,
Beyond the Galaxy, the fabled Milky Way.
What leaps to your mind's eye?
Messier 104, perhaps, the Sombrero galaxy,
Given that I, dazzled by its Mexican resonance,
Dangled the image evanescently before your eyes,
In drafting our unwritten story, years ago?
Sombrero, with its hundred billion stars?

But here is why I'm led to ask the question:
Longing just for you, intelligent being,
Among the endless stars and constellations;
I ponder, nonetheless, the SETI question
And puzzle at the famous Drake Equation.
If there's intelligent life, apart from you,
Worth longing for among the countless suns,
What to make of Fermi's Paradox:
In all that spacetime, where is everyone?
Ah! In the eternity of silence, I still hear
Your singing voice. WE are not alone.

Karl Kraus in love

Timms' *Karl Kraus: Apocalyptic Satirist*,
A bulky tome of some six hundred pages,
Is dense with detail of his life and times:
His obsessions with ink, technology and death,
Absorption in the tussles of his world;
And his acerbic wit, in Café Central.
His faculties turned on humbug and pretension,
Torching, with creative flair, all things that stank;
Inspiring those who thought to innovate,
From Berg to Loos, from Kafka to Adorno.

Yet, as I read, since you were on my mind,
Between Timms' lines, conspiring in my reading,
Nothing so affected me as his account
Of all the tangled love affairs of Kraus,
From Annie Kalman down to Gina Kaus;
But most of all with Sidonie Nadherny—
Itself commingled, through their mutualities,
With love for Mechtilde Lichnowsky,
To whom we still have sixty of his letters,
Though all Mechtilde's letters have been lost.

But Sidonie was the one who captured me,
Perhaps because their passion was discreet.
Sidonie being close to Rainer Rilke,
Whose love, before he died, she cherished greatly.
We lack the letters that she wrote to Kraus,
But have the diaries that she kept for many years.
From these we glean her intimate regard
For the attitude that Karl brought to their union:
Neither love nor sex could be a duty,
But only care and sacramental beauty.

Franz Brentano and us[50]

Now, why did Boltzmann go to see Brentano?
Ah! Now we're riddling with the best of them!
We could be, here, with Gerard Manley Hopkins,
Exploring perceptions, crafting rhythmic verse,
Since they and we all came from Catholic backgrounds.
Brentano, though, was an ontologist,
Who wrote his doctorate on Aristotle:
About the fivefold senses he perceived
Of 'being', or of what 'existing' means;
And the Master's thought on 'active intellect'.

He then became a Roman Catholic priest
And, in his cloth, was heavily involved
In Pio Nono's claim to be 'infallible'—
Ex cathedra, of course, not as a man—
To which Brentano, rightly, stood opposed;
And, losing that debate, gave up the priesthood,
Then the Church entirely, six years later.
Yet, while a priest, he'd done quite brilliant work—
Published after he renounced his orders—
On psychology—the science of the mind.

Do I have, at this point your attention?
Do you start to see why brilliant Boltzmann,
Tormented by the riddles of ontology,
Would have sought Brentano out, in Florence;
And begged of him, in vain, for soothing answers?
Boltzmann couldn't sleep because of migraines,
Yet thought his problem lay in metaphysics.
Brentano's counsel failed to salve his psyche,
For Boltzmann thought there was no 'inner self'.
But ah!—for us—what conversations!

The freedom to aspire

There is no other poet, live or dead,
With whose romantic love, or fervid lines,
I need now fear comparison, it seems.[51]
And who can say as much, who knows their verse?
(As for those who don't, well, what of them?)

I wouldn't claim, of course, to write as well
As Sappho, say, or Ovid or the Bard,
But this I would avow, to you, at least,
That none of them has had the love I know.
That love is yours and ours and that's the point.

It has the richest strains of mutual feeling
Of any passion, exile or recall
That one can find in Sappho's finest fragments,
In Ovid's punished loves or Shakespeare's pain.
I know, for I have read them all.

Sappho's loves, on classic Grecian islands,
Or Ovid's art of love, in ancient Rome;
The sonnets Shakespeare wrote to his Fair Youth,
Or the melancholy verse of poor John Keats,
Astonished, I transcend, in loving you.

Your energy, your beauty and our memories
Have given us the freedom to aspire
Against the very currents of our time,
To every kind of strong and laughing dream
That ever was in venturous souls fulfilled.

Faced with the complexities of love,
We've risen, step by step, to brave the cold
And, warmed by signs that each the other gives,
We've found that as a twosome we are bold;
And have come to see our world from far above.

Whatever is out there[52]

I want to write to you of everything,
Or, rather, whisper of it in your ear;
Exchange it with you through your fingertips;
Have it come alive within your eyes.
Not, just to be clear, between the two of us,
That I'm obsessed with mere atomic facts;
Or even with communicating comprehension.
No, it's you who are the crucial focus here,
As the quintessential other to my being,
With whom I wish to world within my time.

Others won't quite credit this, but you will:
I think of you when reading Wittgenstein,
Or the stunning works of early modern science;
Accounts of Mach or Boltzmann in Vienna;
Their debate on the existence of the atom;
Their insistence there is nothing but sensations;
Their attempt to sweep away all metaphysics;
Their impatience with the thought of Kant and Hegel;
To have done with what they claimed were pseudo-problems—
And how this hit a philosophical wall.

Why you, in such a world of abstract reason?
Well, partly since we met on reasoning's ground;
Partly since you lecture on good thinking;
And partly since you love, what Mach, for instance,
Stood for in his day: progressive thought.
Yet, also, prompted by your invocation
Of 'God, the Universe or whatever's out there'
As being addressable in 'prayer'.
This, pray, is where I'd world you most of all:
In poetry that's metaphysical.

Transcendent conversations

Let there be no doubt that, when you left
The barren Moon, to go and find once more,
The verdant Earth of your own native land,
You broke the cup of bitterness I'd held;
From which I'd sipped the wine of my defeats.

It shattered in my hand and then I felt,
Welling up and pouring out of me,
The need to dream, the need to own emotion
And not to let it die on stiffened lip
Of irony and salted resignation.

How hard it was to meet then, in New York,
To feel, in truth, how distant you'd become;
And then to have to let you go again—
And, two years on, again—from Buenos Aires;
And then once more, from old Hispaniola.

But all these travels generated verse;
That much one can say for them, at least;
Through this, that rendezvous by rendezvous,
By means of laboured and perseverant prose,
The ground was sown with poetries to come.

You it was who made the bold suggestion
That, if I'd help, you'd fly back to the Moon,
To share with me a workshop that I'd done
On the nature of our freedom and the ways
To step into the clearing of our lives.

We shared that work, indeed, and you declared
That in those days of clearing we enjoyed
Transcendent conversations of a kind
That liberated us from where we'd been—
And threw the stars once more before our lives.

Zarathustra and us

When did you first read your Zarathustra?
I did, I recall, when just nineteen;
Two decades shy or so from his descent

From the mountain cave, where he'd reflected
For ten years, in hermetic solitude
On meaning, death and all our cosmic ends;

Before he thought—remember?—that the Sun
Itself, the super-abundant star, would brood,
Had it not those below for whom it shone.

Behold, he then declaimed before the dawn,
I am weary of my wisdom, lacking hands
Outstretched to receive what I might give.

I must go down, like you, behind the Sea;
I must go down, descend into the depths,
I must go down; I must, indeed, go under.

From this mountain cave and solitude,
I must take my leave and find some way
To give away such wisdom as I've gleaned.

Do you remember reading these few lines,
When you were young and still not mountain born?
Before you met Machado and his books?

Oh, I remember well my mountain climb;
The long ascent, free solo, into silence;
The years of learning, harrowed in my cave.

But now I picture you, in Monterrey—
Mount Eyrie, shall we now agree to call it?—
Reading Descartes, thinking of your futures.

Then you, like Zarathustra, came Down Under,
Where I'd become the old man in the forest.
You said that you'd brought fire into my valley.

Museo Larco

My guidebook urged I find Museo Larco,
As I briefly passed through Lima, bound for Cuzco;
On account of its collection of ceramics;
Among which is an 'infamous' curation
Of some 'erotic pots', which, so it stated,
Depicted pre-Columbian sexual mores.

Now, I ask you, having been so tantalized,
Who, in their right mind, could stay away?
Besides, I'd heard, or more precisely read,
In fleeting, candid passages of prose
That what the guidebook hinted might be found
Had flourished long among the free Peruvians.

What I found, within Museo Larco,
Transcended what the guidebook said I'd find
And raised a host of questions in my mind,
Concerned with power, beauty and curation;
The Spanish conquest, the Peruvian nation;
Larco's wealth and his philanthropy.

Yet here, in a discrete, well-lit pavilion,
Were Moche mouldings of the act of love,
With much depiction of fellatio,
As well as diverse acts of copulation;
And skeletons self-pleasuring in the grave.
Imagine, therefore, when that culture lived!

But Larco's fortune came from sugar cane,
A plant whose history's anything but sweet;
His tribute to his father's sponsorship
Of his own life, as antiquarian aesthete,
Exposes the imperial stratigraphy
That yielded all these shards of long defeat.

Agreement over piña coladas

No-one else, I bet, has sat in Panama
As we just did, my beauty;
Well-seated, at Tantalo's roof-top bar,
Sipping the most generous of piña coladas;
Conscious of the history of the Isthmus,
Freshly reminded of its geological,
Or more precisely, its tectonic past;
Conscious of its twofold global function:
Linking continents, linking oceans;
And feeling all this in our finger-tips;
Conscious of our being there as Dasein,
Drinking in all this as our experience,
In animated talk and loving glances;
Bringing all our past into those hours;
Projecting it into our pondered futures.

Didn't we concur, at Tantalo's;
Didn't we design a fresh agreement:
Looking from the old, colonial world
Across to all the towers of the modern;
Didn't we acclaim the tectonic movement
Which, drifting over mantle, under water,
Over the wide Earth brought us here?
Didn't we acclaim the very Isthmus
As our own bridge, our vibrant metaphor;
Knowing the place of bridges in our lives,
Knowing the poetics of our crossings,
Ever since we bridged the Rio Tajo,
Fording it from opposite directions?
We'd dreamed; but there we drank in,
Tantalized, what still might lie beyond.

Heading to Tocumen

'Listo?', you will query me,
Each time it comes to parting;
With a breathtaking briskness
That quietly exudes emotional mastery.

I won't say this time wasn't different.
It was, in my remembering, unique.
It was complete and eloquent,
In pre-dawn understatement.

Out of La Isabella Suites,
Where big Andres, Venezuelan exile,
Had made the pair of us so welcome,
Giving us umbrellas in the tropic rain;

Into the limousine of Jose Leonardo,
Venezuelan exile, also, former oil executive;
We slid, with our light bags
And luminous Tantalo memories.

You, however, took the passenger seat
Initiating a most animated
Conversation with our gentle driver,
Concerning Venezuela and its prospects.

These large men, both alike, have fled
From the plunderers and incompetents
Who pig out, like Napoleon, on your country;
Who've driven millions into flight abroad.

But you are most intent upon returning
With inimitable fire, with unquenchable love;
And so you led the conversation, in the dark:
On democracy and Venezuela's future.

I gently touched your liberated curls.
You turned and smiled, quite unforgettably.

Imagining the Alcantara

We've built a bridge between us, my beloved;
Spun and spanned and sung into being
Out of metaphor and imagining.

Do you remember that morning, long ago,
When, as you slept under my roof,
I found myself teleported to Toledo?

It was a pink dawn and I was looking east
Out the wide window from my writing desk,
Where you would quietly work in later years.

And as the winter sun quite wanly rose,
Inspired by your Hispanicness, I suppose,
I found myself where once before I'd been:

The swirling Tajo, with its fabled crossing,
Came before my speculating eyes,
As the point of entry to a waking dream.

I knew, of course, with wonder, where I was;
It's histories, since the Ice, were known to me;
But its old stones now spoke of other things:

They murmured, like river water, of mutation
And spoke to me in tongues of what might be,
As you appeared across the bridge's span.

It occurred to me, as I then quickly wrote,
That you and I had met in that imaginary
By chance or fateful serendipity;

And so I asked, in very free-form prosody,
Whether we, like hunters, long ago,
Might descend together to the plain.

Why not, I asked your ether self, take aim
At all that may be possible out there?
And so we have—and so have forded fate.

Giles Sparrow's Cosmos[53]

This massive book is full of coloured photos,
Beginning with the numbered inner worlds
From Venus out to Pluto, in our system.

What images! What photographs! What science!
Including graphics of tectonic plates
And studies of our planet's air and water.

Consider what it says of Mercury,
A tiny, racing, charred and barren world—
'Worlded' only by our close attention.

It used be thought of Mercury's solar orbit
That it had simply synchronous rotation,
But the truth is both stranger and more wondrous:

Mercury's day is two thirds of its year;
It rotates thrice in every two full orbits
With curious effects in terms of dawn.

Cloudy, storm-wracked giants hold the void,
Beyond the massive belt of asteroids:
Two hundred million whizzing stones in number.

But let them go, for all their fascination;
Likewise, all the swarms of icy worlds
That orbit wide before one reaches Pluto.

True awe takes flight at interstellar space,
With Sparrow's plates of stunning nebulae
And catalogues of named and fabled stars.

Think Sirius, Canopus and Arcturus,
Giant Rigal, Aldebaran or Betelgeuse,
Of varied spectral types and luminosities.

The distances defy imagination,
Even in the nearer Milky Way;
Yet Sparrow shows us inter-galactic space.

Sao Paolo on foot

Avenida Paulista was once a country road
Cut along a high ridge, looking toward
The hill, where sainted Anchieta and his Jesuits,
Centuries before, built Sao Paolo
To evangelize the ill-fated Guaranis.

Who would guess, from present evidence,
That it had then become
The boulevard of the coffee barons,
When Jardim, east of their height,
Was still a Botanical Garden?

Who would guess now, among the
Serried towers of glass and steel,
That they are so new in provenance;
That this overwhelming conurbation
Is the construction of two lifetimes?

Yet down Avenida Paulista yesterday
I took my way, past all the towers,
Wide-eyed and photographically conscious,
Like a Guarani with a camera;
Blessing myself in the names of

All my most tutelary deities;
Casting my vision like a net
Over all that was redolent,
Coloured, vibrant as sea creatures,
Or scarred with social meaning,

With signatures of opulence or inequity,
From Consolacao to the Casa das Rosas;
Capturing, in that net, the myriad tokens
Of shimmering, arcane thought worlds
Displayed on newsstands in Portuguese—
With you dancing in all my senses.

Flight to Morocco

What a southwestern flight we had, my dove,
Absorbed in starboard, stratospheric views
Of green Sardinian coasts and other islands,
Algeria's starkly arid littoral,
A glimpse of Camus' fabled Oran,
Morocco's striking, watered hinterland
And then descent to Bogie's Casablanca;
Or so it seemed to our flying imaginations,
Little guessing how dull its airport was—
And what would happen down in Marrakesh.

You'd been reading all my childhood poems
Along the way across North Africa,
Exclaiming with delight at my recall
Of picture books I'd read when very young,
As well as more precocious kinds of things;
And so we simply weren't prepared
For barriers to entry or for shocks;
We didn't contact Maximo in time,
Or realize, until it was too late,
That I'd lost my trouser belt in Casablanca.

What followed was half comic, half grotesque:
I could barely hold my trousers up,
As you spoke in Spanish to the Berber guards
Who would not let you come with me
Through Immigration into Marrakesh;
While I, in English, struggled to relate
To Maximo, in distant Malaga,
The unexpected plight that we were in.
I put you on a midnight flight to Spain,
With darkling thoughts of parting, chance and fate.

Without a prayer

It was midnight by the time I reached the riad
And you were gone:
They wouldn't let me have you by my side
In Marrakesh.
I will not readily forgive them that.

Samadi met me in the old medina.
He was cheerful.
He took me to the villa, lit the lamps.
This was a refuge;
But you, beloved; you had been expelled.

What a gross debacle it had been;
How very humbling!
I'd been caught, I ruefully reflected,
With my pants down;
And you, whom most I love in all the world;

Yes, most in all the world, in every way,
Had been sent flying,
Without a hotel booking, to Madrid.
How could this be?
I winced to be so helpless to provide.

The next day I was woken by muezzins:
Their call to prayer.
So, I guess, it goes in all Medinas
But where were you?
I had to learn—and by the swiftest means.

Happily, without recourse to prayer,
Our mobiles worked;
Your competence and general savoir faire
Had kept you safe.
I breathed again and made plans for Morocco.

Marrakesh maze

Why was I in Marrakesh at all?
You know, you know, you know:
To find the ghost of Averroes.

Why that ghost of quiet reasoning?
You know, you know, you know:
He's the cut-out for my rank subversion.

What subversion am I plotting, then?
You know, you know, you know:
Of over serious prophets and fanatics.

What's the plot I have in mind to foil them?
You know, you know, you know:
The glorious fable of the Falcon's flight.

Who was this Falcon, then, and when his flight?
You know, you know, you know:
He fled the Abbasids and conquered Spain.

But why, then Marrakesh or Averroes?
You know, you know, you know:
It's there he lost his copy of the tale.

But how, in that case, has the story surfaced?
You know, you know, you know:
I conjured it from out of Timbuktu.

Timbuktu? So, what's the story there?
You know, you know, you know:
It was hidden, like the imam, 'til our time.

Timbuktu? A hidden manuscript?
You know, you know, you know:
That's the lure of what I'm set to write!

However, Marrakesh did not go well!
I found that the medina was a maze
And Averroes' ghost eluded me, you know.

If you see her

'I want to come to Marrakesh', you'd said
So we agreed you'd join me in Morocco,
Not fly home from Washington instead,
Which allowed the chance for us to go
To Rome, en route.

That shaped my thoughts. It gave me the idea
Of travelling on without you, overland—
So that I could miss you in Tangier;
Proceeding with my fieldwork, as I'd planned,
Once you flew out.

But as explained above, in Flight to Morocco,
You didn't have the passport you required,
Which brought our scheme for touring time undone,
Leaving me alone at once—and tired:
In the riad.

It took a day or so to find my feet.
Without you, being there had lost its charm:
The mosques, the souks, the common Arab street.
Bewildered, I might well have come to harm.
I found my way.

Bob Dylan's famous lines then came to me:
His plaint of poignant loss suffused my brain.
Tangier alone it clearly had to be:
'If you see her, say hello'—again
And again I sang.

The singer's lyrics now became recast,
His motifs and his melancholy mine:
As he had sung, I, too, replayed the past,
Breathing love for you in every line—
En route to Tangier.

High Atlas

How do you get yourself inside
A culture so alien to yours and mine
As Berber Islam,
Or Araby more generally;
As the cities of Morocco,
Or the micro-worlds of the Sahara?

You don't, of course, and nor—
Barring a poet's or an artist's
Dreams of painterly appropriation—
Have I any longing, any thirst,
Any metaphysical aptitude
Or appetite for such a thing.

No, what I bring is just,
Or perhaps entirely unjust,
Blatantly imperial inclinations:
To scan the horizon, assess the wealth,
Compile a kind of Domesday Book
Of writerly, exploitable impressions.

Hence Marrakesh; hence Tangier,
Hence the fast train now between them;
Hence my shameless plundering
Of Bennison on the Almoravids,
On the Almohads and Averroes—
Less, in fact, for benisons than for grid-lines.

But the snow-capped peaks
Of the Berber-kept High Atlas
Take my breath away in transit,
Draw my eyes aloft from the page,
As they held my gaze from the Marrakesh terrace:
Scintillant signs of what was most at stake.

Tangier

I was asked, now many years ago,
As I completed my historical studies:
'Do you see yourself, young man,
When it comes to the world of ideas,
As a priest or an explorer?'

This was six years on
From my impulsive manifesto;
Yet the questioner was,
Of all things, in the circumstances,
An American Professor of Law.

'An explorer,' I responded,
'Every day of the week!'
And here I was: an explorer still,
With countless ventures afterwards,
En route to old Tangier.

The city's very name is redolent
Of exotica, hashish and rent boys,
Extravagances and countless louche affairs;
A history of slavery and violence—
In short, of Rimbaud's dreams.

But I was not in search of sex or hash;
Not being Tennessee Williams,
Not being Truman Capote,
Not being William Burroughs;
I had much rarer plans.

My Tangier was a vantage point
From which to ponder time and tales,
To gaze across the Strait to Andalusia,
With the Falcon's fugitive eyes,
Imagining a stunning scheme of conquest.

From Frankfurt to Singapore

'I've had my first foray in the Maghreb',
I thought, as I flew out from Marrakesh;
Replete with deeply coloured new impressions,
Though depleted by my singular exertions:
Pensive and exhausted.

'I'll rest once I alight in Singapore,
Reflect at ease, compose some bright new verse',
I vowed, as my Lufthansa flight, aloft,
Swept me northward: a poetic Rommel
Taking combat leave.

The vista of the snowy Pyrenees,
The starboard sight by night of Rhone and Rhine,
The gleaming, vast extent of Frankfurt's lights,
The awesome scale of modern Europe's hub,
Framed my outward flight.

Onward, then, to distant Singapore,
I flew, but felt debilitation grow,
Which laid me out in stewardesses' hands,
Feeling aged and all too convalescent.
I slept until the landing.

Blood poured from my nose in Singapore:
As soon as I'd alighted; in the cab;
Again, when I booked in at my hotel;
And once again the next day after breakfast.
I haemorrhaged misgivings.

The E.N.T. at Raffles doubled down.
He charged me, for his service, through the nose:
A captive patient stranded and in need;
But I got through and flew on back to Oz.
Now for bloody poetry!

Aleph was a breathing stop[54]

Aleph, the ox, was first a breathing stop;
And Bayt, where breathing paused, the house.
Gimel, C, was first a throwing stick;
And, with these sparse beginnings, don't you see,
Arose, in time, our fabled A, B, C.

These were the Dalet—door—to all our rhymes
To aeons of delight: exclaimed surprise—
That's E—and peg and fence came next,
Converting objects both to sign and sound:
Like wheel and water, pillar, eye and mouth.

What logic led the goddess to direct
That these assorted objects represent
Her symbols, shaping all articulate speech
Into signs that captured meaning, high and low
And gave the brain a boundless inner scope?

Ah! Semiosis set the spirit free
On inward journeys complex and profound,
Both lending art to commerce in the light
And shadowed subterfuge to courts and time,
Then turning speech to music: metred rhyme.

Have you considered, in your Spanish world,
How linked we are, by sign as well as sound,
To mysteries as ancient as the caves,
To legends that have moved the world around
And resonate in poets' plangent staves?

To visualise and translate into sense
The myriad denotations of these signs
Arranged in chords of shifting mood and tense
Requires a tutored sensibility
Quite Magian in the stars that it aligns.

Gestures, marks and signs

Gestures, marks and signs have—
If one may offer ownership to them—
A history all their own, which,
Captured by our questing modern selves,
Comes back to life by stratified degrees.

They may trace their lineal descent—
An aristocracy of semiosis
As glittering and elegant as Semiramis—
Back through millennia of privilege,
To painted grottos, in the dim and distant past.

The goddess Semiosis is their Muse
And she, perhaps, it was who conjured them
From primal murals daubed on ice age walls,
By long refinement of the fingered brain,
Until they rose as glyphs in ancient times.

Such glyphs, we're told, were shaped, at first, for trade,
Long after settlement, in the warming Holocene,
Of the volatilities of the frozen past
Into the mud-brick towns and fertile fields
Of storied Sumer and rich Pharaonic Egypt.

Yet cuneiform and hieroglyphs of old
Were but the crafted start to self-expression.
Though labouring scribes wrote meaning with such forms,
Imagination sought for nimbler means
To shape by hand what mind and heart conceived.

They say the breakthrough came along the Nile,
Perhaps four thousand years before our time.
And then another thousand years elapsed,
Before Phoenicians made a newer script—
Ancestral to the signs we use today.

Rhythm's roots

Our writing came from painting, it now seems,
But whence is musicality then come?
If signs evolved from Ice Age artists' dreams,
What root was there to song or rhythmic drum?

Break rhythm here;
Defy the hungry ear;
Dump prosody for inquiry,
For no known Muse,
Whatever myth or source you choose,
Will make this clear.

'Whence music?' is the question,
For it's been dubbed the mystery supreme
Of our humanity at core
And, as with reading, so with this
It's only science will yield the bliss
Of deeper understanding.

We must suppose,
For so it goes
With evolutionary theory,
That there was no conceived design
We might retrace
And so align
Our prosody
With old ancestral practice.

The neural root of musicking, it seems,
Was rhythm in our bodies, brains and hands:
Aeons before our art or grammar formed,
Our forebears knapped their stones in time and warmed
To rhythm shared in social hunting bands;
Until, at last, such rhythm filled our dreams.

The making of these signs

Let's go back into the ancient world
And mingle with the making of these signs;
With an educated sense of handiwork,
Of the very possibility of perception,
Memory and the genesis of meaning.

Let's go back into our genome, sweet:
The evolution of the human head
And heart and germinal capacity
To picture not—not for an aeon yet—
Our exquisite love, but mere significance.

Significance at all, I mean to signify:
The crystallisation, in a hunting brain,
Of remembered sentiment and longing
For any other, whose scent or presence
Enlarged upon the pressured life of need.

And then consider how such sentience
Found its way into stumbling utterance;
Into a murmuring or faltering song,
Or into sculpted bone and shape,
Slowly awakening possibility.

Yes, possibility of some…some
Roughly grammared kind,
Ever so slightly inflected,
Dependent more on rude gesture
Than on spoken words or signs.

Ah! Signs? How did they evolve,
These cryptic shapes of Roman make,
In which, with slick technology,
I now communicate my meanings
And sculpted memories to you?

Treatise, tale or ode

How, asks author Stanislas Dehaene,
Apropos of our poetic caper—
In a fine book titled *Reading and the Brain*—[55]
Can obscure black marks, written down on paper
And projected on our retinas, evoke
A universe of meaning quite bespoke?

An inscape shaped by most exquisite rules,
Which must be learned, before we comprehend
What subtle and quite life transforming tools
Such coded squiggles are; for they extend
Our native wit's capacity to learn
Til daisy chains of connotation burn

Not words alone but worlds into the mind
Which, shared and shaped and taken to our hearts
Allow us, each and all, to find
Bright metaphors that generate our arts.
Only recent science, writes Dehaene,
Has opened up these workings of the brain;

Such science is fast moving and still young
But stunningly, it has of late revealed
Whence all our writing systems must have sprung
And how our myriad neurons learn to field,
Decipher, re-encode and deftly use
Those coherent sets of signs our teachers choose

To weave into our infant neural nets;
Though, too often, using pedagogic means
Which leave too much to chance, like making bets
On who will master what and which brain gleans
The deeper possibilities of code
And grows to write a treatise, tale or ode.

Robert Graves on Mallorca[56]

Poetry is housed at Canallun, so Graves decreed—
Once at that faraway home, to which he'd fled
From the scars of war—and domesticity—
With a new muse and a fugitive longing:
To write in devotion, to sing history.

Deia, where he lived, sounds so like goddess;
And there, we know, he wrote his paean to her:
The White Goddess of his fond imagination—
The Moon, the Muse of ancient times;
To whom he could or would not say goodbye.

His grasp of myth was imprecise,
His arguments quite whimsical;
Yet here he walked, each morning,
Through the hills, down to the sea,
Read *The Times* and wrote prolifically.

Here, he later wrote, was such tranquillity
And that was why he made Mallorca home:
The sun, the sea, the hills and olive trees,
Sans politics and superfluous luxuries,
Gave him grace for memoir, myth and verse

I've longed for years for some such Canallun;
A writer's refuge lived in with my muse—
A hamlet with a better Laura Riding—
But could I find it, would you choose
To dwell with me in hiding?

I first read Graves's verse when I was young:
'Love without hope', 'Lost love', 'One hard look';
But now the notion tingles on my tongue
That these soft songs, the poems in this book,
Are our abode—our living Canallun.

In Jerusalem last week

In Jerusalem last week,
Meandering in the German Colony,
I crossed Masaryk Street—
Named for a defenestrated Czech
Of liberal democratic disposition,
Murdered by communist thugs
Three years after 'liberation',
If one can call it that,
From the Holocaust and Nazi rule.
Does that defenestration ring a bell,
In Caracas at this time?
Would you say that that quiet
Naming of a street in,
Of all places, the German Colony;
In, of all places in our time,
Jerusalem of the knives and scissors,
Rings a bell for all democrats?
I felt so, passing by in peace,
And then I chanced upon
A simple, flowered balcony
Above the Hebrew road
That slivers, river-like
Through the German Colony;
And felt, at once, a curled up
Intimacy and partnership with you:
Here was a nook for two minds
Breathing liberty and high aims;
A retreat for warmth and love—
In Jerusalem last week—
But we are now in Caracas!

Easter Someday

They'll take me down, in time, to be interred;
Though who the 'they' will be I cannot say,
Especially if that time is long deferred
And much takes place that's unforeseen today;
But this will hold, whatever has occurred.

By 'this' I mean the vision I have now:
A doctrine of transcendence I can own,
Of all my Logoi come to life and how
They'll rise when angels move the mortal stone—
And bid those in the garden gape and bow.

There are different versions of this fancied tale,
With different groups of women in the garden.
But one is constant, present without fail.
You'll guess who that is. What? I beg your pardon?
The one the male disciples would not hail?

No, no, no! That's quite another story!
It's YOU who figures in my great recension,
As prime and loving witness of my glory,
The Muse of both my works and my ascension;
Not the famous Magdalene called Mary.

Perhaps it's I who caused this slight confusion?
Still, I trust you see the vision that entices
Your writer to indulge in his illusion
In which you bring your loving box of spices
While angels greet the dawn of my profusion.

But though my Logoi rest in diverse graves,
I'd like to think that all who open this
Tome of many hundred loving staves
Will feel that I impart with each a kiss
Upon your mouth—and that such kissing saves.

Epilogue

True companion

'You and I', you wrote, 'aren't mediocre.'
What Goethean boldness oozes from that claim!

That spirit's what you brought to our first meeting
And has me thinking, still, that you're the one.

And let's be clear, it's you who's been, between us,
The more resilient and determined party.

Whatever others say about my talents,
You alone have truly loved me for them.

You have, uniquely, cultivated them
When I'd lost almost all my self-belief;

And, even as you championed my dreams,
You never lost commitment to your own.

With due respect to Christiane Vulpius,
Your love leaves hers entirely in the shade.

You aren't just Christiane to my Goethe;
But, unlike her, a most consummate muse.

This thought had me revert to Zarathustra,
To reflect on what he says concerning friendship:

And, as I read, it struck me forcefully
That you uniquely meet his high criteria:

There's nothing soft in how you've challenged me;
There's nothing but the arrow and the longing.

You've called me on, whenever I was weary;
And awed me with your own heroic deeds.

You've urged that we must both of us think big
And been, at every turn, my true companion.

In short, it's clear that Zarathustra erred,
In saying women are not made for friendship.

Time and Naipi's hair

There can be no finer metaphor
Of the flow of time tumbling
Over the cataracts of all that is—
Of all that is the case, let's say—
Than the majestic falls of Iguazu,
Where three far borders meet.

Above the falls, I briefly stayed,
Ensconced in a bubble of luxury:
The Belmond Hotel das Cataratas;
Giving me the freedom to contemplate
The rich purity of the metaphor;
Breathing the air of time's flow.

The stones there remember Pangaea:
She who was the super continent
For aeons, until the Great Dying,
When Eurasia and Gondwana split,
Furrowing the lands in new ways;
Sundering life's archaic past.

Such time has lapsed in these waters:
A lush confluence of Eden and geology,
Where the Old World's mythology,
Swallowed by the Devil's Throat,
Mingles with the Caiapangue legend
Of Taroba's love for Naipi, long ago.

The river god, M'boi, was owed
Annual sacrifice of a lovely girl.
Taroba defied that and was shaped
Into a tree watered by Naipi's hair—
A tale that might have flowed from Ovid;
But is now ours, my love, to share.

Blue velvet bag

When you sent me the luminous photograph,
You added only, in a brief text message:
'I cannot speak. I have no words'.

In fact, what words could have done justice
To that photograph? To this photograph?
For I'm gazing at the image, as I write.

The softness of the afternoon Valencia light;
The blue, the dark blue velvet, new and clean;
The neatly knotted, binding golden chord

Place your astonishment in centre frame.
The telling tag, so stark, in black and white;
Looked upon by your implicit eyes,

Which wept so copiously before the fact;
Communicated here, by indirection,
A water fall of mute, but liquid words.

This velvet bag, this ceremonial blue,
Offered, shared so silently by you,
Plunged me into mysteries of being.

The tag: 'Cremacion #9994'
And her name, spelled out in Spanish amplitude,
Pointed to the meanings in your mourning—

Unfathomable to those who never knew
The one whose ashes, in their solemn urn
Are now contained within that velvet bag.

She gave you birth, she raised you to be strong;
And having, for so long, withheld affect,
Embraced you in her love, as she lay dying.

Yet your despatch, a golden chorded sigh,
Beneath this blue bound image, was one sentence,
Addressed to me in velvet: 'Please do not die!'

Corngold's Kaufmann[57]

I sat by the café window, in elected light,
With Corngold's life of Kaufmann—
The rounding of my youthful readings—
Set beside my vanilla pannacotta,
With its garnish of reddish summer berries
And a brewed black coffee—
At noon on New Year's Day.

That light, outside, gleamed on all the leaves,
Caressed by the gentlest summer breeze;
While the cloudless sky sealed the scene:
Shining like the serene visage
Of a Grecian deity not at war.
And that easeful shimmering
Bathed the body of the book.

Walter Kaufmann, after all these years—
Who died before his time, at fifty-nine:
Philosopher, humanist, heretic;
Author of the canonical *Nietzsche*;
Preceptor of my restless eagerness
For Bildung, for self-building and worldliness—
Now sat beside my cup, rounded into a life.

What wonders I imbibed, in years gone by,
With each caffeinated sip from this man's books:
On Nietzsche, religion and existentialism,
On Rilke, tragic drama, Kant and Hegel!
And now, as the year turned once more,
I sat with this assimilable distillation
Of what he'd meant to others.

His laved leavings lay in the light
Who'd left life younger than I am now.

Reading *Orlando*

When, at last, I chose to read *Orlando*,
You were a constant presence in its pages:
Garbed in Marousha's trousers, for example;
Arriving at our ghostly assignations
Alone, but cloaked and booted like a man.

Marousha, you'll recall, was very striking;
Orlando's eye was swiftly captivated,
His youthful amour instantly aroused
By the really quite extraordinary allure
Which issued from her whole, seductive person.

But that's not half the reason that I found
Your charismatic presence in the book.
It's how and why the novel was conceived
And dedicated 'To V. Sackville-West'—
An epistle to the gender-bending other.

And, more again, for both these women grew
In households centred on a father's library:
The Sackville one at Knole that Vita knew,
Virginia's the hoard of Leslie Stephen;
To which, by her account, he gave her access.

Each, in girlhood, greedily devoured
All these worlds of letters could divulge
And so acquired a longing for distinction:
To find a place among the mostly male
Authors of the prized, mysterious classics.

You breathed with me, as I read every page,
Like Woolf and Sackville-West we, too, conspire
To revel in a liberated age,
To engender novel narratives, inspire
All those observing us upon life's stage.

Our string quartet in C sharp minor

From our earliest days, formative of trust,
You've been musical, beloved songbird.
You'd speak to me of bitter Sasha's love
Of Mozart, secluded from the wrack
He thought was Russia, in carteled Mexico.

But your character became embodied for me
When, one perfectly sublunary afternoon,
On entering our shared accommodation,
I found you listening, absorbed, to Bach.
Hushing me, you murmured 'This is God!'

How, then, after all our years and travels,
In the context of this artful book of verse,
In the wake of your emotional recital
Of motifs from Beethoven's epic Ninth
To dying Noe, do I put our tale to music?

I feel, in view of all that we've lived through,
And knowing our propensities to dare,
That we might say we live a string quartet;
In fact, no common one, it seems to me,
But Ludwig's late quartet, in C sharp minor.

Your exuberance, your aims and your elan
Would have me postulate a different piece:
A fantasy of love that ends in triumph—
The third, the fifth or ninth symphony;
Or Fidelio, as we transform poor Venezuela.

But chasten your exuberance a little
And listen to this justly famed quartet:
A ceremony framed by grief and mourning,
Drawn from five set plans for seven movements,
In which Beethoven's art found resolution.

Listening to Chopin

The combination of protracted convalescence,
Bouts of exhaustion halting all my projects,
Melancholy news of Venezuela
And wintry thoughts of my relentless aging;
Have me, lately, turning down the lights
And listening intently to some Chopin—
Chiefly to his nocturnes, late at nights—
And feeling deeply privileged, overall,
To be myself, disposed oneirically,
Equipped with such advanced technology;

To have the scope, in quiet, private space,
The means, the education and good grace,
The access to such high fidelity
Recordings, by the Warsaw Philharmonic;
But, not least, our love, my bold, creative muse,
My own George Sand, with her cigars and trousers—
At least if we see them as metonyms—
Whose novels outsold those of Victor Hugo;
Who's been with me to lakes up in the mountains
And taken her composer to Mallorca.

Yet Chopin never wrote a book on China,
Or a book of thirty essays on the West;
Or a book of sonnets, set in B Flat minor;
Or political opinions in the press.
There's much, in short, that Frederic didn't do,
Even with Amanthe Lucile Dupin,
That I've done, in my fleeting years with you
And, having cheated death, perhaps still can.
But when I'm gone, if your lone psyche yearns
For all we were, read these—my own nocturnes.

This book is Chauvet Cave[58]

Did you know that, well within our years,
They found the hidden galleries of Chauvet:
A cavern, love, that stone-fall sealed abruptly
Twenty-seven thousand years ago;
Immuring so its ancient mural wonders?

'Chauvet Cave' are words to conjure with,
Or are once one has come to contemplate
The artistry with which some Ice Age hunters,
Just five millennia before the fateful fall,
Depicted the great creatures of their time.

The subtlety and deftness of their art,
Recaptured from so many years ago,
Must prompt the realization on our part
That these painters, seen in time's long flow,
Were kin and not remote in kind of mind.

That they could apprehend and then depict
The moving forms of hulking Ice Age bears,
The animated shapes of fighting rhinos,
The eyes and mouths of horses, lions' heads,
Makes for startled, time-lapse recognition.

Imprinted on the Aurignacian floor,
At Chauvet Cave, were found the stunning trace
Of one boy's footprints, partnered by a hound,
Who passed that way, a flickering torch in hand,
With wonder etched on his illiterate face.

Imagine, now, you are that vanished child;
My book of verse the opened Chauvet Cave:
What is your torch but wit, or what your wild
Imaginings, at all I here engrave—
And what will be the footprints that YOU leave?

Part two: Discretion

Delphic Deixis

Secret poem

This first poem for you must be a secret,
Since, if I share it with you fecklessly,
I fear that I would simply spook the horses;
When, following our first real conversation,
I'd prefer to play the canny horse whisperer.[59]

You called! You called! You spoke to me;
Declaring how 'fantastic' it had been
That I'd accepted your official invitation,
Eighteen months before, to the iWar forum—
Aye! War forum—but this is love!

Is all, then, fair in love and war? Ah! What
Does fairness have to do with those old games?
All of life's most ancient strategies
Were bundled into how you spoke to me—
Oh, how, since then, my heart has been on fire!

You must have sensed, from what I sent to you,
How ardently, if mordantly, I'd burned,
Before your call and quiet voice
Heaped every kind of fuel upon the fire,
But still consumed my psychic energy.

Now, when I walk, I inhale your gentle warmth,
Like oxygen itself, to feed the flames;
Exhaling, step by step, the doubts and fears
That must attend an unexpected fall
Into longings, raptures, wonders I'd thought done.

You've enchanted me, as hasn't happened
In more years now than I prefer to count.
How so? Ah, in truth, since you embody
Everything that I have ever loved
Of beauty, charm, intelligence and grace.

Yet when I sent facetious lines of praise,
You responded, after giving them some thought,
In such a measured way as to encourage
Leaping hopes of future intimacy
That now have me afraid of writing more!

Ah! Lovely one, if we were in a play,
I'd court your company with clever rhymes;
I'd sing some song like Cohen's 'Hallelujah'[60]
And speak to you of living on the edge;
But this, as we both know, is no mere play.

This is now the forum we both spoke in—
On iWar in the roiling outer world;
In which the schemes of charlatans and powers
Lay traps for the unwary, to undo them—
Transferred to our inner shadow worlds.

Such iWars wrack the inscape of the psyche,
Which fractures into memories, hopes and fears;
Where each of us, as I, will apprehend
The black-clad knights of ghost wars from our pasts;
And so, raise up suspicions and defences.

Your eyes, your smile, the gracious way you move,
The gentle, candid tenor of your voice,
The fact, alone, that you reached out to me,
And spoke of progress on your PhD;
Should set at ease my veteran, wary heart.

Instead, I find I'm pondering the art
Of how one draws such beauty to oneself;
Caresses it and whispers to its wildness—
To win its ease. That's why I murmur:
This first poem for you must be a secret.

Hannah at Marburg[61]

There was a moment, in November 1924,
When Martin Heidegger, lecturing on Plato,
Looked upon the young Hannah Arendt,
A stylish, studious girl, with stunning eyes;
And thought at once, 'If only she, from
Withdrawn grace, would fall towards me'.

They became intimate that winter, but
The poem was written twenty-five years later:
After Nazism, the Holocaust and the war
Had hurled the soft-voiced girl into exile
And he, of the black notebooks, into disgrace—
Yet still I think of you, as he did her.

Fruitful thoughts

You are ripe, I think, and set to fall,
While I await you down upon the ground—
Half-rotten, nowhere left to go.
I'm out of my tree and looking upwards,
Blissfully anticipating that, from withdrawn grace,
As Martin wrote, in nineteen forty-nine,
You'll fall towards me, unable still to cling,
On the brief twig of your mellifluous voice,
Uneaten by the blackbirds of ravenous destiny,
But cutting loose, with passionate exhalation:
Plummeting, on a plumb-line, oh plum, my plum,
To somewhere near my stranded inner boundary.

Rilkean lullaby

I used to walk on solitary beaches
Reading Rilke's poems to the sky; [62]
Especially those in which the poet reaches
For metaphors of poignant memory.

He wrote, back then, to various muses,
Whose warmth he felt most beautifully alone:
The beloved being a direction that one chooses,
Not a captured object cast in stone.

His voice rose as the Moon, on distant loves,
Shining on some space that ached or glowed.
It limned in light their being there in person—
Once, like you, when time had briefly slowed.

Gnossiennes 3

Why did I text you Gnossiennes 3? [63]
To listen to at night and think of me.

Answer with a kiss, when we should meet.
Such music would roll back my long defeat.

His melancholy, meditative tone
Plays my dream of you, when I'm alone.

The liminal Satie, désolé, neglected;
Captured like a bird, recorded, resurrected.

A prolepsis of the mystery that your eyes
Should only now, but only now arise—

So Hesperidean, at the sunset of my being;
With memories folding inward, futures fleeing.

A Greek bearing doubts

Constantine Cavafy[64] wrote a poem,
Called 'Things Ended', in 1911.

I've read it now, with you as a beginning.
It's opening lines declare that we're possessed

By fear and suspicion and desperately invent ways out.
Would you believe me, if I here confessed

That's I'm enamoured of you, but prey to doubt?
The thing is, he then postulated, we're mistaken:

That what one fears is not the danger ahead:
The information was false. We didn't get it right.

It's something else—for which we're unprepared.
I toss and turn and wonder what, at night.

Mercurial beauty

I love Cavafy's 'Sculptor of Tyana':
The way his chosen voice deflects the statues

Not only of historic champions of war
But even of the quasi-mythic eroi:

Fallen Patroclus, ill-fated young Caesarion.
Poseidon and his horses are high art;[65]

Shaped so lightly as to gallop over water;
But he openly declares his most-loved work,

'Wrought with the utmost care and feeling'
Was the vision of a single summer's day:

Hermes, Olympian messenger, of mercurial beauty—
The god of translators and interpreters like us.[66]

Ithaka and I

Ithaka's the goal, but do not hurry:
Such was Cavafy's advice, in his finest poem—
Let it last for years. Enjoy the harbours.

Truth to tell, it's been that way with me:
I've surely been Ulysses, in the fable—
Cast about upon the wine dark sea.

Laistrygonians and Cyclops, wild Poseidon:
Did I bring them, deep within my soul—
When I set out to find a distant love?

Pish! That's all mere psychoanalysis!
I'm journeyed now. I know what Ithaka means—
And you're, perhaps, my final Nausicaa.[67]

Not for me

If I admire Cavafy's 'Ithaka',
Which, pardon me, I actually do, in depth;
There's much about his verse, I have to say,
That I recoil from, in visceral distaste.

He wrote compulsively of male debauchery,
How he admired the morbid and corrupt,
The dissolute recourse to 'sensual pleasure'—
Especially of the secret Grecian kind.

What stirred Cavafy's member's not for me.
Does that make me a homophobe, or prude?
Oh, please! How philistine. How crass! How crude!
I'm not impressed, that's all—and not PC.

Princess and stranger

I somehow doubt you've read *The Odyssey*,
Though maybe I'm mistaken, I concede;
But Nausicaa rises in Book Six,
Luminous, in the brine-scarred hero's eyes.

She was sprung from those who fled Hyperia,
Exiled by the terrors of the Cyclops,
Led by old Nausithous to a haven,
Where he built safe walls and bright new halls.

I'm older far than salt-caked, wrecked Ulysses;
I've travelled further, seen more of the world.
Yet, tossed up on your shore, like him, I'm dazzled.
Naked, I hold out an olive branch.

Old heroes

I'm steeped in the Homeric myths, it must be said:
I'm old, I'm white, I'm Western and I'm male.
I know the wars and wanderings of my kind,
Overlaid in depth on sporting contests,
And read into the tragic crack of nations;
Yet I live on the margins of the world.

You, conversely, come from other roots,
Your heroes, I surmise, fought other wars:
A thousand years of Han and Ming presumption,
Before the French colonial contretemps.[68]
But you weren't born 'til all of that was done—
'Til after Saigon fell. The Reds had won.

Bishop's 'Insomnia'

I don't know if you read Elizabeth Bishop,[69]
Or poetry at all, if it comes to that;
But her eighteen lines of heartache,
Headed 'Insomnia', reflect my present mood:
Like a body of still water, when I dwell
On the inversion of my image in your mind.

I looked, once, in the mirror of my longing;
Dressed in all the confidence you'd written,
Reflecting on your beauty, freshly smitten;
But as your silence fell, the doubts came thronging:
Perspective warped and all that I could see
Was your rejecting hand thrust out at me.

Sextus Propertius and Cynthia

Sextus Propertius wrote of Cynthia: [70]
How he was captivated by her lustrous eyes,
How she placed sweet fetters on his neck,
How her fateful love subsumed all others.

But Sextus Propertius was a stripling boy:
His elegies were written in his youth—
His lungs gave out when he was barely thirty—
So, he never was a veteran like me.

Yet all my youthful loves your voice, your eyes—
As Cynthia's two thousand years ago
Enslaved the callow Latin elegist—
Overwhelmed in amorous dopamine.

You embodied several ghosts

You had no way of being aware
Of the subtle ways in which your loveliness
Triggered traces, blended faces
Of earlier loves, or brief encounters—
From Annabel Coulet, when passing through Bangkok,
To Weili Yang, a decade later, in Hong Kong.[71]

You can't be held in any way accountable
For the lovely ghosts you summoned unawares—
I thought, myself, they'd long been laid to rest—
But everything about you, this past summer,
Summoned that ethereal Sinitic chorus,
Chanting to my psyche, 'She's the one!'

Crystallization

Marie Henri Beyle, pen-name Stendhal,
Author of *The Red and the Black*,
Author of *The Charterhouse of Parma*,
Wrote an analytic handbook, just called *Love*.[72]

His single most original observation
Was that, just as in the salt mines in Salzburg,
A leafless, wintry bough, cast into the workings,
Emerges as a galaxy of crystals;

So, in love, what he dubbed crystallization
Consists in chance, compounding first impressions
Of a woman's (wildly overrated) felt perfections,
Dazzling heart and judgement—like a diamond.

Mistaken about something

The most heart-rending moment of love,
In its infancy, is the realization
That you have been mistaken about something.

That's pure Stendhal! And he added
That a whole framework of crystals
Consequently, has to be destroyed.

Such a thing occurs, Stendhal explained,
If the sufferer from incipient crystallization
Has met with indifference, coldness, even anger.

Which is why, as I assume you'd understand,
I turned again to Stendhal's book on love—
When my courtly invitations met with silence.

Delphic deixis[73]

If the Delphic oracle,
Anachronistic though this sounds,
Had been consulted, in my squalling infancy,
About my fate;

Or if some Sibyl,
Quartered in a cave-like lair,
Had prophesied, with palpable prolepsis,
How comical it would be;

Either would have pointed
To some enchanting nubile beauty, with her hair
Streaming, in her nymph-like, headlong flight—
From a harmless poet.

Daphne and Apollo

In a simpler world, a more coherent one,
Of courtly love and common erudition,
Writing verse like this would be more fun—
And sharing it less prone to inhibition.

Or so it seems to me, as I now muse
On classic myths and ponder which of these
I can most dexterously use—
Not least from Ovid's *Metamorphoses*.[74]

Apollo's cry to Daphne speaks for me:
'You've no idea, rash girl, you've no idea
Whom you are fleeing. That is why you flee.'[75]
But this book *is* the laurel. Are we clear?

Epicurean wisdom

It's not as if I had the least excuse.
After all, I'd long since read Lucretius
And been warned that love is madness—
A sickness that we recognize in others.

Lovers are delusional, he wrote,
And lose the power to make objective judgements.
That was in his poem *The Nature of Things*[76]
Book Four, to be precise—the last few hundred lines.

Given both the merits of the case
And all my long experience of love,
I didn't think that I could fall like this—
In all the ways Lucretius analyzed.

Eugene Onegin

Who'd want Pushkin's brief, erratic life;
Especially his compulsive gambling,
His whoring and his drinking in St Petersburg?[77]

On the other hand, the man did write
Damned good poetry and was acclaimed.
Who'd not want that? *Onegin*, above all!

Tchaikovsky's music really makes it soar.[78]
I've loved the Polonaise since I was young—
Owned Onegin's foolishness and fate.

Do you know the story—how it ends:
Onegin realizing, all too late, that Tatiana,
Whom he'd spurned, was his true love?

Actually, I am Tatiana

Come to think of it, I'm Tatiana,
In that wondrous, lyric tragedy—
My psyche dwelling in a Larin-like estate,
Always reading books and dreaming big.

That's why I was susceptible when you
Stepped into my garden, like Onegin;
Why in your wake, having heard your voice,
I soliloquized, like her, 'I'm all on fire!'[79]

Like her, again, I put my words aside
And swore to lock within my stoic breast
All avowal of mad and ardent passion—
But couldn't hold it in—like her! Like her!

Kraus, Rilke, Sidonie

I would have liked, had it been possible,
The subtlest kind of romancing with you:
The kind that Rilke had with several loves;
Or he and Kraus with Sidonie Nadherny.[80]

You must know tales yourself of subtle love:
Perhaps romantic tales from old Annam?
But it's possible you're entirely unfamiliar
With Karl Kraus, Sidonie or Rilke.

I dream that, like Sidonie, in secret,
You tell yourself the kinds of things she did—
In diaries that she kept for many years—
Of deep regard for their great tenderness.

Nisreen of the orange blossom

Harith crossed a flower-lined portal:
Baghdad University—a future with a fabled past.

For the first time in his life, at seventeen,
Knowledge, music, girls—and alcohol!

He couldn't concentrate in engineering
On anything his good professor said;

His senses overwhelmed by orange blossom—
The perfume of the laughing, lissome girl

Who sat in front of him in every class;
Her chestnut-coloured hair caught in the light.

Before he knew her name, he wrote her verse,
Which, secretly, he'd then leave on her desk.[81]

Beckett's maxim

Do you know the works of Samuel Beckett,[82]
Or the wider genre of absurdist theatre?
Perhaps not. You do influence operations.

In any case, I ask because your silence,
Communicates that, in my acts, I've failed
To find rapport with who and how you are.

Beckett, though, once wrote a striking maxim:
'Ever tried?' he asked and 'Ever failed?
No matter! Try again. Fail again. Fail better.'

That I have failed to win your warmth is patent.
Yet, stuck on stage and feeling quite absurd,
It lights me up to think I've failed better.

Prolepidoptera

You dazzled me,
At the door to an enclosure:
A secret garden full of butterflies.

'What coloured wings!
How gorgeous all the ripe, exotic plants!'
My lips apostrophized, addressing you.

I lingered there,
In those imagined futures,
Gazing at Prolepidoptera.

But, when I turned
Toward the past, you'd taken wing;
My prolepses striking you as moths.[83]

Honesty is the worst policy

I stumbled into honesty,
Despite my best intentions.

To be sure—and, even now,
My fervid, varied, lyrical inventions

Haven't been communicated—
That much honesty would be truly ludicrous.

Still, I stumbled into honesty
By issuing a simple invitation:

Dinner for two at Saigon Secret.
That gave the goddamn scheme away.

When will I learn at last that, in such games,
Honesty is the worst policy?

After Vygotsky

Lev Vygotsky was a Russian Jew
Who died at thirty-seven from TB;
But in his time he learned a thing or two
With some relevance, I think, to you and me.

He came up with the idea of ZPL
Which stands for Zone of Proximal Learning,
Being that within which one learns well—
But I'm thinking, what of Proximal Yearning?

If I, through deft poetic teaching,
Had found a way to coach your cautious heart;
If, thereby, tender thoughts had thus been reaching
That secret Zone in you...Ah! What an art! [84]

The ancient rules

There are some ancient rules to be observed—
In love, in war, in sport—
And, if one's not sufficiently reserved,
Or has not, despite life's course, become the sort
Of masterful move-maker whose deserved
Skills win, well, one's caught.

'Twas ever thus and I have no excuse.
To court or combat is, in fact, to fence.
To play the game of life, one needs must choose
One's ground and tactics well, spare no expense;
And, if the ground's not favourable, refuse—
Decline—to play—with some polite pretense.

Rovelli and reality

While rounding out my thoughts of you, I read
Carlo Rovelli's *The Order of Time*[85], where
The master of spin theory offered me coherence.

The world, he tells us, simply doesn't have
The curved and smooth geometry of Einstein;
Only probabilities of quanta interacting.

So conceived, it's simply a collection
Of interrelated quantum points of view—
You'll grasp how this applies to me and you.

Spin theory is the math of what's not smooth;
While spinfoam is the stuff of seeming time.
'Spinfoam?" I then thought—like lilting rhyme?

Silence is toxic

One can over-interpret words, you know—
Whether written or spoken;
Or even the sending of songs,
Or brief piano pieces by Satie.
I understand your reticence, therefore;
But this silence—prolonged, unpunctuated?

Such silence, my beauty, is quite toxic;
It suffocates and does deliberate violence;
It triggers fractal fretting in the soul—
The fear one's committed some misprision;
And landed, therefore, in the isolator;
Shut away and muted in the dark.

Six hours in conference

After a fortnight in the soundless slammer,
The rumour came that you would soon be coming
To spend six hours in close conference
With a friend of mine, talking reason,
Talking social networks and analysis—
This I learned from him, but not from you.

Are you about to text or call, to draw me
Into the charmed circle of your stay?
Perhaps, at the last moment, your silence
Will be overwhelmed by warm apologies—
And quiet delight at my exclusive invitation?
But where I am there is no hint of this.

Hardly Keats

I'm hardly Keats. He died at twenty-five.[86]
I'm not his 'knight at arms', so palely loitering.

And yet his famous ballad comes to mind,
When pondering my illusions of last summer.

'La belle dame sans merci'? Yes, that's the one;
With all its medieval fantasy:

Of garlands, pacing steeds and fairy song;
Of honey wild, language strange and sleep.

It's true that like his death-pale kings and princes,
I woke in shock, upon a cold hill-side.

But then Apollo rose and, all around,
Glowed fields of song to harvest from the ground.

Saigon Secret

Laughter and a meeting of minds,
The concoction of hilarious scenarios
Over finger food and wine;
Indelible memories of your pink mouth,
The play of light in your melancholy eyes,
Which, perhaps, know Vietnamese fates.

These micro-traces, flowery redolences
Of our quiet hours at Saigon Secret,
Will linger in my heart for many years;
They'll shape the subtle narrative I craft
Of how we angels danced on narrow ground—
But this, of course, is all imaginary.

Re-education camps

I'm assuming you arrived here as a child;
That luck was with your parents on the water,
Fleeing from the Le Duan commissars;[87]
Perhaps that you lost uncles in the camps.

But this, of course, is all the merest guesswork.
You've told me nothing—and never will do now.
So, I'm left pondering some fragments of awareness,
Acquired in my studies of the war.

I'm now in re-education camp—
A serial offender, arrested once again,
Subject to renewed indoctrination,
Regarding what can pass between two people.

Satie, again and again

I listen now, at nights, to Gnossiennes 3,
Drinking Chivas Regal on the rocks;
Sunk, in mood, beneath its minor key.

Its sharps and flats elect the irony,
The mordant rumination that now mocks
How I once looked at what I thought could be.

Again, I sip, again I play Satie:
His plangent, gentle, melancholy's lent
The sound of what your silence means to me.

Again, I listen, working slowly free
Of beauties that are not, of passions spent—
And then I sleep and dream most musically.

Beyond Hanoi

If we'd gotten past that first, unguarded conversation,
In which you spoke so openly of your researches,
Spoke so warmly of my presence in your planning,

If it hadn't been for my disclosed infatuation,
Perhaps we may have spoken of serious things—
Not least of Vietnamese history and of Nguyen Ai Quoc.

Long I was immersed in that marred history,
Even while you, little exile, were a child on these shores;
But now I feel like Ta Thu Thau, the Trotskyist,

A gifted writer and orator, seized by the Viet Minh
In August 1945, in blood-spattered Quang Ngai,
Given a perfunctory trial, taken to a beach and shot.[88]

Imogen and Paul

Frank Tallis nails the syndrome
You seem anxious I might suffer;
Never better than in Chapter Five
Of *The Incurable Romantic* [89] –
The very title chapter of his book,
Whose subject, quite uncannily, is 'Paul'.

Paul, a tripos grad from Oxford, had the lot
And, full of youthful promise, fell for Imogen,
Who, in a timeless tradition, pulled away,
Leaving him bewildered and obsessed.
That'd be disturbing in our context, but
I'm not obsessed and have no youthful promise.

Rational actors

When you declared, in a voice I found
So mellifluous it smothered my critical faculties,
How your researches had led you to observe
That human beings aren't quite rational actors,[90]
I leapt into the Rio da Miel and was stuck—[91]
Yo! The very embodiment of rationality!

Melted by your breathing, I longed for sweet seminars,
Hearing all the sounds from your pink mouth,
While sucking at the breasts of your inquiries.
Rational actors? In a rush of dopamine
I lunged for a passionate copula, impelling you
To flee, as in the myths. Then reason struck for shore.

Quickly forgotten experiences

The only truth in history, wrote the historian—
One I've read in depth on the history of your country,
Or the country, at least, of your beautiful features—
Is that there are no historical truths:

Only an infinite number—this is a direct citation
From his classic, *Vietnam 1945: The Quest for Power*[92]—
Of experiences, most of them quickly forgotten;
A few remembered and elaborated upon by bards.

He mentions novelists, philosophers, priests and others, too.
And so it would have been and still may prove
Of our breathtakingly brief encounter, let's agree:
A quickly forgotten experience—but for this poetry.

Pas de deux

I'd somehow formed the clear impression
That you had come here from Annam.
But veteran China analyst that I am,
I needed a direct and personal confession

Had you, at ease, agreed to dine with me,
At Saigon Secret, I would soon have learned
Your origins, before our talk had turned
To future plans: your sense of destiny.

I might have won your trust, with warmth and grace,
As we danced a pas de deux on song,
Creating a rapport both deep and strong—
Had we had those hours face to face.

A clinical case

Being smitten by you—
Overwhelming and disquieting as it was—
For each of us, briefly—
Showed me I was still alive.

Being smitten by your beauty—
More precisely, if the truth be told,
By your enchanting voice
And your evident, subtle intelligence—

Being smitten by your comprehensive tresses—
As I freely confess I was—
Now occurs as a clinical case
I've suffered, analyzed and recovered from.

De Clerambault syndrome

Gaetan de Clerambault was a French physician,
Who analyzed what's called erotomania—
A syndrome noted even in classical times.

It's a delusional disorder of the saddest kind,
In which a woman, most typically,
Thinks the object of her passion loves her back.

Or rather, her front, if we're more candid:
Not her outward beauty and endowments only,
But the proofs that she provides of being enamoured.

You know, by now, that had you been besotted,
No-one would have found this fault in you—
But neither shall they—thanks!—in amorous me.

What Lucretius wrote

Lucretius was an Epicurean and wise,
Beyond the scope of classical physiology,
With regard to sexual passion and its causes.

Why would he not have been, when the symptoms
Have been evident to dispassionate observers
Since any myth or folklore one might know?

Lucretius was an Epicurean and wise:
He dwelled in theory, not in folklore only—
Atomism at his fingertips and poetic skill.

His dissection of infatuation long ago—
Of how we fall for beauty and what follows—
Remains quite priceless—re-read now.

Oberon's potion

I suffered—even you will now agree—
A veritable mid-summer night's dream:
Productive both of roundels and of faery songs.

Remember Oberon's flowery words to Puck:
'I know a bank where the wild thyme blows,
Where oxlips and the nodding violet grows'?

Here's a test of just how literate you are:
Do those two lines flow on through eglantine
To the enchantment of Titania and the rest?

We both know now that Oberon's secret potion
Played me as an ass for a brief, wild time.
But you? Titania? You'd no such notion.[93]

Malvolio

Malvolio was induced to play the fool,
Puritan though he was—a downright prig.
The household staff, for sheer, malicious fun,
Gulled him, as the Bard expresses it,
Into the groundless, gartered and absurd belief
Olivia loved him—as he fondly, madly hoped.

I'd play Malvolio in theatricals for free,
As Alec Guinness did or Herbert Beerbohm Tree,
For *Twelfth Night*'s just been acted out in me:
Maria and the others capering with glee
Within, Olivia, my cross-gartered brain.
Oh! 'Take the fool away!' I say again.[94]

Let's briefly imagine

Let's, briefly, presuppose you hadn't fled,
Hadn't frozen in the headlights of my interest,
Then dashed off, in your maidenly discomfort,
Seeking the river; turning into this laurel.

Let's briefly imagine, as I kiss the trembling
Bark of your arboreal mutation,
That we'd spoken, at the dinner I'd proposed,
Of mutual constraints and all life's ironies.

I might have called you Merline, as Rilke called
His artist muse, young Baladine;
I might have spoken of the *Duino Elegies*
And how the Earth's transformed. Let's just imagine.

Baladine Klossowska

For Christmas 1920, Rilke's love,
The Polish artist, Baladine Klossowska,
Gave him Ovid's *Metamorphoses*—
A French translation, set in prose, not verse.

And, when she gave him space, the following year,
She left a postcard, pinned upon the wall
Opposite the poet's writing table,
Of Orpheus in song, beneath a tree.

He'd been depressed for years until that point,
But Baladine's bestowal of these gifts
Released the poet's spirit in a storm:
His famed *Duino Elegies*—and *Sonnets to Orpheus*.

Rilke's grave monument

But Merline's gifts of Ovid and of Orpheus,
While they were what sprang up in Rilke's verse,
Did not impart the inward form or feel
Of the sonnets that his unleashed muse composed.

A tree arose! Yes, that—quite certainly,
Across—O pure transcendence!—from his desk.
But the felt cohering of the seer with song
Was for the girl, the dancer, who had died.

Vera Ouckama Knoop, at just nineteen,
Daughter of friends from Rilke's Munich days,
Who'd played with his child, Ruth, before the War,
Plucked true singing from his narrow lyre.

Duino dialogue

I long to ask—and would, if you would talk,
Leap back into litheness and warm voice,
Out of the tremulous rind of this resistant laurel;

If we could be at Duino, like the poet;
If, like him, I then cried out up there—
Would you, in place of angelic orders,

Take me, heart, into a great existence,
Where beauty of the kind that swept my psyche,
Would still disdain to cryptically destroy us;

Where, more at ease than the enciphered beasts,
In our deciphered world, we might converse
Of how to unconceal each other's fates?

Hypothetical only

You were never mine to lose
And can't be held accountable for how
Your voice, so warm, so pure and gentle,
Drenched my aging mind in dopamine.

Yet, even so, the Thracian adder bit,
If not your ankle then my shapely hope,
Plunging my wholly hypothetical Eurydice
Down to an Underworld of bloodless norms.

What option had I, then, if not to sing,
As I have done herein, before Persephone;
And draw, at least, the phantom of my love
Along an upward path—not looking back? [95]

Near Methymna's walls

Obviously, of course, I can't assume
Of you—or any given reader—that you know
Book Ten of Ovid's *Metamorphoses*,
With all its famous tales of mythic love.

But that's of no account, since now it's broken,
This Orphic hope of song and transformation:
Dismembered by the raving mob of maenads,
Who've overwhelmed my wooing of the trees.

In any case, what counts is Book Eleven:
The legend of how Orpheus' severed head
Sang its way down Hebrus to the Sea—
And thence to Lesbos, near Methymna's walls.

Orpheus dismembered

The secret didn't keep and you were spooked.
So much for my whispering and stealth!
Your horse sense, if you'll pardon the expression,
The wildness of your beauty, saw me coming.
Tame you? Not a chance! You're off and running!

It's funny, though, how this occurred,
Since all I did was send an invitation:
A far less frightening thing, I would have thought,
Than writing, as I had, of being dazzled
By your beauty, grace and high intelligence.

Was it the very idea of Saigon Secret,
Of cooking up a neat scenario
To camouflage my patent love for you,
To bottle up, in private conversation,
The poetry your virtues had uncorked?

It seems I'll never know, as you've declined
Not only a romantic assignation,
But communication, since, of any kind.
You've not reached out, as you had said you would;
And promptings haven't done me any good.

You flew in, did your work and disappeared—
All on radio silence, as I'd feared.
You worked so close to where I live and breathe,
So close that I could almost feel your warmth,
Despite the ice of your relentless muteness.

Do you realize how you plunged me into Werther,
Into every kind of febrile mood;
Into fighting demons—yes, those black-clad knights—
That clutched, like zombies, at my tender throat?
I can't believe that this was your intent.

Well, anyway, I pressed the reset button;
I blew the zombies off and went to bed,
Refusing to go down in World War Zed.
Executive judgement pushed you off with them
And set me free to turn back to my work.

Or so I thought. But when my Android beeps,
I jump to see if it's a text from you.
This against my sombre better sense—
And traumatized, deep memory of the past—
Insisting that it simply isn't true.

Two days you were here: Thursday, Friday;
Working with my friends, across the road—
Those fortunate and undeserving bastards!—
And, right throughout, I longed for you to call;
That, breathlessly, you'd come here late and fall

Into my bewildered, aching arms
And kiss me, shedding tears, in your confusion,
As we tumbled up the stairs and into bed;
Confessing you're distracted and conflicted:
That it was and wasn't love from which you'd fled.

I dry your tears and kiss your murmuring mouth;
I kiss you everywhere and, overwhelmed,
By all my pent-up longing so fulfilled,
I chant to you a Rilkean lullaby—
Among sweet heaps of soporific herbs.

Such thoughts have made these days an Easter passion,
If not exactly of the Christian kind;
More a dismembering, in the pagan fashion,
By the maenads of your silence, cruel and blind,
Of Orpheus, for his singing to the wind.

Part three: Passion

This Floating Shell

Prologue

Before breakfast

You are in the interrogation room, sweet lady;
Your limbs spread, in tremulous bewilderment,
When I ask, 'Would you care for a little
Cunnilingus, before I bring you breakfast?'

Other words dance on the tip of my tongue,
But how will you receive them, lying there?
Ah! Truth to tell, your labia minora long,
Do they not—don't lie!—for my longing?

For my wondrous palabrations; for such
Discursive flickers of my subtle tongue;
To divulge wantonly their red assent;
To disgorge a joyful concordance

Such that your unuttered ecstasy will come
To seem entirely unambiguous and unfeigned.
For all we tested, boxed and cunning linguists
Well know that art can overlay apparent pleasures.

Will you, therefore, lie in such a cause,
Or pause to heed, or better yet, receive
Not the questioning only, but the lingering parole:
The suggestions, dancing and darting lingually,

That I put to you, between your parted sighs?
For believe me that this masked interrogation
Has been invented, given vent; has only
Been breathed into the imaginary,

Tabled, laid before my eyes, made
The occasion for such fluid ejaculation
By the stimuli, the caressed potentialities
Rumoured forth from your own lips.

Not, I grant, quite lit-orally, but arising,
Budding, at your bidding. Breakfast, then?

Pink silk dress

You surely knew, when murmuring to me,
Of your luncheon in a pink silk dress—
And what you might not wear beneath it—
There, in your imaginary Paris,
Among big men and the affairs of state,
The feelings your alluring hints would stir.

With that soft stroke, run like a poet's hand
Over your still firm and nubile breasts,
You plunged my primal brain into a frenzy,
So that the poet's hand was seized upon
By tropes remembered from Anais Nin,
And drawn towards that most diaphanous dress.

How did you accomplish this in innocence?
Surely, as with the sending of those songs,
Like 'You can leave your hat on'—meaning
Never mind the rest, except stilettos—
Or, earlier, those 'Bette Davis eyes'
Cast upon me, saying 'You are mine!'

We'd only just been talking Oliver Sacks
And how your deft, chameleon evasions
Tantalize the analyst in me;
You'd just exclaimed, in your so ravishing voice,
How very much you actually love his work,
When there alighted, on my unsuspecting brain,

Like one of Nin's disarming little birds,
Those murmured words, so delicately spoken,
'I'm wondering what colour under wear
To put on underneath my pink silk dress.
Should I, perhaps, wear none at all?'
Oh! Instantly, I was your sexual slave!

Ecstasy itself

Ecstasy itself takes just this form,
When one's beloved sighs 'You said my name!'
Exclaims in wonderment at what's transpired,
'Wieder, wieder, wieder, Feuer!' Flame.
Again, again, again, for I'm on fire!'
That moment, angel, never let it pass!

You pressed your point: 'I want your voice again.'
The sighing sound of being deeply loved
That so transfigures human carnal congress,
Is what, at last, we lit upon this morning,
Listening so intently to the breathing
Of the other in our coupling, lost in wonder.

You sent me Clapton, singing Dylan's song
'Knock, knock, knocking on Heaven's door'
And then, as if some adept in the school
Of sexual love, declared with startling fervour,
'Teach me, guide me, show me everything.'
Ah! That, from beauty, is the call of life!

'Hold me close and whisper things to me,
My heart, the maker, mender of my name!'
We are embodied beings, full of longing,
Poets, both, upon the burning shore,
Where Shelley lingered, lost and passionate,
Composing, now, our Epipsychidion.

I know there is an ancient school of wisdom,
Which counsels us against Romantic love,
Insisting that its passion cannot last.
But what are all such Buddhist tropes to us?
Life is brief, but here and now we know
What ecstasy there is in being loved. We glow.

End to End

Dream Godiva

You volunteered that you are my Godiva,
But does that make me Mercia's Leofric,
Or do I have the fate of Peeping Tom?
Either way, I'd watch you ride through Coventry![96]

Your glorious hair, so long, so glossy, falling
Loose about your shoulders and your breasts,
Is, for me, the very stuff of legend,
The 'gift of God', as eyes on you agree.

'Ego Godiva Comitissa diu',
She wrote, it's said, though churlish pedants quibble,
'Istud desideravi.' Is that so?
Have you inscribed those words upon my heart?[97]

You speak of Ovid

It struck me as incredibly romantic
That you likened me to Ovid, lost in Pontus,
In exile from the palaces of Rome,
Banished for his amours and his errors.

Not just because you're over there, in Paris,
While I am beached in Tomis, far away,
But rather for the depth it indicated
In the reading and the thinking that you do.

Ovid's *Art of Love*, his *Heroides*,
The fables in his *Metamorphoses*,
His *Fasti* and *Epistulae ex Ponto*
Are ours now, all, to kiss and tell.

Count Henri Marie Raymond

You'll understand, I trust, if I confess
That, short and hobbled artist that I am,
Sketching out ideas in my bohemia—
Montmartre of the fabled demi-monde—

Rich in my inheritance of graces:
The redolence, the traces of Toulouse,
Drunk with coloured ancestries but wry,
Unable to be sure I'll live much longer,

I'm stunned to know, my glowing, long-haired beauty,
That I, amid all this, had caught your eye;
I'm summoned by your urge that I be stronger
And make fulfilling you my primal duty.

Catullus 101[98]

Do you think it's faintly possible
That the music of a journey long ago,
Across the seas, traversing many countries,
In Latin verse that ends with 'atque vale',

Could come to sing, but also haunt our longings?
That seeking me, across those centuries,
Having learned too late of my demise,
You might arrive for my poor obsequies;

Alight with love for this, your brother poet,
To find no more than mutam cinerem,
Then offer me a vigil in your grief
And weep, at last, for all that might have been?

Reading 'Epipsychidion'

It's strange, you know, that though we venerate
The poetry of Byron, Keats and Shelley,
We generally recoil from their excesses,
Their thees and thous and soaring rhetoric,
Such as Percy Shelley's flight of fire:
'I pant, I sink, I tremble, I expire!'

Yet, when I hear your panting, living voice
Murmur words of moist and ardent passion,
When I read the words you write to me,
Or listen to the songs you cast my way,
I live, then, Shelley's high, Romantic line:
'I am not thine. I am a part of thee.'

Fortunate foundling

Oh Lady Godiva, how did you find
The way to take this foundling on your horse,
Enfold me in your naked, tender arms
And slip my lips behind your golden locks,
To suck in secret on your splendid nipples,
Hungry, like a wolf cub in the cold?

Your breasts bring forth the very milk of life,
Released to quench my yearning at the source,
By raising up my warm and tender head
Which you caress with gentle, royal hand,
At which I sigh with such full ecstasies
That Peeping Tom, in envy, is struck blind.

Goethe and you

I wasn't raised to read erotic verse
And never heard of Goethe, while at school.
Sex was quite verboten and, what's worse,
My parents hoped I'd be a holy fool.

If only I had read his *Roman Elegies*,[99]
When bursting with the juice of life, in youth.
Propertius, too, and Ovid—all of these.
I'd then have had a different gospel truth.

Instead, conflicted, I lived with unease;
Guilt-racked and uncertain what to do,
Hedging against sin and foul disease.
Until I learned my Goethe—and found you.

From Ovid to Goethe

Naïve erotic verse is classical.
It's what the free-willed Greeks and Romans wrote.
Though, even then, sweet Eros clashed with order,
As Ovid found, for writing *Art of Love*.

He was a kind of ancient Alfred Kinsey,
Exploring how the Romans took their pleasures.
Though he did so in poetry, not prose,
Enchanting and enlightening at once.

But all such verse is best when breathed together,
As you and I both know and long to do.
And Goethe's finest work brought antic Ovid
Into modern life, for me and you.

Bath and Trav

You called me, Violetta, as I bathed,
Inspiring a rendition of Brindisi:[100]
My sighing song of longing and of passion.

Now I cannot bathe without the thought!
But you are off in Paris, with Douphol—
A jealous man of wealth and violent temper.

Ah! Mia traviata, do not stray.
Don't say that our love has come too late!
'E tardi' isn't what I want to hear.

Tell the Baron that you love Alfredo;
That I'm your poet. He can be your friend.
That's the way the opera's meant to end!

Ovid on SMS

Just suppose your Ovid had a phone
And consequently didn't have to pine,
Or send epistulae to Rome by boat.

He could call or text you, all the time;
And, more important, you could send him love—
In sexy voicemails, naughty messages.

That'd cut the distance down a lot
And, frankly, stir the exiled poet's pot.
What say you, muse? A good idea or not?

I'm teasing you, of course. We've both got phones
And your bewitching voice, seductive notes
Are the air in which your poet floats.

Camille Claudel

The family of Camille Claudel were reptiles.
At least, her mother was, her brother Paul,
Poet of some note and diplomat. Oh, and
Her envious little sister, young Louise.

Auguste Rodin seduced and then betrayed her,[101]
Claude Debussy sought her love in vain.
'Sakuntala', she then carved in solitude,
Expressing so, in stone, her inner journey.

You, I fear, at times, are like Camille:
Ripe with love and genius, but alone.
Oh, come to me and gift me with 'The Waltz',
Lest I weep, as fond Debussy did.

Before dawn

You long to wake, you wrote from far away,
Beside me, in the hour before dawn.
As it is, you hardly seem to sleep,
But I now lie alone, before daybreak,
Imagining you recumbent in my bed
Beside me, with your long hair in a bun,
Above the nape that I'd so gently kiss,
While running one forever tender hand
Along the glorious curve of your right hip,
Listening, in silence, to your breathing,
Until you roll and draw my fervid lips
Down upon your mouth and wondrous breasts.

Faustina and Rome

Goethe found fresh love in Ewige Roma:[102]
A widow called Faustina set him free.
Though Rome Eternal be a world itself,
If not for love, it wouldn't be a world.

Thus he wrote, in *Roman Elegies*:
Great Rome itself, sans love, would not be Rome.
Not, at least, the city of Catullus,
Or Ovid, in the days that he lamented.

While Goethe found Faustina, I found you.
Sure, he wrote his poems while with her—
In bed and not in exile, as I am.
But, with your love, I have no need of Rome.

D. H. Lawrence

You've read so well; you must have read your Lawrence—
David Herbert, not the Seven Pillars—
And, knowing you as rainbow, gypsy lady,
I imagine you'd an eye for what's 'obscene':
What got his novels banned or expurgated,
Until the famous trial, in nineteen sixty.

But here's what strikes me most, at this remove:
Far more than Lawrence, you have stirred my senses,
Rousing me from cold, platonic torpor,
Encouraging the fire and passion of sex.
You make me feel I'm Lady Chatterley—
And you her potent lover in the garden.[103]

Delete the WAVs!?

I fancy Goethe would have tried this out:
Mutual self-pleasuring by phone.
In fact, when I was spent—remember this?—
I texted 'Oh my god! Now Goethean poetry!'

You texted back, 'I felt you throb inside me,
Moving, like the life-force deep within.
Now, drenched by who you are, I feel renewed.'
If that's not sex, we don't know what sex is!

But now you'd have me scuttle all our WAVS,
Not least your own, in which you sigh with pleasure,
Or murmur, 'Cum to me! My cunt's on fire!'[104]
That I can't. They are a priceless treasure!

War of Shadows

Curiously, I thought, for one like you,
So attuned to world affairs and wars,
When I avowed I'm reading Gorenberg's
War of Shadows on the SIGINT game
During World War Two, especially Egypt,
You snorted that such stuff is mere old news.

But, that aside, as I got into it,
I found a tale of espionage you'd love:
Hermione Ranfurly, on the lam,
Crossing Africa to get to Cairo,
Then landing work, to stay there, as a spy.
You're like her, I think. You've wings. You fly.

Sancerre et Renoir

The luncheon that you had—do tell me more.
Not the pink silk one, sans underwear;
The broad-brimmed hat and pressed white linen dress,
The best Sancerre, you texted, in the region.

I can only form impressions of you, here:
Pixils, daubs, Pissarro pointillism,
Where I'd prefer a painting by Renoir,
Of you at ease, with colleagues, in the country.

His 'Luncheon of the Boating Party'. Oui?
With Charigot, his mistress, on the left:
A Tilla Durieux, Sancerre in hand.
Oh, never mind. I'll paint you. Understand?

Genital hypertrophy

Perhaps your thing's too large, you gently quipped,
Referring to a stalling SMS—
Then giggled by emoji, straight away.

Would you giggle, if in fact I had
The genitalia of Toulouse-Lautrec,
Whose nickname, 'Tripod', frankly, says it all?

He was, actually, shorter far than me:
Eight inches so. I swear, I tell the truth.
But not, I must confess, just genitally.

Heavens! That'd cause a girl to gasp—
To think me so much larger than the count.
Don't panic, though. I'm well within your grasp!

Proust's muse and mine

Proust, remember, during the Great War,
Corked and slowly dying from disease,—
A lung malfunction, not from mustard gas
Inhaled in any dugout at the front—
Immersed himself in memories of things past,
Lingering in his Parisian bed.

Famously, his muse was madeleine,
Whose subtle taste made moons of bitten orange;
And I, while ill, delighted in his prose,
Resting and reflecting on my years.
But now I'll put my past to better use,
Inspired by you, my late and glorious muse.

No drop wasted

After that remark, I've got to plunge
Back into the poems of Propertius,
Looking for his scattered hints or clues
Of any such enticement by his muse;
And into Ovid's brilliant, amorous verse,
Sceptical that, even there, I'll find

Intense, alluring passion of the kind
Compressed into the words you've sent to me:
'I will not let you waste a single drop,
No perfect drop, my darling, of your seed.
From now on, every drop of you is mine.'
Did Cynthia give Sextus such a line?

Never in my youth

If anyone had told me in my teens
'Prepare, my lad, for glory after sixty.
Then you'll find your culminating love!'
How could I have answered with decorum?
Like exclaiming simply 'Heavens above!'
Yet here I am and glory is upon me!

Count the many deep infatuations
That punctuate the record of my years,
The fecklessness, the follies and the tears:
The toll's been grave of many passions spent.
But you, against the odds, bright Evenstar,
Fulfil that oracle beyond all dreams.

Charlotte Corday strikes

Anatole France's novel, nineteen twelve,
The gods will have blood (*Les dieux ont soif*),
For which, in part, he won the Nobel Prize,
Had once, on its Penguin Classic cover,
A painting of Marat, slain in his bath:
Marat, Jacobin, assassinée.

Charlotte Corday struck the killer down.
Jacques-Louis David gifted us the scene.
Her honorific, coined by Lamartine,
Became 'the Angel of Assassination'.
Why does all this come to mind right now?
You've slain my past, Charlotte—and in the bath!

BBHM

Of many songs you've sent to win my heart,
Few can rate with 'Big, Bad, Handsome Man':
Imelda May, the big band singing tart
Avowing love for some dull Mick or Stan.

But who he was is simply not the point!
Your sending her amused me to the core.
It blew my mind, like some sweet smoking joint,
Set me laughing, wanting more and more.

Could I really be your kind of guy?
Is romance with me what you've really planned?
Does Aphrodite have me in her eye?
Then take me, muse! O take me by the hand!

Priapus in the garden

In the Prologue to his *Roman Elegies*,
Goethe celebrates the blooms of Eros,
But turns on hypocrites who'd blight his garden.

Famously—this passage long got censored—
He set Priapus as the prickly guard
Of Nature's fruits, his red staff rearing hard.

Punish those, the poet instructed him,
Who'd slander or despoil what's growing here—
With one quick thrust of that thing up the rear!

Thus the sage of Weimar, in his time.
But now the Garden's ours to till and sow.
Priapus stands and scented zephyrs blow.

No-one from nowhere

'I do not want,' you sniffed, 'to be an icon,'
A celebrity pursued by paparazzi,
An image fixed in other people's minds.

I understand. Well, who could disagree?
Such status strips one of all privacy,
As Philip Seymour Hoffmann once observed.

But then you added something quite disturbing:
'I am no-one,' you exclaimed. 'I'm from nowhere.'
Betraying emptiness in your inner self.

How could such a woman, self-possessed,
A paragon of beauty, wit and masque,
So see herself, bereft of worldedness?

This fleeting moment

I somehow can't believe that this can last—
This secret, sighing, virtual affair.
The songs, the WAVs, the texts at dawn.[105]
I can't imagine where it's got to go.
Certainly, we're exercising freedom,
But, sweet thing, we have so little time.

Still, in our fleeting moment, I rejoice
That you, who long so much for poetry,
Have exercised so singular a choice,
In courting my supposed polymathy,
Enchanting me with your exquisite voice;
Declaring I'm your big, bad, handsome man.

Cosmological optics

How do you view the cosmos, may I ask?
Or what, on Earth, inspired your startling words,
'Shut your mouth, you don't know anything!'
When I extolled the atoms and the void?

We really need to have a conversation
About the things that ultimately matter,
About the void that seems to lie beneath
The easy grace and wit of your demeanour.

Don't you know that I stand with Lucretius,
Or better still, with Einstein, Planck and Hubble?
The optics, looking outward, are quite clear,
But look within, for there you are in trouble.

Remi nepotes

Catullus seemed to know his Lesbia's secrets,
Going by his frank and scurrilous verse.
Remember him addressing Caelius
About 'our Lesbia', whom, he said, he worshipped?

'Nunc', he snorted, 'in quadriviis et angriportis
Glubit magnanimos Remi nepotes'.[106]
That's best left, between us, in the decent
Obscurity of the classical language.

But your Catullus doesn't know your secrets,
Only that you've glossed them with the claim,
You've occupied the company of fellows
For a very long time—and all are grateful.

If I were Abelard

I think I am as bright as Abelard
I know for sure I've suffered more calamities,
Though not, perhaps, the cut by Fulbert's men.[107]

His advantage was he lived in Paris,
Even if, back then, it bloody stank.
It really wasn't what it's since become.

Teaching there he met young Heloise,
The brilliant, polylingual, passionate
Muse that any man like him most needs.

But then he gave her up to convent life,
Devoting all his time to dialectic.
If were him, I'd be your troubadour.

The Three Graces

The cover image for *The Erotic Poems*,
The Penguin Classic paperback of Ovid,
Lifts before our eyes a classic sculpture:
Aglaia, Euphrosyne, Thalia,
The celebrated, rightly loved Three Graces,
Naked, in white marble, at their bath.

Beauty, charm and elegance they are,
Attendants of the goddess Aphrodite,
Whose cult, though long suppressed, returned to life
In the Renascence of Western art.
Botticelli, Raphael and others
Painted them. But you bring them to life!

Musée Rodin

Have you been there yet? Perhaps with Douphol?
I'd love to gaze with you upon its wonders,
Immersed in the profound erotic art
Of Rodin, maestro, sketcher, mentor, sculptor.

It's many years since first I passed its doors,
A young and earnest student on the move,
A reader both of Balzac and Flaubert,
A Rastignac of sorts, at Pére Lachaise.

Seeing Rodin's work, then, was a dream
Of stepping into higher worlds of meaning.
It's traces faded with the passing years,
But now you *are* his sketches and his sculptures.

Leave your hat on

What did you have in mind in sending Cocker
To sing his classic, 'You can leave your hat on'?
The woman he undressed was someone else,
Until your act embodied her for me.

All at once, I saw your apparition,
Lavish hat, stilettos, little else.
Well, frankly, not a stitch, to my delight:
You caught the beat and danced in front of me.

When you let down your long, luxurious hair,
I might as well have been on LSD;
And when you climbed, at last, upon the chair,
I rose to where you clearly wanted me.

Your Ovid

I'm certainly your P. Ovidius,
At least as far as exiled amour goes;
Exiled, note, from your sweet Aventine,
Where I'm politically on the nose.
What do they say, my love, in Palatine
Parties, or in Circus conversations,
Concerning your poor poet? I suppose
They snigger at his long humiliation,
Remarking drily, 'After all, he chose
The wrong side in the court of great Augustus.
That was a fatal error, Heaven knows!
But living on the Euxine? How invidious!'

Tall priestess

It has to be said
You loom like Jerry Hall,
Over the little rock star
You seem to take me for.

What's not to like?
You've all her attributes:
Legs that go on forever,
Sexiness to up and die for.

Me? Well, that's another matter!
But if we took it quietly:
Poems, not smash hits,
It just might, just might work.

Rommel of the heart

Erwin Rommel was quite undeterred
By cautionary principles of strategy.
His boldness at the front was legendary.
With his eye on Alexandria,
Despite his patent lack of potent forces,
He threw himself at Cyrenaica.

I'm a bit like that, it must be said.
I'm prone to seize the moment, dash ahead,
Hurling promises across the desert,
When I know the distant, glittering prize
Lies just beyond a poet's Alamein.
Defeated once this year, I'm back again.

These walls of Rome

Lucius Domitius Aurelianus
Was, at one time, lord and master:
Dominus et Deus he was called.[108]

Rising from the peasant soldier ranks,
As master of horse, leader of men,
He pulled the crumbling Empire back together.

Famously, he crushed Zenobia,
Then made her walk the Via Triumphalis
Bound, by his command, in chains of gold.

But signally he built new walls round Rome,
Before assassins struck him down, in Thrace.
Such walls, my love, are all my poetries.

The bed of your voice

There's something in the timbre of your voice
Which utterly enchants this poet's brain:
A quality of gentle femininity,
Unspoiled by any artifice or guile,
Breathing forth such unaffected beauty,
Articulating literate, moving thoughts,

That every memory I have of love,
Every redolence of roseate care,
Every perfume, every balm of life,
Seems scented in my listening to you speak;
Until it seems that, with your voice,
I'm on a bed of opiate ecstasies.

Like and unlike

How did Dylan Thomas walk the street,
At least when he was not completely legless?
The classic doomed and drunken, brooding poet,
He never could find decent, well-paid work,
Or make a cheerful life with hapless Caitlin.
He foundered, fully wrecked, in Greenwich Village.

I only ask because today I walked
The quiet avenue I've made my own,
Brooding on my lot—sans alcohol—
Mulling on the bitterness that comes
From poet's moods and chronic lack of coin,
But joyful in the bounty of my muse.

It isn't easy

In one of your more plaintive, honest moments,
Fending off my probing of your past
Concerning other men and your adventures,
You touched the tender feminist in me,
Declaring that it really isn't easy
To be a woman in a world of men.

Not least the world of high finance,
Where you, through D, elected a new life,
Riding on the ego and the fortune
Of an alpha male who's lacked the mere good taste
To cherish, much less nourish, your fine virtues,
Which so enchant the beta man in me.

Your languages

Your fluent use of quite colloquial German,
Dropped into a glowing use of English,
Hinted, I assumed, for want of knowing,
At what you dubbed, in wry off-handedness,
Your heritage as a crypto-Hun.
Then the Latin. That's been simply dazzling.

But with your high heels firmly planted
Among the staff at D's deluxe château,
Which you have dubbed the palace of the Count,
You often send me messages in French.
Ah! My charming, polylingual muse,
What tongues you have! What languages you use!

Midnight in Paris

We both say we love Woody Allen's film.
The question we've agreed we must discuss
Is why we fancy vanishing at midnight
Into an imagined cityscape

Where Dali, Scott Fitzgerald, Gertrude Stein
Paint and drink and talk up different worlds
And bring alive the past exotica,
The rich alterities we might prefer.

In some ways, it's like reading well-loved books,
But Allen raised an existential question
Regarding the allure of other times:
Why would *you* flee now, when I am here?

Pharaoh's dreams

You know, at least, a little of the Bible.
Do you know, then, Pharaoh's troubling dreams
Of seven kine and seven ears of corn;
How it was only Joseph who could read
From these signs a forecast of the famine
That lay ahead for thriving, well-fed Egypt?

I am Joseph now and you are Pharaoh,
Dreaming and in doubt what it might mean.
Let Joseph speak of how to lay up corn
Against the dearth that surely is to come.
Oh let me be your provident *traumspieler*,[109]
My poetry our store against great need.

Theseus ponders

At times, you make me feel I'm Theseus:
A prisoner sentenced to the Labyrinth,
A sacrificial offering to you,
As consort to the King of the Aegean.

At other times, although you seem remote,
I feel as though you'll play my Ariadne
And, after I have slain the Minotaur,
Will come in wild hope with me to Naxos.

But you're the Queen of Gnosis, not of Gnossos
And each of us is well aware that myths,
Whatever names have been pronounced on us,
Are open to our hermeneutic use.'

Dido and the knife

I was thinking, I'd remarked to you,
Just floating an idea past my muse,
Of writing you a cycle of new poems
Based on Ovid's *Heroides*—what say?

'That sounds pretty right', was your response,
So true to who you are and how you think.
And so I threw myself into his verse,
Pondering, 'Where do I find you here?'

I found myself, two days ago, in Dido,
Angry at the fleeing prince, Aeneas,
Fingering my fatal Trojan blade,
Lamenting that I'd offered you my kingdom.

Fucking to Wagner

Your subtleties and glamour drew me first,
Your golden garb and glowing, blue-green eyes,
The claims that you were highly educated
And travelled to exotic destinations.

But then you sprang upon me, Straussian woman,
The wholly unexpected declaration
That you, the golden girl with emerald eyes,
Were actually a Wagner kind of chick.

You liked, you upped and said, with stunning candour,
Fucking to the sound of Wagner's operas.
So there! And we were hardly yet acquainted.
Now I know you meant just what you said.

So nice to come home to

You've sent me songs, from very early on,
And, plainly, chosen them to serve your aim,
Which was, it's clear, to make this poet yours.

None of them was better fit for purpose
Than the cover version of Cole Porter's
Song 'You'd be so nice to come home to'.

The cover was by Nina—Ms Simone—
But listening to it I could hear your sighs,
A longing for the simplest kinds of pleasure,

In private quarters, canopied in trust.
That was long before we'd ever spoken,
But now informs our every tryst and turn.

Our labyrinths

I wish that I could pacify your fears
Which have you wander in the Labyrinth
Others, back in Athens, say exists
At Gnossos, where, supposedly, you rule.

You know that isn't so. It's all projection.
Yet, there are times you truly seem confined
To mysteries set in dark Minoan script,
Which I must needs decipher in my mind.

In any case, when you are not with me
And I lie in my blue Minoan bed,
I also feel I'm in the Labyrinth –
Or even that I am the Minotaur.

Oxyrhynchus fragments

No-one in their tidy mind believes
That any set of poems tells the story
Accurately or completely of
The lives and thoughts of poets or their muses.
That's why scholars write biographies,
Though even then there's stuff that's unrecorded.

In fact, the felt life of such pairs
As you and I have recently become
Will vanish without fail in desert sands
Of desiccated time and long neglect.
My poems for you, therefore, must soon become
Like Oxyrhynchus fragments found in Egypt.[110]

Kay Summersby

Would you prefer that our discreet affair
Remain a matter only between us?
Assuming we ourselves are not forgotten,
As others quickly are, once they're interred,
Would or would you not want to be known
As the muse of my erotic verse?

There's precedent aplenty for concealment.
Here's one I just lately chanced upon:
Kay Summersby and Dwight D. Eisenhower
(Lovers, it would seem, in World War Two),
Who left so little trace of what they did
That even now historians disagree.

After the tryst

The smallest gestures have such resonance,
When our imaginations are engaged.
Your note, just yesterday, about our tryst:
'It felt that we were really making love,
You here, me there, our bodies brought together.'
The sending of it! That was such a gesture.

But, more than that, your precious note spelled out
That it had only been an intuition,
Until I'd sent you loving poetry,
Celebrating secret ecstasies.
'Now' you wrote, 'with these sweet words from you,
I know what I'd intuited was true.'

Aspasia

I like to think of you as my Aspasia,
But who would think of me as Pericles?
Socrates would be a better fit.

But never mind, it's you I want to flatter,
By drawing on my polymathic learning
To cast you in a role that stands apart.

Since she, the striking beauty from Miletus,
Was famous for her intellect as well,
Her mastery of rhetoric, her wit

And, nota bene, for the ease and grace
With which she kissed her Pericles in public—
The Muse, in fine, of Athens' Golden Age.[111]

Not wanting the day

Stirring, after only five hours sleep,
The blinds still drawn, no hint yet of the dawn,
I felt your presence in my rumpled bed.

Truly, it was palpable, your body;
More precisely, you were all my thoughts,
My manhood pressed against your perfect belly,

My John Donne hands a roving round your hip,
My eyes, my mouth a dwelling on your face,
The latter moving down to kiss your lips.

So vivid was your presence in the shadows
That I looked not for light of day to come,
But longed for darkness such as this to last.

Summer's day

They say, you know, that Shakespeare's famous sonnets,
Despite his several boasts in some of them
That they would last as long as men can breathe,
That they'd be read as long as eyes can see,
And, being so, they would give life to 'thee',[112]
Were actually incidental to his life.

He saw them as a private set of lyrics
For circulation only among friends.
And never dreamed—of this I feel quite certain—
That his summer's day would come to seem,
Outlasting all rough winds and scorching eyes,
The very 'thee' that YOU have now become.

Better than Christiane

Reading Goethe's *Roman Elegies*,
Unless you know his story inside out,
You might assume they're simply set in Rome;

When actually he only wrote them later,
Back in Weimar, where he'd set up home
With Christiane, fifteen years his junior.

She's the one who set his Eros free,
Much to Charlotte's anger and dismay—
Just as you have liberated me.

But Christiane can't compare with you
In stature, learning, wit or, I aver,
Where all the arts of Eros are concerned.

Catastrophe imagined

When you declared you'd be three days sans phone,
Somewhere at a party south of Paris,
Perhaps in Orleans or Aquitaine;

When I imagined all that might occur
In those three days, in limousines and lodgings,
Making merry with Douphol and friends,

Given that this month has been so sweet
In your inimitable company
And soaring to the music of your voice,

It came to me that I might lose you there,
Not to Douphol, but catastrophe:
Some fatal misadventure on the road.

Birthday bash in Bordeaux

'I'll be AWOL', you announced by text,
'Until the morrow. Therefore lickedy split.'
Giving Douphol, so your text declared,
His early birthday present in Bordeaux.

That sounds very good, I said, for him.
So Aquitaine it is—full bottle, too.
Ah! The lucky man, to be away
With my beloved muse, among the vines.

I wonder, as I ponder his good fortune,
Whether he delights as much as I
In all your wit and dazzling erudition,
Or how you've curled him round your little finger.

Dante and Petrarch

If Dante had received from Beatrice,
Or Petrarch, from the Laura of his sonnets,
The SMSs you have sent to me,
How would those great humanists have acted,
How inflected their great poetry?
Boccaccio, I'd say, might offer clues.

Imagine Dante's *Divine Comedy*,
With Beatrice anything but chaste,
Winking at the poet and enticing
Him to Aphrodite's paradise,
While Petrarch's endless vows of sublimation
Became a whirling dance of ecstasies.

Against the wall

You called me, as I strolled home from the mall.
I paused, to put your voice on speaker phone.
And stood, while we conversed, against a wall.
Listening with care to your concerns,
Feeling I was somehow Leonard Cohen,
Talking with his fabled Marianne.

Your longings and your doubts put us on Hydra,
With me, your poet, reassuring you
That, truly, we are free and can invent
The love we seek, in our most private moments,
Since we, alike, are alchemists of time,
Transmuting what's improbable to gold.

Philaenis and the saints

Philaenis may have been apocryphal,
But still her famous handbook did the rounds
For many years, until the rising Church
Suppressed her text on sexual positions:
As reading—well, as viewing—
Matter quite unfit for holy Christians.

It was a sort of Grecian *Kama Sutra*,
As you rightly guessed when I suggested
That you Google it, while dreaming of Greek islands.
And then, of course, I mentioned Cohen's album,
Various Positions, which I'll share
With you when next we are on Hydra.

All I need

Since we dispose, between the two of us,
Of everything that Western civ allows:
Art and music, literature and science;
And since, by clear agreement, we arouse
Each in the other, all but uncontrolled
The longing to awaken before dawn

Satiated, warmed and oxytocined,
By fulfilment of our mutual passions,
Cuddling up and murmuring in the dark,
What need have we, though it now be the fashion,
Of artificial sexual stimulation?
The magic of your voice is all I need.

The true sex organ

The true sex organ is between the ears;
Some brain parts have, in fact, to be turned off,
In either sex, releasing inhibitions,
For the addictive neurochemicals
To effect the frenzy called orgasm.
Alas, the bar's been high within my head.

Before you laid concerted siege to me,
With all your songs and wit and sexiness,
I'd manned the castle of my sombre mind
With iron guards of brooding scepticism:
An aging poet's mordant irony.
Before, before—a fading memory!

Were I Elon Musk

Musk, to some subordinate, they say:
'Impress me and remember I could be
Sipping mai tais with a super model,
Naked and alluring. So why you?'

That's the man who wants to die on Mars;
A master of the universe, no less.
As well as maker of electric cars.
A billionaire. An icon of success.

If I were him, would I strike such a pose?
I'm not inclined to think I really would.
It's you, no supermodel, that I chose
And being *with* you is my cosmic good.

I will, we will, he will

Could we complete so heady an exchange
As poetry for loving impregnation?
Certainly, the seed you plant in me,
Of beauty and linguistic sub-creation,
Might, in long tradition, seem enough,
Without you bearing lovely progeny.

And yet, when I declared you make me pregnant,
With poetry that burgeons from within,
And asked is this not counterpart to you
Taking in my seed to grow a child,
You responded with a phrase that awes me still:
'Oh my poet, I will—we will, he will!'

OSINT and our privacies

You're haunted by the thought that they'll find out
The things we've sighed and shared with one another,
That swept the globe in images and WAVs.

And even more—so strangely in a muse
Who's said to me that she used to collect
Nutcracker men and always left them sated—

That those who love you most would all be shocked,
If OSINT or my verse should make them public:
The privacies that we have generated.

Yet you have said yourself and I agree
We haven't done a thing to be ashamed of.
I treasure every word that we have uttered.

Emanuele Severino and nihilism

Severino was a Gnostic of some kind,[113]
Parmenidean heretic of Being,
Who made the most fantastical of claims
Concerning metaphysics and ontology.

Read, in some fine villa in Toulouse,
The Essence of Nihilism, his key book.
He used to teach in Venice, for his sins,
Prognosticating gnomically to Linceians.[114]

Every state of human life, he taught,
Does not partake of death, but is eternal,
Though God and reason tell us otherwise.
I plunder him to find it's true of us.

We have little time

Like every lover, long since passed away,
Their passions withered, organs gone to dust,
Being still alive, on this spring day,
This culminating, greening Primavera,

I write to you, with animate urgency,
Insisting we've no time to dissipate,
But must conjoin our love with cogency,
For noon has passed and it is getting late.

We have discovered wit in one another
And we surely, for its sake, must seize our chance,
Though brief our hours may be, they're ours to dance
And kiss the beauty each sees in the other.

Dichtung und Wahrheit[115]

What is truth and what is poetry,
Amid the flux we cannot comprehend,
The ethical irrationality
Of what the nihilists, in their presumption,
Deride as our late capitalist world;
And all our tumbled wet dreams of romance?

Well, 'What is truth?' was jesting Pilate's question.
Playing Jesus, I declare, 'For this
I was born and came into the world:
To find your love and lavish mine on you.'
Let me die for saying so. I'll rise.
That, Astarte, is my poetry.

All that you desire

'I think that's what I wanted from the start',
You wrote to me, when I raised the idea
Of finishing a single book of verse
For you and making love to you just once,
But to the highest pitch of sexual congress,
So that I could die a happy man.

But you were being most ingenuous,
While I was being quite ironical;
For, if the truth be told, I want you all
And not just once, but to the crack of doom;
While you desire more than this again:
To be my only muse and greatest love.

Our child is Voluptas

'You should have a son', you said to me,
Implying that you'd give yourself to that
Fulfilment, Psyche, of your womanhood,
Before the Moon should wane and leave you barren.

That compliment would overwhelm my judgement,
Being Eros, were we wed and able
To contemplate and fruitfully enact
The sacred deed of human reproduction.

But think, beloved Psyche, of our state
And bow with grace before the fate we are:
Our child must be the poetry I write,
Inspired by you and loved—as young Voluptas.[116]

Epilogue

Love of one

Love of one, wrote the philosopher,[117]
Is a piece of barbarism, for
It's practised at th' expense of any others
(Likewise with the love of just one God),
Yet you claim that you're a one-man girl.

So, who is it to be, then, you in Paris?
The philistine of ample appetite,
Who has you on his arm at fine soirees,
Who fills your fine apartment with fresh flowers,
Enables you to drink pichon lalande

And chateau patris every other day,
To gossip of propinquity to 'power',
Chatter of arcane affairs of state,
Go riding in Provence, like some French heiress,
Pretend you've secrets not vouchsafed to moi?

Or the poet you have so long courted,
To whom, as you have written (don't deny it),
That you wish you could come home to him,
To lie with him before each day arises,
Knowing he will kiss you on the mouth?

You've even gone so far as to demand
That I rework my poems for another,
Pretending that I wrote them all for you,
Altering their patent dedication
To an Asian, not a European muse.

So it goes and so it ever has.
I'm hardly so unworldly that I fail
To comprehend your delicate dilemmas.
Fortunately, I am no barbarian
And cast a mordant eye on your affairs.

Cupid, Psyche and the West Wind

'Re-read', you wrote, 'the tale from Apuleius,
Of Cupid, Psyche and the hidden palace.
Their narrative is rather close to ours.'

I loved you for that literate suggestion
And bought *The Golden Ass* in fresh translation,[118]
Thinking to recover what you'd meant.

But Finkelpearl and Singer left it out
Of what, I learned, was an abridged edition,
Keeping just the stuff on animals.

So, back I went to Brewer's *Phrase and Fable*—
And, of course, to Wikipedia—
Looking for some clues to your dark meaning.

Cupid—that is Eros—teaches Psyche
The lesson that *sans* trust there is no love.
Were you implying I can teach you this?

The background to the story, you remember:
Is Aphrodite's jealousy of Psyche
For her mortal beauty and the way

A goddess who could not abide a rival,
Sent her son by Vulcan (that is, Cupid)
To slay the hapless Psyche in her sleep.

But Cupid fell in love with her instead
And took her on the West Wind to a palace,
Where he'd come to her invisibly at night,

So that she would love him tenderly
For who he was and not some godlike features,
Making tryst by voice and poetries.

Well if, as you've declared, our narrative
Resembles what's related in the fable,
How does it end for us? What was your point?

This floating shell

Few things have endeared you more to me
Than our exchange concerning Botticelli:
Your claim, which I believe, that some official
Declared he'd seen you framed in the Uffizi—
Specifically 'Nascita de Venere',
The birth of Venus, rising from the sea.

I responded, as you will recall,
That I would really love to see you painted
After that famed figure found on Melos,
Sculpted from the purest Parian marble,
Not by Praxiteles, it now seems,
By a lesser light from Antioch.

You quipped back—a piece de resistance—
That, when push comes to shove, you'd rather float
In some great shell (like Venus in the painting).
I laughed aloud, rejoicing in your wit,
Your erudition and your irony.
I vowed, at once, that that would be the title

Of this book of ribald, loving poems,
In which I've sketched a first approximation
Of how you first arose off my Cythera,
Redolent of Phryne swimming nude,
Or of Campaspe, whom Apelles painted,
In the nascence, not the renascence.

The scallop shell's the symbol of the vulva
And well I know, now, that is where you float,
Yet, my living, breathing Aphrodite.
You're anything but just a pretty picture.
No form of plastic art could do you justice—
But possibly my verses have come close.

Endnotes

Part I

1 For several billion years, from the origins of life on Earth, all life consisted of single celled organisms: prokaryotes were those that reproduced by cloning and there were no others for the first couple of billion years. Then eukaryotes evolved, which were far more sophisticated and could swap genetic information, thus pioneering what would become sexual reproduction and also a division of labour, enabling the evolution of larger, complex organisms. The poem's playfulness derives from the idea of exchanging information whether sexually or verbally and the nature of life.

2 A great deal of our evidence about human evolution comes from fossils discovered in the Olduvai Gorge in Tanzania. An archaic species of hominin was *Paranthropus Boisei,* which Mary Leakey dubbed 'Nutcracker Man', because she reasoned that the stone tools shaped or 'knapped' by that species, more than 2.5 million years ago, were for cracking the hard shells of nuts, among other things. In the poem the species name is divided into the female Paranthropa and the male Boisei. Refinements in the art of knapping stone tools led to a breakthrough about 1.5 million years ago, with a new species, *Homo erectus,* shaping impressive, leaf-shaped hand-axes. The poem is a satire on the clash between innovation and 'practicality' in human culture.

3 Frances Burton's *Fire: The Spark That Ignited Human Evolution* is the source for the first stanzas of this poem. She argues that our hominin ancestors were very likely using fire in various ways long before the building of actual hearths and that this shaped the cognitive evolution of the genus *Homo,* which culminated in our species after millions of years.

4 Archimedes (287-212 BCE) was a brilliant mathematician and geometer who was among the many Hellenistic scientists that broke new ground, in the 3rd century BCE, as regards the actual physical nature of reality and the laws that govern it. He was a citizen of Syracuse, then a wealthy and powerful Greek city state in Sicily. It was besieged by the Romans, under their general, Marcellus, in 212 BCE, during the Second Punic War (218-202 BCE). When the city fell, Archimedes was killed by a Roman soldier.

5   Lucius Licinius Lucullus was a Roman general who, returning to Rome from wars in the east with a huge personal fortune, built a fabulous villa on the Pincian Hill, just outside the old walls of the city and within it gardens and an elite library. He married Clodia Metelli, but she was notoriously promiscuous and did not perform her wifely duties. The poem is a whimsical reflection on the ironies of human relationships and the place in them of wealth and property.

6   This poem has deep personal roots. The first poem I wrote for the muse of Part I was called 'Ancient Bridge' and it took the famous bridge at Toledo as a metaphor for our meeting. That poem hangs on my living room wall to this day. When the story *Darkness Over Love: A Complete Fiction* began to take shape, it began with Fenimore and Margarita meeting in Toledo, in April 2004, only a short while after the notorious Madrid bombings. In 2018, she and I visited Spain together, starting in Madrid and then making our way to Toledo and Cordoba. Both the poem and the story had been written by then and we spent a whole day stepping through the Fenimore and Margarita tale in Toledo. It was an extraordinary experience.

7   This poem is based on the characters in Gabriel Garcia Marquez's novel *One Hundred Years of Solitude* and it uses them to make wry remarks about Garcia Marquez's life and politics.

8   This poem is based on the funeral of Yury in Boris Pasternak's famous 1957 novel *Doctor Zhivago*.

9   This poem is a villanelle, a very demanding form of poem, which has its origins and derives its name from rustic verses of medieval times. Perhaps the best-known villanelle of the past century has been Dylan Thomas's 1951 lyric, which begins

>   *Do not go gentle into that good night,*
>   *Old age should burn and rave at close of day;*
>   *Rage, rage against the dying of the light.*

Thomas himself may have raged, but he died of alcoholic poisoning at the age of just 39, not getting close to old age. My own philosophy is very different. This villanelle was written both as a reflection on the challenges of building and sustaining genuine intimacy with a beloved other and as a retort to the claim by the Catholic theologian Augustine of Hippo, in the 5th century CE, that love of a woman (or any other) was a distraction from the love of God, which dispersed one's self or soul. Hannah Arendt, of whose work I have long been an admirer, wrote her doctoral dissertation in Germany, in the late 1920s on the concept of love in St Augustine. It is a fine and scrupulous piece of work. It was the immediate source of my inspiration for writing the poem. But writing a villanelle was simply a whimsical idea, a challenge to see whether I could turn the trick.

10 While this poem is a slight reworking of a poem by Dietrich Bonhoeffer about his incarceration and separation from his beloved young wife, it entered into my work both because, in *Darkness Over Love*, Fenimore was reflecting on his relationship with Margarita through the story of the Bonhoeffer family, while I was using the fictional story of Fenimore and Margarita to get perspective on my relationship with the woman to whom the whole of Part I is addressed, from whom I had become separated in late 2007, but with whom I would meet here or abroad at long intervals in the years that followed.

11 This, is a slight reworking of a poem by Dietrich Bonhoeffer, written by him during his imprisonment by the Nazis in 1944. It was composed in the context of a story I was writing at the time for the muse of *Darkness Over Love*.

12 This poem takes as its raw material and turns into an extended metaphor the life of the French architect Le Corbusier, as set out in rich detail in Nicholas Fox Weber's *Le Corbusier: A Life* (Alfred Knopf, New York, 2008), which I read that year, when I was making the strenuous adjustment to Muse 1's departure from our shared home, never, I suspected, to return. It is, clearly, an attempt, at least, to find a heroic inspiration in what was, at that time, a feeling of deep loss and desolation. As it turned out, the heroic ethos brought into being a remarkable and mutually inspiring relationship and an extraordinary range of enriching, shared experience, over the following decade.

13 This poem is fairly self-explanatory, but a delightful coda to it is that I emailed it to the author of *Proust and the Squid,* Maryanne Wolf, in Boston, more or less as soon as I had written it and she emailed back within the hour saying she found it delightful, was just about to go to deliver a lecture and would, with my consent, share it with her class.

14 Marcel Proust's *In Search of Lost Time* is a reading experience every thinking and sensitive person should have. Unfortunately, its sheer length (some 4,000 pages published in English in six volumes) deters most people. I read it during the cancer years, when I was forced to rest a great deal. But I also read Alain de Botton's *How Proust Can Change Your Life* (Picador, 1997) and Roger Shattuck's splendid study *Proust's Way: A Field Guide to In Search of Lost Time* (Norton and Co., New York, 2000). Shattuck's fifth chapter 'Proust's Binoculars' lucidly explains the relationship between memory, cognition and understanding, or the generation of meaning. The link is seeing things twice (experience and recollection) and magnified by distance. Seen this way, life ceases to become a confused and arid series of meaningless events and can become a polysemic narrative, as Proust's life did in his writing. My poetry has been an attempt to generate such meaning by capturing experiences, both as they occur and as they seem to me in the longer context of my experience. This specific poem marked a turning point in my appreciation of what I had been through with an exceptional person and what it could mean if I kept reflecting on it and communicating with her.

15 This and the following two poems are reworked from several of a cycle of twenty-one poems I wrote in March 2008, called *The Neruda Variations*. Those poems, which took Neruda's *Twenty Love Poems and a Song of Despair* as their reference point, were my emotional catharsis as I struggled to deal with the perceived failure of my relationship with the closest partner and lover I had ever had. I worked both from Neruda's Spanish original, in the edition she had given me and also the English translation by W. S. Merwin.

16 One of half a dozen reasons why this relationship came apart in 2006-07 was that I had become psychologically scarred by earlier failures in love and unable to trust or give myself to a partner. Only after Muse 1 left did I find my emotions erupting in a cathartic manner. Listening to Sinatra sing 'If You Go Away' (and also to Dolly Parton singing 'We Used To'), in 2008, I burst into sobs and cried, something I have only ever done a handful of times in my entire adult life. I felt grief and

loss. Ultimately, this was therapeutic. The writing of the poetry was a freer and freer outcome of that therapeutic experience and gave expression to my high regard for the woman I had loved and lost, but who grew close to me again as the years passed and we worked at the relationship. *Lyrical Epigrams* would become my attempt to really give that expression and do her justice.

17 'Manuela' is not the name of the muse of Part I. It is a figure of speech for the need I was addressing and the vision I had regarding what had taken place in 2007-08. It was only over a decade or so that the vision spelled out in it, of meeting and parting, again and again, in the clearing for being that we created, would come to pass. In a sense this poem helped to bring that possibility into being.

18 This poem is a simple expression of my rejection of otherworldly religion. It was written at a time when it was by no means clear how much longer I would live. A charming moment occurred one day, in 2015, when one of my younger sisters had called in to see how I was and to prepare me a meal and I read her the poem. 'That's fantastic!' she exclaimed. 'Who did you say wrote that?'

19 This poem is really meant to be sung and the refrain is imagined as being made the subject of a saxophone riff. But the underlying meaning has to do with the famous legend of Theseus and Ariadne, as narrated within the poem. I really had come to see my departed companion as my Ariadne, who had urged me to become the writer and poet I longed to be and set me free to do that, not least by leaving me to pursue her own dream of a career in her native country. When my book *The West in a Nutshell* was published, in 2009, it was dedicated to her, with an inscription in Spanish declaring 'for my Ariadne, with her thread of gold. Never Naxos but always love in Athens.' The poem takes that sentiment and turns into a kind of jazz lyric.

20 So many have been my failures in conventional love that I have never had children. This poem was written as a reflection on the imagined idea of having had a son. It was inspired, in part, by Rilke's famous lullaby, but is very different in intonation. Only when Muse 3 came on the scene, a decade after this poem was written, would the idea of actually having a son with a woman I loved surface as an alluring idea.

21 This song, as it were, arose out of spending time with my estranged partner in Buenos Aires, in 2010. My love for her remained strong, but she had become rather distant at that time and it would be six years before that shifted to a deeper intimacy, by then on a new foundation. 'Fusion' gave expression to my longing for an erotic intimacy that had evaporated and would not, in fact, return—until Muse 3 won my heart in 2021.

22 Ovid's *Metamorphoses* is one of the master works of Western literature and has been popular and influential ever since it was published two thousand years ago. No book had a greater influence on Shakespeare than this one. I have four different translations of it in my personal library and have believed for decades that, had I been given a 'real' education, a close study of this book in the original Latin as well as in translation would have been an integral part of it. That didn't happen. Like almost everything of value in my education, it was something I had to discover for myself and explore on my own time. One of the most touching moments in the development of my intimacy with Muse 3 was when she remarked, with that easy grace of hers, 'you remind me

of Ovid in exile on the Black Sea' and, even more, when she described me as her Ovid. Her own immersion in the classics is one of the things that drew me to her as a stunning muse.

23 Sappho was dubbed, in the ancient world, the Tenth Muse, an extraordinary honour, both because she was the only mortal human being to be so honoured at any time and because she was a woman, not a man.

24 This is a Sapphic ode. The only one I have written. And it is about Sappho. I enjoyed writing it, not least because I had been to the Aegean and could imagine the settings. I visited Istanbul in 2006, Lesbos in 2011 and Santorini in 2013. The poem was written after the third of those sojourns, which came towards the end of a field trip in the Mediterranean for the novel *Darkness Over Love*, which I was deeply immersed in at the time, but which was not completed, owing to the fact that, on returning from that journey, I discovered that my melanoma, long confined to my right leg, had metastasised and I was in trouble. I prepared and published, instead, a truncated version of it, thinking that, otherwise, all my work might end up being wasted.

25 The seven songs of Queen Nefesh come from a long fable made up by Fenimore Moneghan for Margarita Henderson y Mendoza, the fictional pair in the story *Darkness Over Love*, as set out by his executor, Tom Emerson, in Appendix B to the posthumously published Notebooks of Fenimore. Emerson himself speculates about the origins of the story and deduces that it derived from a visit Fenimore and Margarita had made to Egypt, in April 2008, and Margarita's gift to Fenimore of Daniel Levitin's *The World in Six Songs: How the Musical Brain Created Human Nature*. He pointed out that, as Fenimore revised the tale of Raneb and Nefesh, he had become increasingly ambivalent about who had actually composed the seven songs: Raneb for Nefesh, Raneb's court sage Urhotep or Queen Nefesh herself. But he revealed that Margarita had inscribed inside the gift copy of Levitin's book the words: *Yo quiero que escribes, para mi, seis canciones del cerebro musical que evoquen nuestra entranable visita a los Valles de los Reyes y las Reinas, Margarita, 14 Abril 2008*: I want you to write for me seven songs of the musical brain evoking our entrancing visit to the Valleys of the Kings and Queens. Margarita, 14 April, 2008.

26 Helen Vendler *Dickinson: Selected Poems and Commentaries* (Belknap Press, Harvard University, 2010). See, also, Alfred Habegger *My Wars Are Laid Away in Books: The Life of Emily Dickinson* (Random House, New York, 2001). It was an extraordinary life in several ways, marked by her exploration of the decay of doctrinal Protestantism and her very private attempt to delineate a personal lyrical vision of meaning and truth.

27 James Romm (ed) *The Landmark Arrian: The Campaigns of Alexander* (Pantheon Books, New York, 2010). Alexander wintered in Gordion in 333 BCE. The account of the cutting of the knot is to be found in Book II Section 3: 1-6. Pierre Briant *The First European: A History of Alexander in the Age of Empire* (Harvard University Press, 2017) is a thought-provoking reflection on the significance of Alexander's epic conquests for modern Europeans, as they debated the morality and geopolitical merits of empire building in the 18th and 19th centuries. Alexander was generally depicted as rational and benevolent and the Ottoman Empire as the modern counterpart to the Persian Empire that Alexander had conquered long before.

28 My PhD fieldwork, between late August 1984 and April 1985, took me on a journey—my first overseas travel—from Hawaii and Los Angeles to Mexico City, San Salvador, then, retracing my steps via Mexico City and LA, to Sacramento, Seattle, across to Ann Arbor, Michigan, then to Pittsburgh, Allentown, Washington DC, New York and Boston, then back to Washington DC, before embarking on a skimming journey through London, Paris, Rome, Athens, Bangkok, Hong Kong and Tokyo to Manila. El Salvador was in the throes of civil war in October 1984, when I arrived there. The following trio of poems are attempts to capture a few of the experiences I had while there. My journals contain many more.

29 The whole series of poems set in Rome or about the decline and fall of the Roman Empire was triggered by a brief visit to Rome with Muse 1, en route from Washington DC to Marrakesh, in early February 2019. The pivotal ones are 'Being in Rome' and 'Pantheon', which best capture the sense of intimacy, but 'Love Among the Ruins' casts us back to the sack of Rome, as if we had been there and survived that catastrophe—then departed for a farm in Africa (itself, of course, soon thereafter overrun by the Vandals). That touch was thrown in chiefly because she loved the Robert Redford/Meryl Streep film *Out of Africa* and would often dreamily recite the evocative words from Isak Dinesen's journal, 'I had a farm in Africa'.

30 Michael Kulikowski *Imperial Tragedy: From Constantine's Empire to the Destruction of Roman Italy AD 363-568* (Profile Books, 2019).

31 Jens Malte Fischer *Gustav Mahler* (Yale University Press, 2011) is perhaps the best biography of the composer. Alma Schindler enters the story in Chapter 22.

32 Roger Shattuck *Proust's Way: A Field Guide to In Search of Lost Time* (W. W. Norton & Co., New York, 2000) is a splendid introduction to Proust. Shattuck (1923—2005) was a very fine literary critic and sage. His books *Forbidden Knowledge: From Prometheus to Pornography* (1996) and *Candour and Perversion: Literature, Education and the Arts* (1999) will concern us later, in Part III.

33 Richard Holmes *Shelley: The Pursuit* (1974) is my chief source on the poet. He had a sojourn in Rome in 1819, more or less exactly two centuries before Muse 1 and I visited the great city. On 8 July 1822, he set out to sea on his yacht the *Don Juan*. A storm blew up and, caught in it, Shelley refused expert advice to accept rescue or at least reef his sails. His yacht foundered and he drowned.

34 This poem is pretty much a history of my relationship with Muse 1 and is best read in conjunction with several others, not least 'The pact we've formed' and 'Shrovetide', in order to get some idea of how hard we worked on companionship, over many years in the midst of wide geographical separation, lack of sexual affinity and my prolonged illness. The remarkable thing is that we achieved so much.

35 Simone de Beauvoir *Prime of Life*, the second volume of her four-volume autobiography (Penguin, 1962, reprinted 1979) p. 135:

> *Raymond Aron was spending a year at the French Institute in Berlin and studying Husserl simultaneously with preparing a historical thesis. When he came to Paris, he spoke of Husserl to Sartre. We spent an evening together at the Bec de Gaz in the Rue Montparnasse. We ordered the specialty of the house, apricot cocktails. Aron said, pointing to his glass, 'You see, my dear fellow, if you are a phenomenologist, you can talk about this cocktail and make philosophy out of it.' Sartre turned pale with emotion at this. Here was just the thing he had been longing to achieve for years—to describe objects just as he saw and touched them and extract philosophy from the process.*

The incident is so well known that it found its way into the title of Sarah Bakewell's book on existentialism *At the Existentialist Café: Freedom, Being and Apricot Cocktails* (Vintage, 2017).

36 This poem was prompted by a reading of Thomas W. Laqueur's remarkable study *Solitary Sex: A Cultural History of Masturbation* (Zone Books, 2004). In his Acknowledgements, at the very beginning of the book, he evokes his mentor Lawrence Stone as having declared in the late 1970s 'that someone really should find out why what he called the hysteria about masturbation appeared so dramatically in the eighteenth century, at a time when, he thought, all signs pointed to a great acceptance of sexual pleasure...I wish that he had lived to see my account of a problem he pondered.' But just as this book of mine was about to go to press, Chantelle Otten's book *The Sex Ed You Never Had* (Allen and Unwin, 2021) was released. She writes: 'As a sexologist, I tell people to masturbate in different ways to help with a variety of sexual concerns...Masturbation is both a privilege and a right. It's a fantastic way to relax your whole body and de-stress, as it reduces the stress hormone cortisol...which can make self-pleasure particularly useful just before bed for an excellent night's sleep. Sweet dreams!' (pp. 110-11).

37 Judit Frigyesi *Bela Bartok and Turn-of-the-Century Budapest* (University of California Press, 1998) is a beautiful book and one that made a profound impression on me a generation ago. I had long been fascinated by George Steiner's little book *In Bluebeard's Castle* (Faber, London, 1971) and by Bartok's dark opera *Bluebeard's Castle*. Indeed, before Muse 1 arrived, in 2004, I had come to see myself as a kind of Bluebeard, immured in his castle and unable to find love. I played the opera for her one day and read out a passage from Frigyesi's book about the opera being a theatrical metaphor. She declared on the spot that we were never going to listen to that opera again. I subsequently came to see her as Judith to my Bluebeard.

38 Peng Ming-min (born 15 August 1923) is a noted democracy activist, advocate of Taiwan independence, and politician. Arrested for sedition in 1964 for printing a manifesto advocating democracy in his native Taiwan, he escaped to Sweden, before taking a post as a university teacher in the United States. After 22 years in exile he returned to become the Democratic Progressive Party's first presidential candidate in Taiwan's first direct presidential election in 1996. His book *A Taste of Freedom: Memoirs of a Formosan Independence Leader* (Taiwan Publishing Co. Irvine, California, 1972) is a classic. I was privileged to meet him in the Presidential Palace in Taipei and to receive from him a personal copy of the book, some twenty years ago. He is now 98 years old and the threat once again hangs over Taiwan of violent subordination to a mainland based Chinese regime. Muse 1 and I visited Taiwan as the guests of the Taiwanese Foreign Ministry, in 2006.

39 Wei Jingsheng *The Courage to Stand Alone: Letters From Prison and Other Writings* (Viking, New York, 1997) is a valuable record of this man's brave defiance of the Chinese Communist Party. His October 1979 trial speech, reprinted in Appendix II of that book (pp. 213-226) is a classic defence of liberty against tyranny. An illuminating introduction to the hopes of students and many others in China in the 1980s that political democratization would come about soon is Merle Goldman *Sowing the Seeds of Democracy in China: Political Reform in the Deng Xiaoping Era* (Harvard University Press, 1994), written and published after the crushing of just such reforms and hopes in Tiananmen Square on 4 June 1989—on the orders of Deng Xiaoping.

40 Liu Xiaobo *No Enemies, No Hatred: Selected Essays and Poems* (edited by Perry Link, Tienchi Martin-Liao and Liu Xia, Belknap Press, Harvard University, 2012) is the remarkably eirenic record of the thinking of this man, who was incarcerated and slowly killed by the Chinese Communist Party for his liberal democratic activism.

41 Albert Camus (1913-1960) was one of the towering moral figures of the mid-20th century because he refused to subscribe to the Left-wing cant that held up Marxism-Leninism as liberating and defended the Soviet and Maoist regimes against the West. Less conservative than Raymond Aron, he stood chiefly in contrast to Jean-Paul Sartre, who remarked as late as the early 1970s 'the revolution will come through Moscow or not at all' and 'the problem with the French Revolution was not that they killed too many people, but that they didn't kill enough.'

42 Anna Politkovskaya *A Russian Diary* (Harvill Secker, London, 2007) gives us Anna in her own words. Masha Gessen *The Future is History: How Totalitarianism Reclaimed Russia* (Granta, London, 2017) provides a broader background to the context in which Anna worked and was murdered. Steven Lee Myers *The Rise and Reign of Vladimir Putin* (Alfred Knopf, New York, 2015) also covers this ground very well. See especially pp. 307-14 on the killing of Anna P. Anders Aslund *Russia's Crony Capitalism: The Path from Market Economy to Kleptocracy* (Yale University Press, New Haven and London, 2019) is required reading on the subject of the things Anna P was struggling against like a rip tide.

43 This poem was written on a visit to Caracas, in 2016, and inspired by the direct experience of the prestigious public park on Mount Avila—which had been nationalized by the Chavista government—running out of piped water because the water utility had broken down and unable to import bottled water because the regime had wrecked foreign trade. In form and rhetoric it was inspired by Osip Mandelstam's Stalin epigram, which got him arrested and sent off to the GULAG, where he died, in 1938. See Robert Littell *The Stalin Epigram: A Novel* (Simon & Schuster, New York, 2009).

44 Daniel Ellsberg *The Doomsday Machine: Confessions of a Nuclear War Planner* (Bloomsbury, 2017) is a remarkable and chilling book. He remarks that when, in 1964, he and his senior RAND Corporation colleague Harry Rowen came out of a cinema where they had watched the newly released black comedy *Doctor Strangelove*, they agreed that what they had seen was essentially a documentary.

45 This poem was based on the story of Yesenin's life recounted by Martin Sixsmith in *An Unquiet Heart: A Poet in Love and Revolution—A Novel* (Scribner, 2019).

46   Diogenes Laertius lived in the 3rd century CE, though it is unclear when he was born and when he died. He wrote a two-volume set of concise biographies of the Greek philosophers. Nothing is definitively known about his life, but this two volume work *Lives and Opinions of Eminent Philosophers* has long been a principal source for the history of ancient Greek philosophy. He often repeats information from his sources without critically evaluating it and frequently focuses on trivial or insignificant details of his subjects' lives while ignoring important details of their philosophical teachings. He also sometimes fails to distinguish between earlier and later teachings of specific philosophical schools. However, unlike many other ancient secondary sources, he generally reports philosophical teachings without attempting to reinterpret or expand on them, which means his accounts are often fairly close to the primary sources. Due to the loss of so many of those primary sources, which were still available to him in the 3rd century, but were lost as the Roman Empire disintegrated, his has become a valuable reference work on the history of Greek philosophy.

47   It was only in the 1830s that geologists began to compute just how old the Earth is and only in the late 20th century that plate tectonics was accepted as defining how continents moved and changed shape and position over aeons. The perspective so gained is known as Deep Time and it eviscerates all the myths and legends of every human culture on Earth that postulate stories about how the Earth began and its age and formation. See Douglas Palmer *The Atlas of the Prehistoric World* (Summit Press, Rowville, 2004) and especially pp. 22-23 for the shape of the continents—Gondwana, Laurentia and the Panthalassic Ocean—420 million years ago. This was where I got the idea for 'some Silurian Nureyev' dancing across the Panthalassic Ocean, which was far larger than today's Pacific Ocean. On the development of the theory of tectonic plates, see James Lawrence Powell *Four Revolutions in the Earth Sciences: From Heresy to Truth* (Columbia University Press, New York, 2015), Part II Continental Drift and Plate Tectonics.

48   In 2016, the Rolling Stones performed before a vast crowd in Havana, at the end of their America Latina Ole Tour, by special arrangement with the US and Cuban governments—and on Good Friday, to the discomfort of the Vatican. Charlie Watts was still alive and drumming and the concert, dubbed Havana Moon, was a huge success. Sasha Allen had joined the band for the Latin America tour and performed spectacularly in a duet with Jagger singing Gimme Shelter. Jagger, on stage, called her La Encantadora, the Enchantress.

49   David N. Schwartz *The Last Man Who Knew Everything: The Life and Times of Enrico Fermi Father of the Nuclear Age* (Basic Books, New York, 2017) is a good introduction to this Promethean intellectual figure. On the paradox in question see pp. 37 and 364. It was a back of the envelope calculation that, if there was intelligent life elsewhere in the cosmos, we should have heard from it by now, given the age of the universe.

50   Franz Brentano *Psychology From an Empirical Point of View* (1874, Routledge 2015), with its 2015 Foreword by Tim Crane, is a good introduction to the life and thought of this fascinating freethinking individual. Crane remarks 'it is arguable that, at the beginning of the twenty-first century, his work is more scrutinised and debated than it has been for at least a hundred years.' The book published in 1874 consisted of the first two volumes in a planned six volume magnum opus. The other four volumes exist in draft form, but were never published.

51 This poem was written about two years before the poems in Parts II and III of the present book and yet it rings truer now than it did then, precisely because of the intensity of the feelings aroused by the muses of those later poems.

52 Karl Sigmund *Exact Thinking in Demented Times: The Vienna Circle and the Epic Quest for the Foundations of Science* (Basic Books, London, 2017) was the book that prompted this little bit of verse. We certainly live in somewhat demented times in the early 2020s and the sciences are rampant now in a way they had barely begun to become in the 1920s.

53 Giles Sparrow *COSMOS* (Quereus Publishing, London, 2007) is a superb, large-format book full of magnificent photographs and images of the solar system and the galaxy, as well as galaxies beyond. The detail concerning just the solar system is fabulous. The whole book is a superb illustration of how very much we, as a scientific species, have learned since Galileo put his eye to a telescope just over 400 years ago.

54 David Sacks *The Alphabet* (Hutchinson, London, 2003), Johanna Drucker *The Alphabetic Labyrinth: The Letters in History and Imagination* (Thames and Hudson, London, 1999) and Denise Schmandt-Besserat *How Writing Came About* (University of Texas Press, Austin, 1996) were among the inspirations for this and the next few poems, which are just whimsical reflections of a writer on the origins of his chief instruments.

55 Stanislas Dehaene *Reading in the Brain: The Science and Evolution of a Human Invention* (Viking, 2009). This is a brilliant book. Every literate person should read it, but above all every teacher of reading and literature.

56 Jean Moorcroft Wilson *Robert Graves: From Great War Poet to Goodbye To All That 1895-1929* (Bloomsbury, 2018) is a good source on the background imagery here. Graves only arrives on Mallorca with his muse Laura Riding in the last chapters of the book and there is much to come in what one anticipates will be two further volumes in Wilson's biography.

57 Stanley Corngold *Walter Kaufmann: Philosopher, Humanist, Heretic* (Princeton University Press, 2019). His title deliberately echoes Kaufmann's sub-title for his book on Nietzsche: *Philosopher, Psychologist, Antichrist.*

58 Jean Clottes *Return to Chauvet Cave: Excavating the Birthplace of Art: The First Full Report* (Thames and Hudson, London, 2003). On the footprints of the youth and hound see pp. 34-38.

Part II

59 Horse whisperer: A horse trainer who adopts a sympathetic view of the motives, needs, and desires of the horse, based on modern equine psychology. Horse whisperers are people who are able to calm horses and work with difficult to train horses. ... One becomes a horse whisperer by developing an innate sense of the animals. It is one thing to be able to work with a horse, but it is quite something else to do it with the gentle actions of a horse whisperer. *The Horse Whisperer* is a 1998 American film directed by and starring Robert Redford, based on the 1995 novel *The Horse Whisperer* by Nicholas Evans. Redford plays the title role, as Tom Booker, a talented trainer with a remarkable gift for understanding horses, who is hired to help an injured teenager (played by Scarlett Johansson) and her horse back to health following a tragic accident.

60 Few lines from this famous song are more celebrated than 'All I ever learned from love was how to shoot at someone who outdrew you'. But the opening two verses have always been the ones I love most. And, in the present context, the second has particular resonance:

> *Your faith was strong but you needed proof*
> *You saw her bathing on the roof*
> *Her beauty and the moonlight overthrew ya*
> *She tied you to a kitchen chair*
> *She broke your throne, and she cut your hair*
> *And from your lips she drew the Hallelujah*

Erotic attraction, of its nature, embodies a tension between what might be called secular enactment or defeat, on the one hand, and transcendent experience on the other. Cohen's great song is an anthem about this.

61 Hannah Arendt (1906—1975) was a brilliant young woman of Jewish background who went to Marburg to study philosophy, drawn by the rising reputation of a young professor there called Martin Heidegger (1889—1976). She was eighteen when they met. He was thirty-five. They had a love affair which was unforgettable for each of them. It is well covered by Daniel Maier-Katkin in *Stranger from Abroad: Hannah Arendt, Martin Heidegger, Friendship and Forgiveness* (2010). She loved him for the passion that he brought to thinking about existence—why there is anything at all and what it means to be a conscious being in a world one has not made. He loved her for her beauty, her intelligence, her intense interest in the same questions that rivetted him. It was some months after they first encountered each other, in his seminar on Plato's *Sophist* that, February 1925, he approached her and asked him to his office. As Maier-Katkin relates:

> *At the end of class one day at the beginning of February 1925, Heidegger approached the stylish young woman with stunning eyes who sat in the seminar room taking careful, thorough notes and asked her to come and see him in his office. The days are grey, wet and cold in Marburg at that time of year and the old buildings were chilly and damp. When she came to his office, Hannah was wearing a coat, buttoned to the collar and a hat with a large brim against the rain and cold. He asked about the lectures and about the philosophers she had been reading; she answered briefly in a soft voice, sometimes*

in Greek and Latin. She looked away demurely, but he took her in with his eyes and years later admitted to Hannah that he had retained the image of a shy girl quietly answering his questions all the rest of his life.

For each of them, the love affair that soon began remained a defining experience for the rest of their lives—for half a century. He would declare that she had been his muse, the inspiration for all his greatest work. She would ever afterwards think of the affair as having defined passionate love for her, even when she found other deeper and more enduring love.

I have known this story for many years. I fell under the allure of Hannah Arendt myself in the mid-1980s, reading about her in the biography *Hannah Arendt: For Love of the World* by Elisabeth Young-Bruehl (1946-2011). Arendt's doctoral dissertation, completed after she and Heidegger had gone their separate ways, was on the idea of love in the theology of St Augustine. That was a profound meditation and had a major influence on me, when I acquired it in English translation, in 1998. Heidegger, meanwhile, in 1927, published his pathbreaking *magnum opus*, or the first part of what was at that time intended to become his *magnum opus: Being and Time*. That, too, I have read—as well as numerous commentaries on it. The 1920s, in short, were the years of the intimacy of Heidegger and Arendt. However, when the Nazi Party was catapulted into power in 1933, Heidegger became an active Nazi and Arendt became a refugee. She survived the ordeal and the Holocaust and by 1941 was safe in New York. He, between 1931 and 1941, kept a private journal, which he called *The Black Notebooks*, in which he recorded his thoughts of the era. When finally published, long after he died, they became and remain the subject of great controversy. This poem arose against that background.

62   Born René Karl Wilhelm Johann Josef Maria Rilke, the poet Rainer Maria Rilke (1875—1926), was of Bohemian-Austrian origin, but travelled widely in Europe, including Russia, Spain, Germany, France and Italy. In his later years, given the upheaval caused by the First World War, he settled in Switzerland. Rather like his contemporary Martin Heidegger, he was deeply preoccupied with the existential solitude and dilemmas of the conscious self and the creation of meaning and authenticity. His greatest work came in a creative burst in 1922, after a number of years of depression and strandedness, under the influence of his last and greatest muse, Baladine Klossowska: *Sonnets to Orpheus and Duino Elegies*. Hannah Arendt loved poetry and not least that of Rilke. It's easy to believe that, had she met him, in 1924-25, she would have been drawn to him as she had been to Heidegger—except that he was a decade and half older than Heidegger and fell ill in 1925 with the leukaemia that would kill him, at the age of fifty, the following year.

63   Erik Satie (1866—1925) was a French composer and pianist in the late 19th and early 20th century Parisian avant-garde. His work was a precursor to later artistic movements such as minimalism, repetitive music, and the Theatre of the Absurd, while his 1917 coinage 'furniture music' would presage the development of background and ambient music. The Gnossiennes are several very short piano pieces that he composed in the late 19th century. They are in rather free time and were highly experimental in form, rhythm and chordal structure. Both the form and the term were invented by Satie. Gnossiennes, though a neologism, would appear to hint at Gnosis and Gnosticism. It has been suggested that, if existentialism had a theme tune it might well be Gnossienne 3.

64 Constantine Cavafy (1863—1933) was a Greek poet, journalist and civil servant who spent much of his life in Alexandria, Egypt, the ancient Hellenistic capital. His consciously individual style earned him a place among the most important figures not only in Greek poetry, but in Western poetry as well. He only wrote 155 finished and published poems, though dozens more remained incomplete or in sketch form. He was homosexual and much of the poetry is homoerotic. But he is best known for poems evoking the classical world whether in myth or history. Perhaps his most famous poem is 'Ithaka', which makes the case that it's better to journey than to arrive, if only because 'arrival' either means the terminus of life (death), or retirement from active endeavours, in which case the richest things that one will have are memories. The present cycle of poems might be seen as embracing this wisdom—exploiting the emotional journey for all it was worth, rather than being attached to a specific outcome, which, it quickly became apparent, was most unlikely to eventuate anyway.

65 Patroclus, the young lover of Achilles, in Homer's epic *The Iliad*, who is killed in battle by the Trojan champion Hector, who is himself, in turn, slain, famously, by Achilles; only for Achilles himself to then be slain by Hector's young brother Paris, whose elopement with Helen from Mycenae had started the Trojan War to begin with. Caesarion was the son of Julius Caesar and Cleopatra, murdered on the orders of Augustus, the nephew of Julius Caesar and, by 31 BCE, when his armies defeated Mark Antony and Cleopatra, master of the Mediterranean world. Caesarion was eliminated lest he be held up by rebels as the true heir of mighty Caesar. Poseidon was the god of the oceans.

66 Hermes was originally a phallic god but evolved over the centuries into the messenger of the gods of Olympus. Zeus gave him this role, providing him with a broad-brimmed hat, winged sandals and a *caduceus* or herald's staff. But around this figure, over the centuries between 300 BCE and 1200 CE, there grew syncretistic fables and finally whole systems of ideas. Hermeticism is the common name for philosophical speculations supposedly based on teachings of Hermes Trismegistus (a Hellenistic combination of the Greek god Hermes and the Egyptian god Thoth). In 1964, Frances A. Yates advanced the thesis that Renaissance Hermeticism, or what she called 'the Hermetic tradition', had been a crucial factor in the development of modern science. While Yates's thesis has since been largely rejected, the important role played by the 'Hermetic' science of alchemy in the thought of such figures as Jan Baptist van Helmont (1580–1644), Robert Boyle (1627–1691) or Isaac Newton (1642–1727) has been amply demonstrated.

Throughout its history, Hermeticism was closely associated with the idea of a primeval, divine wisdom, revealed only to the most ancient of sages, such as Hermes Trismegistus. In the Renaissance, this developed into the notion of a pristine or ancient theology, a single, true theology given by God to the first humans; traces of which may still be recovered from ancient systems of thought. Thinkers like Giovanni Pico della Mirandola (1463–1494) supposed that this 'ancient theology' could be reconstructed by studying (what were then considered to be) the most ancient writings still in existence, such as those of Hermes, but also those of Zoroaster, Orpheus, Pythagoras, Plato, the 'Chaldeans', or the Kabbalah. My poetic use here of the name of Hermes draws on this millennial idea of preservation, recovery, inquiry and translation.

67 In Homer's great epic *The Odyssey*, set after the Trojan War, when the surviving hero of that war, the wily Odysseus, is seeking to find his way back to his spouse, Penelope and his young son Telemachus, at Ithaka, on the western littoral of Greece, Nausicaa (pronounced naw-si-kay-a, with the emphasis falling on the second syllable), is the princess daughter of King Alcinous and Queen Arete of the

Phaeacian kingdom called Scheria, where Odysseus is cast ashore shipwrecked in Book Six. She is, as Betty Radice expressed it in her wonderful glossary *Who's Who in the Ancient World* (Penguin, 1971), 'the heroine of a particularly human and charming episode' in the epic.

Nausicaa 'has done the family washing in the river mouth and is playing ball with her maids when Odysseus appears after his shipwreck. She receives him with dignity, when her maids run from his nakedness, gives him food and clothing, and takes him home to her father; and rather sadly sees him sent on his way home to his wife' after a wonderful feast in her father's halls, in which Odysseus shares tales of his epic adventures—in Books Seven to Twelve. Based on those tales, there have even been claims (by Samuel Butler and Robert Graves) that Nausicaa herself was the true author of what we know as *The Odyssey*. Odysseus, when he first encounters Nausicaa, declares to her, 'I look at you and a sense of wonder takes me.'

68   The 'muse' of these poems, the 'Nausicaa' of the iWar forum, is of Vietnamese origin. To be precise, she is Sino-Vietnamese. For a thousand years and more the Vietnamese fought Chinese suzerainty, finally shaking it off during the Ming dynasty (1368—1644), which is all the more remarkable since the early Ming were expansionist and were succeeded by the enormously aggressive Qing (1644—1912) who brought Central Asia, Tibet, Mongolia and Manchuria into the Chinese Empire, where they had never been before.

The French arrived in the 19th century and colonized Indochina, including Vietnam, ruling it from 1885 until the Japanese overran it in 1940. The communist Democratic Republic of Vietnam was declared by Ho Chi Minh in August 1945. The French then attempted to turn back the tide in an eight-year neo-colonial war that met with defeat by 1954. The Americans then picked up where the French had left off, attempting to prevent the unification of Vietnam under Communist rule. They failed and withdrew. Saigon, the capital of anti-communist South Vietnam, fell to the Communist armies in April 1975. Many hundreds of thousands of people fled Communist rule and large numbers of them perished at sea in their bid to escape.

69   Elizabeth Bishop (1911—1979) was an American poet. For an analysis of her poem 'Insomnia,' see William Waters *Poetry's Touch: On Lyric Address* (2003) pp. 43-46. A two-volume anthology of Bishop's poetry and prose was published in 2011 by Farrar, Straus and Giroux, New York. Originally published in her poetry collection '*A Cold Spring*', in 1955, 'Insomnia' can be found at p. 68 of the anthology of her poems. Waters comments, in a characteristically acute and sensitive analysis of this poem:

> *...no signal before the last line reveals that the poem is not uttered within the self alone. Heartbreak is in a sense about the I-you relationship, but talk of heartbreak need not therefore take the form of address. Rather, address to the unloving partner takes on, formally speaking, a special pathos, since in the courageously sustained appeal to the beloved are already present the vulnerability of the speaker, the yearning for reciprocal intimacy, which is, or may feel like, the radical of all address, and the anguished suppression of that same yearning.*

It need hardly be said that this speaks to where I found myself as I wrote this cycle of poems—including experiences at times of insomnia.

70   Sextus Propertius (45—15 BCE) was an elegiac poet of the age of the Emperor Augustus who wrote four books of elegies—sad love poems, basically—the first two or three centring on his passion for one Cynthia, whose lustrous eyes and aloof demeanour caused him agonies. He died very young and was less acclaimed in his time than he has since become. His Cynthia poems, however, have had a lasting influence, not least since the invention of printing and the Renaissance. Propertius published a first book of love elegies in 25 BCE, with Cynthia as the main theme.

A second, larger book of elegies was published perhaps a year later. A third book came sometime after 23 BCE. Its content shows the poet beginning to move beyond simple love themes, as the poet grows tired of the demanding but fickle Cynthia and implies a bitter end to their torrid love affair. Book IV, published sometime after 16 BCE, displays more of the poet's ambitious agenda, and includes several aetiological poems explaining the origin of various Roman rites and landmarks. In short, his love poems for Cynthia were all written and published when he himself was in his early to mid-twenties.

71   Annabel Coulet was a French-Vietnamese woman of great beauty and dignity, whom I met in a brief visit to Bangkok, in late March 1985, on my way from North America and Europe to Japan, during the fieldwork for my PhD. We spent a long morning in conversation before she asked me how long I would be in Bangkok. I was leaving within hours. 'When will you be back?' she inquired. In fact, I have never been back. But I have never forgotten her beauty or our conversation. Weili Yang was the daughter of a Chinese scholar, Richard Yang, who, in the 1990s, ran a think tank in Taipei. He, in his youth, decades before, had been private secretary to the great Chinese liberal and philosopher Hu Shih, during the years of Chiang Kaishek's dictatorship.

That led to Richard and his wife being exiled from Taiwan in the 1960s and 1970s, the pressures of which finally destroyed their marriage. I met Weili at a conference in Hong Kong in 1994 that her father had organized. I was instantly smitten and sought ways for the next several years to move to Hong Kong so that I could court her, but I was unable to engineer the move. I have, however, always remembered our conversations—and her captivating beauty, including her voice. She was, at the time, a highflier at Price Waterhouse. She later married a British merchant banker. They chose not to have children, I was informed, because they wanted the freedom to travel.

72   Marie Henri Beyle (Stendhal) (1783-1842) has been a model for my own approach to matters both of the world and of the heart. Perhaps all that need be said here is that, for all the vulnerability and fecklessness he exhibited in his passion for Mathilde Dembowski, he was a man of many parts and his novels set the bar of realism high for future French novelists such as Flaubert and Zola. Even in *Love*, it is clear that he was analytically fascinated by what had happened to him and determined to pin it down diagnostically—while celebrating the high feelings and longings that it had involved.

I relate to that in the present case, perhaps more than ever before in a life of romanticism and writing. In *The Charterhouse of Parma*, he depicted a 'hero', Fabrizio, who was swept along by world affairs and was unable to take their measure or have any effect. Finally, he withdrew into a monastery. Though that option has largely been abandoned in our time, in Stendhal's recounting it foreshadowed the dilemmas of many would-be activists of the 20th and 21st centuries who flounder around, unable to get purchase or find an authentic vocation.

73 *Delphic Deixis* is the title of this whole cycle of poems, as well as of this specific one. Why? What does it mean? The word oracle comes from the Latin word oraculum, which means both a prophecy made by a god (or priest) and the place where the prophecy is given. Delphi was the most famous place in the classical world where such prophecies were to be heard or received. It was, in classical times, and well into the Roman Empire, a remarkable site. It included a Temple of Apollo, the Castalian spring, a theatre, a hippodrome, a stoa and various other public buildings. It lasted for over a thousand years, from archaic Greek times (around 700 BCE) until the late fourth century CE, when Alaric the Goth is said to have sacked it (in 396 CE), during his invasion of Greece—fourteen years before he famously sacked Rome itself. After centuries of ruin and neglect, it is now a major archaeological site.

The oracle was the Pythian priestess who delivered her pronouncements (famously ambiguous ones) in a state of ecstasy. Deixis is something much less ambiguous. The word means pointing or demonstration, from the ancient Greek word *deiknumi* (to show) or *deiktikos* (capable of proof). What is being implied is that the poetry may seem at times 'Delphic', but it is deictic—it points to what has happened and what it means. This short poem 'Delphic deixis', spells out with mordant irony the specific meaning in the poet's mind: his personal fate might, he suggests, have been pointed out by the Delphic oracle (or by the famous Sibyl, at Cumae, south of Rome, which was also a classical oracle) long ago, in a way that makes sense of what has just happened to him—and has long been happening to him. And, in any case, he identifies with Apollo (in the pursuit of Daphne) and there was a Temple of Apollo at Delphi.

74 Publius Ovidius Naso (Ovid) was one of the greatest of the Latin poets, two thousand years ago. Many of his books remain classics right down to the present, not least among them his *Metamorphoses*, in fifteen books, relating the mythopoeic story of the world from its creation to the rise of the Roman Empire. No book had a greater influence on Shakespeare than this one. I have long had four different translations of it in my library, including the 1567 one by Arthur Golding that Shakespeare himself would have used and the far more recent ones by Charles Martin (2004) and David Raeburn (also 2004).

Ovid himself was exiled to the Black Sea coast by the Emperor Augustus, at least ostensibly because his love poetry was deemed subversive of the conservative moral order; though it is well known that he had got himself somehow caught up in political intrigues that put him out of sorts with the Emperor. In exile for the rest of his life, he kept writing brilliant poetry, including his great work on the Roman calendar, the *Fasti*. But there is no better narrative or poetic introduction to classical mythology than Ovid's *Metamorphoses*. It is from them that my use of the tales of Daphne and Apollo and Orpheus and Eurydice are borrowed. His love poetry, of course, has also long been an inspiration. He was a remarkable poet, though his father is said to have retorted, when the young Ovid declared he wanted to be a poet, 'A poet? Not even Homer ever made any money out of poetry!'

75 Ovid *Metamorphoses*, translated by Charles Martin, Book One, lines 710-11. But here is Raeburn's translation of the passage, a little before that, in which Apollo is first smitten by Daphne:

> *Phoebus caught sight of her, fell in love and longed to possess her. Wishes were hopes, for even his powers of prophecy failed him. Think of the flimsy stubble which burns in a*

> *harvested cornfield and think of a blazing hedgerow fired by a torch which a traveller*
> *has carelessly brought too close or dropped behind him at daybreak. So was the god as*
> *his heart caught fire and the flames spread through to the depths of his soul and passion*
> *was fuelled with empty hope.*

So it goes in such cases. So it was with me.

76 Lucretius *The Nature of Things* (Penguin, translated and with notes by A. E. Stallings, 2007) is a remarkable book, written in the last decade of the Roman republic, by a man who seems to have died shortly afterward—reportedly by his own hand and, if St Jerome is to be believed, because he had taken a love potion that chemically drove him mad. That would have been one of history's, or at least of literature's most sublime ironies. But his book is an erudite and lucid rendition into verse of the atomist philosophy first conceived by Democritus (460–370 BCE) and written up at length by Epicurus (341–270 BCE), in his multi-volume treatise *On Nature*.

It has only been in the past hundred years or so that atomism has come into its own. Yet these classical thinkers had the daring and imagination to espouse it as a system of ideas more than two thousand years before the instruments and mathematics had been developed that could drive home the inquiry and demonstrate what they had been guessing at. For a splendid introduction to the philosophy that arose out of their speculations, see James Warren (ed) *The Cambridge Companion to Epicureanism* (Cambridge University Press, 2009). Suffice it to say, no-one before the contemporary era offered a more lucid or succinct analysis of sexuality than did Lucretius, who based his thinking not on myths, as Ovid would after him, but on a coherent if speculative materialism or physiology.

77 T. J. Binyon *Pushkin: A Biography* (Alfred Knopf, New York, 2003). Alexander Pushkin (1799–1837) is Russia's most famous and best loved poet. He was an admirer of Lord Byron and sought to become Russia's equivalent. He succeeded in almost every way. He declared quite early in his short life, 'the whole aim of life consists in this: everything on earth is done to attract the attention of women.'

78 Peter Ilyich Tchaikovsky (1840–1893) is, perhaps, to Russian music what Pushkin is to Russian poetry. And the two come together in Tchaikovsky's wonderful opera *Eugene Onegin*, based on Pushkin's famous Byronic epic poem. In the story, Tatiana Larin, who lives on a quiet country estate with her mother and her sister Olga, meets and is smitten at once by Eugene Onegin, the friend of Olga's beau Vladimir Lensky. Unable to restrain herself, Tatiana writes a passionate letter to Onegin declaring that she knows him to be her destined partner and guardian until the grave. He coolly distances himself from her and then mischievously flirts with Olga to tease Lensky.

The latter, in a jealous rage, challenges him to a duel and is shot dead by Onegin who then becomes haunted by Lensky's death and travels abroad unable to find peace of mind. When he returns to Russia, he finds that Tatiana has married an aging military officer and is the toast of high society for her dignity and elegance. He realizes that he made a terrible mistake in spurning her years before and throw himself at her feet. She confesses that she is still in love with him, but turns him away saying that there can be no going back to the past. She is married and will not break her vows. Onegin collapses in despair, bemoaning his cruel fate.

79 In Act 1, Scene 2 of *Eugene Onegin*, Tatiana sits at her writing table saying 'Ah what's the matter with me? I'm all on fire! I don't know how to begin!' Then she writes passionately to Onegin:

> *I write to you—and then? What more is there to say? Now I know it is within your power to punish me with disdain! But if you nourish one grain of pity for my unhappy lot, you will not abandon me...*

Then she pauses to soliloquize:

> *Oh yes, I swore to lock within my breast this avowal of a mad and ardent passion. Alas, I have not the strength to subdue my heart!*

So, she resumes writing:

> *Why, oh why did you visit us? Buried in this remote countryside, I should never have known you, nor should I have known this torment. The turbulence of a youthful heart, calmed by time, who knows? Most likely I would have found another, have proved a faithful wife and virtuous mother. Another?! No, not to any other in the world would I have given my heart! It is decreed on high. It is the will of heaven: I am yours! My whole life has been a pledge of this inevitable encounter. I know this: God sent you to me. You are my keeper til the grave!...As soon as you arrived I recognized you. I almost swooned, began to blaze with passion and to myself I said: Tis he! Tis he!...*

The sublime dramatic irony of the opera is Onegin's final appeal to her, in which, years after her letter, which he had spurned, he bursts out passionately with almost her own words:

> *Oh, do not drive me away; you love me! And I will not leave you! You will ruin your life for nothing! This is the will of heaven: you are mine! All your life has been a pledge of our union! And be assured I was sent to you by God. I am your protector to the grave...*

But it is too late. Tatiana is now beyond Onegin's reach or recall.

80 Edward Timms *Karl Kraus: Apocalyptic Satirist—The Post-War Crisis and the Rise of the Swastika* (Yale University Press, 2005) describes the relationship between Kraus and Nadherny beautifully. Kraus's love life was complex, not simple or saintly, which is perhaps why he interests me so much. There were certainly women in his life, in an erotic sense, other than Sidonie Nadherny; women such as Gina Kaus, Mary Dobrzensky and Mechtilde Lichnowsky. He corresponded with these women. He wrote poetry to them. He dined with them. He holidayed with them. He did not marry any of them.

Kraus was especially protective of his relationship with Sidonie, Timms tells us, but believed that 'being in love with more than one person may be an enriching experience.' His relationship with her waxed and waned, but was rich and full of intelligent freedom. Perhaps nowhere more succinctly does Timms capture this than at p. 216:

> *He experienced the relationship with Sidonie as a mystical union which redeemed him from the condition of 'forsakenness'. For both lovers, an intense bereavement had shaken their faith in divine benevolence, and Kraus's poetry suggests that they responded to each other as if to a mystical reincarnation of the beloved person they mourned. For Sidonie, he is to be the emissary if not the replacement for her dead brother Johannes.*

> *For Kraus, she has removed the shadow thrown by the death of his first beloved, Annie Kalmar. Love and faith are fused through the 'mysterious radiance of sexuality'...for Kraus it is the eros inherent in the most intense I/Thou relationships that gives access to a sense of the divine, and his poems celebrate the indwelling presence revealed through the union of male and female.*

Kraus, however, was both a man of mature years by this point and a highly sophisticated intellectual. Not everyone is capable of the kind of erotic/mystical union he had with Sidonie.

81 This poignant little story comes from Margaret Coker's *The Spymaster of Baghdad: The Untold Story of the Elite Intelligence Cell That Turned the Tide Against ISIS* (Viking Penguin, 2021) pp. 15-21.

82 Samuel Beckett (1906–1989) was one of the major figures in 20th century letters, writing in both French and English. He is regarded as one of the prominent figures in the 'Theatre of Absurd.' Some of his best-known works include, 'Happy Days,' 'Waiting for Godot,' 'Not I,' 'Murphy,' and 'Krapp's Last Tape' amongst various others. He was also awarded the 'Nobel Prize in Literature' in 1969. I stumbled upon this quote from his work on the arm of the Swiss tennis maestro Stan Wawrinka, during the 2014 Australian Open and was so impressed by it that I wrote an op ed for *The Age* the day after he defeated Novak Djokovic in the quarter final—the first time he had defeated Djokovic in fifteen attempts. He went on to win the Australian Open that year.

83 Prolepsis is anticipation or representation of something before it actually takes place or exists. Lepidoptera are moths and butterflies. The playful combination of the two words in this poem ought be fairly self-explanatory. The idea simply occurred to me in pictorial form one morning and the words followed from the picture of the enclosure.

84 Lev Semenovich Vygotsky (1896–1934) died tragically young, given his precocious contributions to the theories of language, mind, education and cognitive development. See his essays in *Thought and Language* (MIT press, 1962). According to Vygotsky, the zone of proximal development is 'the distance between the actual developmental level as determined by independent problem solving and the level of potential development as determined through problem-solving under adult guidance or in collaboration with more capable peers.' I have substituted 'learning' for 'development', which others also do at times, without distorting Vygotsky's meaning, but in order to be able to rhyme it with yearning.

I read Vygotsky's essays in 1981, in the midst of doing my History honours thesis on the student rebellions and general strike in France in May 1968. It had struck me by then that there was no discernible theory or philosophy of education being applied in the Faculty of Arts of Melbourne as regards what constituted a sound liberal education or how to most efficiently and creatively teach students anything at all. Alas, I discovered that this was even more the case when I commenced graduate school at the Australian National University in 1983. As for how security vetting and intelligence analysis were done, when, with a freshly minted PhD, I applied to work for and in due course did work for the Defence Intelligence Organization, that's a subject for another time and place.

85 Carlo Rovelli (born 1956, so the same age as I am) is a distinguished Italian theoretical physicist.

The Order of Time (Penguin, 2019) is a delightful and extraordinarily lucid explanation of special relativity and the nature of time. The three parts of it are headed, respectively, 'The Crumbling of Time', 'The World Without Time' and 'The Sources of Time'. Rovelli explains why our intuitive sense of time is as illusory as our intuitive sense that the earth is flat or stationary or that we are standing upright in space or that the Sun revolves around the Earth. It's a bravura performance. He then explains how we construct a meaningful sense of time within the intuitive world we inhabit and how to reconcile this with the realities of physics. It has long been my opinion that our poetry has to embrace this and other magnificent achievements of modern science, not proceed as if it existed in some world apart. But that doesn't mean abandoning our literature or our narratives of meaning. It means deepening them and transforming them—over time!

86 John Keats (1795—1821) like Vygotsky and Propertius and countless other people, died young of tuberculosis. He was a brilliant poet and his achievements at such a young age are awe-inspiring. His younger brother Thomas Keats died of tuberculosis aged just nineteen, in 1818, even before the poet. His output, given his early death was staggering and remains so. But the quantity would be less remarkable if it were not the case that the output was so consistently of the highest quality, also. He is among the most famous English Romantic poets, along with Byron and Shelley, if only because all three were so very young when they died and he the youngest of them all. 'La belle dame sans merci'—the fair lady without mercy—is among his most famous poems. It has deep roots in medieval and Provencal poetry. I subvert it here, not merely out of caprice, but because what I claim is what in fact happened—leaving aside the mythic evocation of Apollo. But I did feel 'Apollonian' in rising above the problem that confronted me in this matter.

87 Le Duan (1907—1986) was the grim political leader who succeeded Ho Chi Minh and led North Vietnam to victory over South Vietnam in 1969-75, then closed the country off from the outside world and confined hundreds of thousands to re-education camps by way of introducing orthodox communism to the territories that had for three decades resisted it.

88 Tạ Thu Thâu (1906—1945) was, in the 1930s, the principal representative of Trotskyism in Vietnam and, in colonial Cochinchina, of left opposition to the Indochinese Communist Party led by Nguyen Ai Quoc (Ho Chi Minh). He was executed by the Viet Minh in 1945, in a political purge in which they eliminated a great many political figures whom they saw as potential threats to their monopoly of power. Clearly, here, I am identifying with him as someone given a perfunctory trial, taken out and shot. Let's call that poetic license.

89 Frank Tallis *The Incurable Romantic and Other Tales of Madness and Desire* (Basic Books, New York, 2018) is a book that I chanced upon at the most opportune possible time. Tallis explores a lot of territory and does so with admirable humanity and objectivity. You might say he was plumbing the deep water into which I was in some danger of falling.

90 This was a remark she made to me in the phone conversation that I found so enchanting. Her PhD researches, somewhat stalled, had led her to this provisional conclusion. 'Ah!' I exclaimed, 'Now you're talking my language. I'd love to discuss this further with you!' Those conversations, it seems, will never happen.

91   Rio da Miel—River of Honey.

92   This is the title of a book by one of the mentors of my own PhD inquiries, David G. Marr, a former US Marine Corps intelligence officer in Vietnam, before the escalation of the war in 1965, who, determined to get to the root of the war, learned Vietnamese, married a Vietnamese woman and devoted his life to the history of the Vietnamese revolution. I read all his books and reviewed this one, when it was published—which was after I had completed my PhD.

93   This whole poem, of course, plays with the plot in Shakespeare's *A Midsummer Night's Dream*, in which love and jealousy are theatrically explored by the peerless Bard. Oberon's potion is administered to Titania in order to make a fool of her, by having her fall in love with some uncomely creature—Bottom, who has been given ass's ears and other features of a braying beast. In the play Titania falls in love with and dotes on him—which is his midsummer night's dream. I made a bit of an ass of myself, but Titania did not, in my case, fall for the ass. Plainly, Puck hadn't been able to anoint her with Oberon's potion.

94   Here is another peerless Shakespearean comedy. The punchline has a twist, though. It is Olivia who says, of Malvolio, 'Take the fool away'. To which her jester responds, 'You heard the lady: take her away!' Merely the poet being puckish, of course.

95   I have refrained from commenting on most of the poems dealing with Rilke, Baladine and Orpheus, but a little explanation may be helpful here. The myth of Orpheus, as recounted by Ovid and widely attested elsewhere, is that he fell in love with Eurydice, but she was bitten on the ankle by a poisonous adder and died. She went down to the Underworld, to Hades. Orpheus, grief-stricken, went after her to find her and plead with the gods of the Underworld, Hades and his spouse Persephone, to release her back to the world of the living. His singing was so enchanting that it was agreed she could return to the Overworld to live with him—but he had to leave the Underworld and trust that she would come after him. If he looked back, he would lose her forever. He held to this until the last moment, but then could not restrain himself, desperate to know whether Eurydice was behind him or had been detained. He turned—and she vanished.

It was after this that Orpheus wandered distraught in Thrace until he was set upon by wild women, the maenads and torn to pieces. They cast his severed head into the river Hebrus, but it floated down the river still singing. It finally floated out into the Aegean Sea and across it to the shore of the island of Lesbos, where it was beached. The blood and spirit of Orpheus then rubbed off on the soil of Lesbos, which would, in the centuries that followed, become the well-spring of lyric poetry in Greece and the Ionian world. The various elements of this tale are woven into several of the poems that follow, including the final stanza of the last poem, which takes its title ('Orpheus dismembered') from the tale. Thus, Orpheus competes with Apollo for the role of dominant trope in the cycle. Both are used to suggest that the very trauma of overwhelming passion and rejection have generated the poems that form this cycle. The poems might be considered as the membra disjecta of Orpheus or the laurel tree into which Daphne herself was turned in order to elude the love of Apollo. They have felt in the writing like the former, in the finishing like the latter.

Part III

96 Lady Godiva was a late Anglo-Saxon noblewoman, who actually died at some point after the Norman Conquest in 1066. She was the wife of Earl Leofric of Mercia, and was a patron of churches and monasteries. She is chiefly famous for a legend dating back to at least the 13th century, in which she rode naked—covered only in her long hair—through the streets of Coventry to gain a remission of the oppressive taxation that her husband, Leofric, imposed on his tenants. The name Peeping Tom for a voyeur originates from later versions of this legend, in which a man named Thomas watched her ride and was struck blind or dead.

97 Lady Godiva's signature, 'Ego Godiva Comitissa diu istud desideravi' ('I, the Countess Godiva, have desired this for a long time'), appears on a charter purportedly given by Thorold of Bucknall to the Benedictine monastery of Spalding. However, this charter is considered spurious by many historians. In the poem, obviously, the signature is appropriated for intimate purposes.

98 Peter Green *The Poems of Catullus* (University of California Press, 2005) must be close to the canonical modern translation of the poems of Gaius Valerius Catullus (84-54 BCE), who has achieved immortality and wide influence based on a single book of poems, of which '101', an elegy about the death and cremation, for which, after a long journey, he had arrived too late, of his brother is one of the most famous. He also wrote 25 love poems, in strikingly different moods, for a muse he called Lesbia, but who, by scholarly consensus was Clodia Metelli. Poem 101 is only ten lines long. The key phrase is 'let me address in vain your silent ashes' (et mutam nequiquam alloquerer cinerem).

99 Johann Wolfgang von Goethe (1749-1832) was a German poet, playwright, novelist, scientist, statesman, theatre director, and critic. His works include plays, poetry, literature and aesthetic criticism, and treatises on botany, anatomy, and colour. He is considered to be the greatest German literary figure of the modern era and is also widely regarded as one of the last 'Renaissance men'—a polymath who was able to range across the full breadth of both the human and natural sciences of his time. His *Roman Elegies* are a set of erotic poems he wrote in 1788, following his Italian journey. Several of them are so risqué that they were omitted from published editions of the elegies for many years. Several of the poems in *This Floating Shell* partake of that risqué character, but have been included in defiance of prudery and hypocrisy.

100 Giuseppe Verdi's *La Traviata* is one of the most famous and well-loved operas in the repertoire. The title literally translates as 'The Fallen Woman'. It is a tragic tale about the Parisian courtesan, Violetta, who tries to leave the life she knows behind, in an attempt to finally find true love. That true love is Alfredo Germont. But she is constrained by Alfredo's father, who forbids their love. She is also courted by one Baron Douphol, who is jealous of Alfredo and challenges him to a game of cards, which Alfredo wins. Violetta warns him to be wary of Douphol's jealous and violent temper. That leads to a breach between them, but one that is healed in one of the opera's finest arias, when Violetta sings of her love for Alfredo. There is duel between Douphol and Alfredo, in which the former is wounded. Alfredo and Violetta are reunited, but she dies of tuberculosis, in the melodramatic nature of opera—the 'song of love and death' as Peter Conrad dubbed it.

101 Camille Claudel (1864—1943) was a French sculptor known for her figurative works in bronze and marble. She died in relative obscurity, but later gained recognition for the originality and quality of her work. She has been the subject of several biographies and films. She started working in Auguste Rodin's workshop in 1883 and became a source of inspiration for him. She acted as his model, his confidante, and his lover. She never lived with Rodin, who was reluctant to end his 20-year relationship with Rose Beuret. Knowledge of the affair agitated her family, especially her mother, who already detested her for not being a boy and never approved of Camille's involvement in the arts. As a consequence, Camille was forced to leave the family home. Rodin turned against her, she ended up in poverty and her family had her committed to a psychiatric hospital.

102 German meaning Eternal Rome.

103 When D. H. Lawrence was writing *Lady Chatterley's Lover*, he was living with his partner, Frieda, in Italy. She was having an affair with another man, while Lawrence himself was suffering from erectile dysfunction. Doris Lessing (1919—2013), in an Introduction to the novel very late in her life, made two remarks that I can't help citing here, given their relevance to the poems in this cycle: 'Lady Chatterley', she wrote, 'is as alive in the popular imagination as is naked Lady Godiva riding on her horse through Coventry, hiding behind the curtains of her hair.' And, some pages later, 'I have used the words fuck and cunt freely in this piece, because Lawrence wanted to rescue them from the lexicon of "dirty words" and make them stand for a healthy respect for sex.'

104 See previous note! This is where the work of Roger Shattuck is very pertinent. In *Forbidden Knowledge* and then *Candour & Perversion* he offered us two fine sets of essays on questions of art vs decadence, eroticism vs pornography and the boundaries of permissible knowledge. The questions involved are profound and complex, admitting of no easy rules or sweeping judgements. But the issue raised here is that of the use of 'obscene' words in love poetry and the use of them, in particular, in the disclosure of private conversations between consenting adults. The simplest answer to those who would find the few instances of such language in these poems objectionable would be to say that such objections are confused and perhaps hypocritical. The exclamations in question pertain to the very nature of physical sexual passion and ought be considered in poetry as they are in daily life, a basic part of the lexicon of desire. I do not apologize for using them—as the poems themselves make plain. But I do not for one moment intend them to compromise or degrade the image of the woman I love.

105 WAV: Waveform Audio File Format (WAVE or WAV due to its filename extension; pronounced 'wave') is an audio file format standard, developed by IBM and Microsoft, for storing an audio bitstream on PCs. It is the main format used on Microsoft Windows systems for uncompressed audio. The usual bitstream encoding is the linear pulse-code modulation (LPCM) format.

106 Catullus 58A—a five-line poem, which I will not translate even here.

107 Peter Abelard (1079-1142) was a medieval French philosopher who had a famous love affair with one of his students, Héloïse d'Argenteuil, which led to her being sent to a convent and him being castrated. She subsequently wrote him letters reflecting on the nature of love, while he concentrated, even in his replies to her, on philosophical dialectic and church affairs.

108 The Emperor Aurelian ruled the Roman world for just five years (270-275 CE), but won an astounding series of victories and put the cracking Empire back together again, when it was coming apart at the seams, both East and West. He rebuilt the city walls at Rome, which had been demolished by Augustus almost 300 years before, since dark and dangerous times had returned. In short, he was walling in what most needed to be protected and defended. Hence the poetic metaphor.

109 Traumspieler = dreamplayer

110 Oxyrhynchus fragments are a group of manuscripts discovered during the late 19th and early 20th centuries by Bernard Pyne Grenfell and Arthur Surridge Hunt, at an ancient rubbish dump, near Oxyrhynchus, in Egypt. There is a huge mass of them, of which only a tiny sample has thus far been curated and catalogued. The material ranges from the 3rd century BCE to the Muslim conquest of Egypt in 640 CE. Only about 10% of what has been sorted out is literary in nature. Most are codes, edicts, registers, official correspondence, census-returns, tax-assessments, petitions, court-records, sales, leases, wills, bills, accounts, inventories, horoscopes, and private letters. Most are in Greek, but some are in Egyptian hieroglyphics, Coptic, Latin or Arabic. There are also a small number in Hebrew, Aramaic, Syriac and Persian.

111 Aspasia (470–400 BCE), according to Plutarch, writing 500 years later, attracted the most prominent writers and thinkers of the time, including Socrates, to her salon, which became an intellectual centre in Athens. She grew up in the Ionian city of Miletus, but lived out her adult life in Athens. Vincent Azouley, in his *Pericles of Athens* (Princeton University Press, 2018) provides a wonderful account of how besotted Pericles was with Aspasia. He would visit her house twice a day, just to talk with and kiss her, scandalizing ancient writers. In fact he lived with her for several years and they had a son. Such were the beauty and intelligence of Aspasia that she is reputed to have schooled Pericles himself, the master of Athens, in both rhetoric and sexual pleasure. There is also a theory that she was the original of the fictitious Diotima in Plato's *Symposium*, who taught Socrates his doctrine of transcendent beauty.

112 Shakespeare Sonnet 18, 'Shall I compare thee to a summer's day?/Thou art more lovely and more temperate/…So long as men can breathe, or eyes can see/So long lives this and this gives life to thee.'

113 Emanuele Severino (1929-2020) In 1970, the Vatican's Congregation for the Doctrine of the Faith ruled that Severino's ideas were not compatible with Catholicism, since Severino's belief in 'the eternity of all beings' eliminated the need for a Creator God. However, he was awarded the gold medal of the Republic for cultural merit by the Italian President. In April 2019, less than a year before he died, Severino was interviewed by the then Italian premier Giuseppe Conte, who described him in glowing terms as an eminent focal point of international philosophy. His book *The Essence of Nihilism* was originally published in Italian in 1972. His was a strange epistemological or ontological position, rooted in the claim by the Pre-Socratic Greek philosopher Parmenides that there cannot be any nothing since what is nothing cannot, by definition, exist. Therefore all being must be eternal. He spent a lifetime elaborating this arcane idea in numerous books, teaching in Milan and then in Venice.

114 The Academy of Lynxes or Linceian Academy is an Italian institution originally founded in the early 17th century to forward scientific inquiry and philosophical speculation, even in opposition to the Catholic Church. It was suppressed during the Counter Reformation, but revived in the late 19th century, after the Italian state had been united and the Papacy confined to the Vatican. In my unfinished novel *Darkness Over Love: A Complete Fiction*, Fenimore Monaghan and a small group of brilliant Harvard graduate students form their own Academy of Lynxes in the 1980s, directed at pooling their specialist studies to arrive at a consilient worldview, i.e. one that reconciled the physical and mathematical with the human sciences.

115 *Poetry and Truth*—the title of Goethe's autobiography.

116 In the myth of Cupid and Psyche, they end up having a child called Voluptas (Pleasure).

117 Friedrich Nietzsche *Beyond Good and Evil* (Penguin, 1981) #67 'Love of one is a piece of barbarism, for it is practised at the expense of all others. Love of God likewise.'

118 Lucius Apuleius *The Golden Ass* (edited by Peter Singer and translated by Ellen Finkelpearl, Text, Melbourne, 2021). The Cupid and Psyche tale, however, was omitted by Peter Singer, rather frustratingly, because of his singular focus on animal rights. It's about the overcoming of obstacles to the love between Psyche (Soul or Breath of Life) and Cupid (Desire) or Amor (Love, Greek Eros), and their ultimate union in a sacred marriage. Although the only extended narrative from antiquity is that of Apuleius from 2nd century CE, Eros and Psyche appear in Greek art as early as the 4th century BCE. In this poem, the central motif is Cupid's attempt to show Psyche that love must be built on trust and not illusion or infatuation.

Acknowledgements

This book may never have been published at all but for the generous sponsorship of my friend of forty-seven years, Tim Norton. Certainly, it would not have been published in this lavishly illustrated version. If the book, to be available in hardback, soft covers and Kindle, takes off, this will make him known as a patron of the arts. Regardless, I am deeply grateful and hope that he and his partner Joanne will feel proud of the book in years to come.

The second person who has made an invaluable contribution to the creation of *The Three Graces* is, of course, Ingrida Rocis. Having begun with drawings for what was originally to have been a book called *Lyrical Epigrams* (now wholly subsumed within Part IC of this book), Ingrida became, in the course of 2021, a witness to my breakout romantic obsessions and poetry. As the latter became first *Delphic Deixis* and then *This Floating Shell*, she became both my closest confidante about the emotional dilemmas I encountered and the increasingly passionate illustrator of the culminating affair with Muse 3. It has been a remarkable creative partnership and one which has beautifully graced this book.

A similar vote of thanks belongs to Pasiphae Seferis, for her years of friendship and encouragement of my poetic endeavours. But above all for the conversations we had about *This Floating Shell* and the possibilities for a unique book bringing the poems for three diverse muses together between two covers. Whatever my crass jokes in Cancun about her exotic name, she is not by any means full of 'bull' or unnatural lusts or sorcery. She is an architect and sommelier of taste and distinction, whose friendship and counsel I value more than ever.

The manuscript was shared, in full, as soon as it had been assembled, with both Muse 1 and Muse 3, though not with Muse 2, for reasons explained in the Preface. Both read it with keen appreciation, and each was magnanimous in conferring her emphatic approval, despite the intrusive presence of the other (and another) within the same covers as love poetry for her. That alone was remarkable. But I must acknowledge here the profound role each of them has played in my life: the first by long, slow influence and affection; the third with a revolution of the heart that I never anticipated, and which has immeasurably enriched me as a man and as a poet.

The poetry was also read by a number of other friends, notably including Ingrida Rocis, who was so inspired by the poetry that she created a wonderful set of drawings and watercolours in response to it. I would particularly to thank Rod Moran, Nick Fabbri and Joe Lo Bianco for their interest in and encouragement of the verse as it flowed from my pen. Their enthusiasm for my creative endeavours was a great inducement to keep going. Rod, in particular, read the whole of *Lyrical Epigrams* and the whole of *This Floating Shell* and was extravagant in his praise for the work.

This is the eighth book I have published through Echo Books, first when Ian Gordon created the press (which I used to call my 'Aldine Press', after the Renaissance publishing house of Aldus Manutius and his heirs in Venice between 1494 and 1597) and now under Marcus Fielding. Each book is a treasure, even if still, in the public domain, a largely hidden one. Peter Gamble has been along for the ride from the start and has overseen the design of a succession of handsome, complex books with artwork of various kinds. My gratitude to him and Marcus for this one is deep. It has given me a book which Muse 1 has declared to me is 'the best book you have written so far' and which Muse 3 confided to me she thinks is 'quite wonderful'.

I have been in complete remission from cancer for almost four years now, but that was a long battle (2004-18) and all my books have been published against that background. I must, therefore, once again, express my gratitude to Dr. David Speakman and his colleagues at the Peter MacCallum Cancer Centre for their years of expert labour that kept me viable and able to write. They credit me with an immune system they would love to be able to bottle. But unaided it surely would have been overwhelmed sooner or later. Instead, I lived to see *The Three Graces* emerge into the light of day. That alone was worth staying alive to accomplish and to witness.

Index

Abelard, Peter 302
Alaric the Goth 91, 103
Alcaeus 39
Alexander the Great 94, 106
Allen, Woody 315
Aphrodite xxxiii, xxxiv, 163, 295, 303, 333, 351
Apollo 227, 241
Archimedes 8
Arendt, Hannah 207
Ariadne xviii, 32, 318
Arthur, King 63, 72
Aspasia of Miletus 327
Aurelian, Emperor 90, 310
Autopoiesis xx, 109
Averroes 180, 182
Beatrice (Portinari) xxviii, 333
Beauvoir, Simone de 115
Beckett, Samuel 229
Beethoven, Ludwig 200
Bishop, Elizabeth 217
Boltzmann, Ludwig 157, 167, 169
Brentano, Franz 157, 167

Byron, Lord xix, 87, 275
Caesar, Julius 67, 70, 82, 105
Camus, Albert 126, 127, 178
Carrera Damas, Herman 164
Catullus, Gaius Valerius 274, 284, 301
Cavafy, Constantine 211
Chavez, Hugo 133
Chopin, Frederic xxvi, 201
Churchill, Winston 146
Claudel, Camille 282
Clodia Metelli 9
Cohen, Leonard 206, 334, 335
Cynthia (muse of Sextus Propertius) 218, 292
Dante Alighieri xxviii, 67, 333,
Daphne 223
Darwin, Charles 61, 157
Dickinson, Emily xxiv, 60
Donne, John 328
Douphol, Baron xxvi, xxix, 304, 331, 332
Dylan, Bob 181, 267
Egypt 186, 317, 323
Einstein, Albert 21, 235, 300

Ellsberg, Daniel 134, 135
Epicurus 143, 144, 145
Fagan, Brian 59
Fermi, Enrico 165
Freud, Sigmund 116
Gilgamesh 57, 160
Godiva, Lady 271, 277, 374
Goethe, Johann Wolfgang von xxviii, xxxi, 124, 195, 278, 279, 284, 287, 297, 330
Grahame, Kenneth 76, 77, 78, 80
Graves, Robert xxiv, 190
Hadrian, Emperor 88, 103, 106
Hall, Jerry 308
Hamlet 58, 137
Hannibal 100, 101, 104
Hardy, Thomas 79, 80
Heidegger, Martin 115, 207
Hölderlin, Friedrich xvi, xvii
Horace III, 83
Jagger, Mick 163
Jerusalem xxv, 191
Kafka, Franz 153, 166
Kama Sutra 335
Kaufmann, Walter 198
Keats, John 88, 168, 238, 275
Kraus, Karl 166, 227
La Traviata xxvi
Laura (de Noves) xxviii, 333
Lawrence, D. H. 285
Lehrer, Tom 108
Liu Xiaobo 123
Lorca, Federico Garcia 13, 14
Lucretius 224, 249, 300

Marrakesh 102, 178, 179, 180, 181, 182, 184
Mahler, Gustav 108
May, Imelda 295
Michelangelo 88
Nadherny, Sidonie 166, 227
Nausicaa 213, 215
Nefesh, Queen 45
Nehamas, Alexander xx
Nero, Emperor 75, 86
Neruda, Pablo xxiii, 26, 114
Nietzsche, Friedrich xix, xx, xxi, 88, 112, 139, 157, 198
Nureyev, Rudolf 154
Odysseus (Ulysses) 57, 134, 213, 215
Orlando 68, 72, 110, 149, 199
Orpheus 38, 39, 253, 254, 257, 259, 260
Ovid (Publius Ovidius Naso) 36, 168, 196, 203, 248, 253, 254, 257, 272, 278, 279, 281, 284, 292, 303, 307, 319
Polo, Marco 70, 81
Porter, Cole 321
Propertius, Sextus 218, 278, 292
Proust, Marcel 21, 109, 291
Psyche/psyche xvi, 22, 23, 104, 114, 132, 150, 151, 167, 201, 205, 219, 226, 254, 346, 350
Pushkin, Alexander 225
Renoir, Pierre-Auguste 289
Rilke, Rainer Maria xxvii, 166, 198, 209, 227, 252, 253, 254, 260
Rimbaud, Arthur 84, 183
Rodin, Auguste 282, 304
Rommel, Erwin 184, 309
Rovelli, Carlo 235
Sacks, Oliver 266

Sappho 39, 40, 87, 168

Satie, Erik 210, 236, 241

Schmeisser, Jorg xxiii

Shakespeare, William xxii, xxiv, xxviii, 58, 60, 67, 74, 165, 168, 329

Shelley, Percy Bysshe xvii, xxxi, 88, 90, 111, 267, 275

Simone, Nina 321

Stalin, Josef 64, 136

Steele, Timothy xxiv

Stendhal 220, 221

Stilicho 103

Stravinsky, Igor 154

Tallis, Frank 243

Tangier 181, 182, 183

Ta Thu Thau 242

Thomas, Dylan 312

Thoth 45, 48

Toulouse Lautrec, Henri de 273, 290

Vendler, Helen xxiv, 60

Verdi, Giuseppe xxvi

Vortigern 63

Vulpius, Christiane 195, 330

Vygotsky, Lev 233

Wagner, Richard 157

Waters, William xxiv, xxvii, xxxI

Waugh, Evelyn 72, 113

Wei Jingsheng 122

White Goddess xviii, xxiv, 190

Wittgenstein, Ludwig 156, 169

Woolf, Virginia 68. 72, 148, 199

Yesenin, Sergei 136

Zarathustra xx, xxi, 139, 147, 171, 195

www.ingramcontent.com/pod-product-compliance
Lightning Source LLC
Chambersburg PA
CBHW041409300426
44114CB00028B/2963